WITHDRAWN

LAURA CARTER

W9-BYP-177

TELEVISION AND THE RED MENACE

The Video Road to Vietnam

J. Fred MacDonald

PRAEGER

PRAEGER SPECIAL STUDIES • PRAEGER SCIENTIFIC

New York • Philadelphia • Eastbourne, UK
Toronto • Hong Kong • Tokyo • Sydney

Library of Congress Cataloging in Publication Data

MacDonald, J. Fred.
 Television and the red menace.

 Bibliography: p.
 Includes index.
 1. Broadcasting—Political aspects—United States—
History. 2. Broadcasting policy—United States—History.
3. Television broadcasting of news—United States—
History. 4. World politics—1945-   . 5. Vietnamese
Conflict, 1961-1975—United States. I. Title.
HE8689.8.M33   1985   959.704'31   84-18302
ISBN 0-03-001063-2 (alk. paper)
ISBN 0-03-001029-2 (pbk.: alk. paper)

Published in 1985 by Praeger Publishers
CBS Educational and Professional Publishing,
a Division of CBS Inc.
521 Fifth Avenue, New York, NY 10175 USA

© 1985 by J. Fred MacDonald

All rights reserved

56789 052 097654321

Printed in the United States of America
on acid-free paper

For my wife, Leslie W. MacDonald—
as always, her judgment and encouragement
have been indispensable

PREFACE

Dear Mr. President:

In my humble way I am writing to you about the crisis in Vietnam. I have a son who is now in Vietnam. My husband served in World War II. Our country was at war, but now, this time, it is just something that I don't understand. Why?

—letter from a Midwestern woman read by
Lyndon B. Johnson at his press conference
on July 28, 1965

The Vietnam War has often been called a television war. This is to suggest that the protracted conflict in Southeast Asia was telecast with gory immediacy into American living rooms, thus allowing viewers to evaluate the progress of battle. Never before, it is claimed, has a public so closely observed its military in deadly action. Never before had a home-front audience had so much information with which to praise or condemn the course of war.

Few doubt that TV played a role in the progress of the Vietnam War. Some have maintained that the war ended because years of video exposure turned American public opinion against the commitment. Others have argued that the presence of TV cameras and journalists inhibited military commanders conducting the war. In recent years, moreover, the critique of television and its role in the war has become more specifically focused on the Tet offensive of 1968. Here, some have alleged, TV reporters turned an enemy defeat into victory, misled domestic public opinion, and broke the resolve of Americans to endure continued warfare.

Whether hawkish or dovish in their orientation, however, all arguments about the Vietnam conflict treat the importance of television once the war began. And whether marking that beginning as the Tonkin Gulf resolution of August 1964 or "Operation Rolling Thunder" (the bombing of targets in North Vietnam) in February 1965, the relationship between television and the war is generally dated from Lyndon B. Johnson's decision to escalate U.S. involvement in Southeast Asia.

Few, if any, have maintained that TV played a crucial role in getting the United States into the Vietnam War. Few, if any, have suggested that there was a link between what was seen on television in the 1940s, 1950s, or early 1960s, and the development of a national mentality able to accept without much questioning a bloody and inefficient conflict in the Asian jungle. And few, if any, have maintained that commercial TV—whether as entertainment, public service, or news programming—conditioned the American people for almost two decades to tolerate an unwanted and unexplained land war far from home.

This book attempts to fill this gap in understanding the relationship between television and the Vietnam War. Rather than blame the distortions of TV for popular distaste for the war, this book argues that years of misrepresentation on television actually led the American public toward that battle.

From its beginnings in the late 1940s, video fed the nation a powerful menu of propagandized, persuasive programming. In informational and escapist TV Americans were presented an interpretation of life in which a good "us" was forever defeating, in 30 or 60 minutes, an evil "them." Government officials used free television time to justify their policies. Broadcast journalists also helped in the persuasion, frequently offering the news as an "us against them" report bordering upon advocacy journalism. Cold War entertainment shows—ranging from football games and "Victory at Sea" to "The Phil Silvers Show" and the juvenile "Rocky and His Friends"—heightened militaristic values and lavished praise on the American military establishment. Further, the Defense Department helped its own image, making its own TV shows and providing free film, equipment, manpower, and expertise to civilian TV producers of whom it approved.

Patterns of propaganda and misrepresentation would be easily recognized in Soviet television programming. There, where state controls are stringent and there are "official" lines of thought, an American viewer would quickly discern the persuasive content in a situation comedy about fun and high jinks in the Red Army, or documentary series lauding the prowess of the Soviet Navy in World War II, or even a children's show in which foolish American spies were perpetually thwarted by a heroic Russian squirrel and his friend the moose. Perhaps it has been harder for Americans to notice such manipulative content in their own television fare.

Even into the 1960s, when the public grew increasingly aware that its government was waging undeclared war in Vietnam, the political persuasion continued. Now there were more spies than ever, more "happy democratic military" sitcoms, and more presidential exploitation of video than in the previous decade. The 1960s gave TV audiences more documentaries about victories in World War II, and more war dramas than ever in broadcasting history.

Thus, as President John F. Kennedy escalated the American military involvement in Southeast Asia into a guerrilla war against Communism, and as President Johnson raised troop levels to over half a million, the majority of the American people asked few questions. For years they had seen TV heroes fighting evil men, many of them specifically designated as Communists. There had also been many series showing how easily war could be won. Even TV news lacked the detached objectivity needed by a free citizenry seeking information with which to make choices.

Why the Vietnam War? It remains an unresolved question. During the conflict, political and military leaders offered more rhetoric than substance when they answered the query. These leaders uttered slogans such as "Free World versus Red Empire," "national honor," and "keeping our word to friends who have invited us into their country." As for the Communist enemies—the Southern rebels of the National Liberation Front and the Northern troops of North Vietnam—they were explained in clichés such as "Red blueprint to conquer the world," "monolithic, Godless Communist expansion," and "puppets of Moscow and Peking." While such phraseology may have had a certain appeal, a Gallup poll in 1967 revealed that only 48 percent of the American people "knew" why the United States was waging war in Vietnam.[1]

In theory, unpopular national policies cannot long endure in a democracy. Yet, American involvement in Southeast Asia began as early as the presidency of Harry S. Truman. Certainly, during the eight years of Dwight D. Eisenhower, the United States operated in unstable Indochina. The American role in an active military struggle commenced in the Kennedy era and lasted until 1973. Throughout the 1950s, however, most Americans were unaware of their nation's involvement in the crumbling French empire. But in the following two decades after 1960, GIs would kill and die in an open conflict that drained domestic fiscal resources, shattered moral unity, and destroyed the innocent disinterestedness popularly attributed to the conduct of American foreign affairs. Moreover, all this was sanctioned without recourse to a constitutional declaration of war by a Congress representing a citizenry reluctant to undertake foreign military entanglements—a people who as late as 1941 detested the Nazis and their Fascist allies, but still preferred noninvolvement in World War II.

In answering "Why the Vietnam War?" the writer must contend with its corollary: Why would an isolationist and generally honorable people accept a chronic, undeclared, ill-explained foreign war? The answer lies less in the secret decisions of presidents and military leaders and more in the influence of the new communications medium, television, from its infancy in the late 1940s to the emergence of the full-scale Vietnam War by the mid-1960s.

Undoubtedly, the propagandistic thrust of Cold War TV impacted upon a relatively pluralistic culture. Whether from political, religious, philosophical, or nationalistic influences, some Americans held preconceptions about the East-West struggle that no amount of video persuasion could alter, or needed to alter. Despite impediments erected by government and society, it still was possible in these decades to encounter conflicting points of view on the Cold War. However, in a nation growing dependent upon television for its information as well as its entertainment, foreign magazines and newspapers, shortwave broadcasts from overseas, and unbiased books about the world situation were news sources for only a small minority of citizens. Mass America loved and trusted TV. The overwhelming majority of the nation saw and understood the world through television. It was in this relationship between the mass audience and politicized video that the acceptability of the Vietnam War was fashioned.

To be effective, propaganda need not deliver unanimity. What is important is that enough of the manipulated believe—that they "buy" the interpretation of reality being communicated. And just as surely as TV can sell a particular brand of mouthwash or the radial tires of a certain company, it can sell ideology and political policies. Politicians have always appreciated the leverage afforded them by broadcasting. In an earlier time radio was exploited by heads of state from Adolf Hitler to Josef Stalin to Franklin D. Roosevelt. With its melding of sight and sound, television enhanced the manipulative potential of broadcasting. Indeed, Cold War television unrelentingly sold a view of the world—of the noble American role in it and of the destructive subterfuge that was Communism. In this light the Vietnam War seems inevitable because two decades of TV had programmed Americans for such a confrontation.

In writing this book I have relied on the printed sources traditionally important to the reconstruction of television history, particularly *Variety, TV Guide,* and *Broadcasting*, three journals offering a comprehensive view of the video industry. However, the TV historian must deal ultimately with actual programs. This I have accomplished by exploiting my private archive of filmed and recorded TV shows. Since there is no published catalog of these holdings, whenever possible I have cited the dates of their original telecast.

I have been assisted in my research by many people. One of the most inspirational is unknown to me. In 1971 H. J. Kuiper of Gronigen, Holland, sent me a postcard on which was a frightening picture of bodies of people killed in the Vietnam War. On the back my correspondent had written, "What will you tell your children when they ask why you tolerated this war?" In great part, this book explains why I and millions of other Americans tolerated that war.

In more tangible ways, I wish to thank those film and sound-recording collectors who have preserved the history of broadcasting where academic libraries have been remiss. Among those upon whom I relied are J. David Goldin of Sandy Hook, Connecticut, who has always understood the value of recording the present in order to preserve the past, and Larry Urbanski of Chicago, who has found and shared with me some of the richest examples of TV history. Les Waffen of the National Archives was also strategic in providing sound recordings.

Other collectors who helped immeasurably include Harold Doebel, Maury Crane, Barbara Watkins, Omer Whayne, Veto Stasiunaitis, Ernie Rethschulte, Joe Sarno, Scott Zuniga, Bill Morgan, Ward Olander, Richard Manegre, Irv Abelson, Ralph Scull, Stan Margolis, and Kay Salz.

Dr. Alan Blum, editor of the *New York State Journal of Medicine* and a good friend, was singularly helpful. I thank him. I am also grateful to the academics who gave me advice and direction: Bernard S. Bachrach of the University of Minnesota, Todd Gitlin of the University of California at Berkeley, Lewis A. Erenberg of Loyola University of Chicago, and Samuel Betances and C. David Tompkins and Brad Baker of Northeastern Illinois University. I also thank Michael Marsden and Jack Nachbar of Bowling Green State University and of the *Journal of Popular Film and Television* for permission to reprint from my article "The Cold War as Entertainment in 'Fifties Television" (vol. 7, no. 1).

My gratitude is also extended to Nell Musolf and Florence Levy, secretaries for the department of history at Northeastern Illinois University, who spent much of one summer typing manuscript pages.

Finally, I wish to thank my wife, Leslie, for her perceptive ideas and criticisms of this work, and her unflagging support for my research in the history of popular culture. This book is dedicated to her.

CONTENTS

LIST OF TABLES

1

THE EMERGENCE OF POLITICIZED TELEVISION

Television and the Cold War became popular realities in the United States at exactly the same time. With its promise of improving the lives of Americans through wide-ranging programming, TV emerged as a technologically possible and financially affordable mass medium in the late 1940s. Simultaneously, the nation began to experience the generalized political, social, and military fear that resulted from the international rivalry between the United States and the Soviet Union.

Both manifestations were long in arriving. Television had been decades in the making. Throughout its gestation period in the 1920s and 1930s, the medium was heralded as the future arena for free inquiry and inventive diversion, a forum for improving the popular mind as well as entertaining and uplifting mass society. The Cold War, too, had been incubating for decades. And now, in the years immediately following World War II, it condemned the nation to an uncertain future replete with distrust, inhibition, and hatred of an enemy abroad and at home.

The Cold War emerged on several levels. As a geopolitical phenomenon, it was that rivalry between the United States and the Soviet Union—the two nations that finished World War II as superpowers while Western Europe and its colonial empires were fundamentally weakened—on which the balance of world power and the future of global peace rested. As a philosophical struggle it was that contest be-

1

tween liberal-democratic Western society, with its modified capitalistic economic systems, and the Communist Eastern world, with its authoritarian government and collectivist socioeconomic arrangements. And as an unsophisticated struggle for the allegiances of men and women, in the popular American view the Cold War was that struggle between the tyranny of the Iron Curtain and the liberty of the Free World. Again in the American view, it was a moral duel against Communism, an ideology that was despotic, atheistic, and anti-American.

With the end of World War II, almost three decades of development had prepared television for popular acceptance. Ahead were several years of industrial retooling to produce transmission equipment and video receivers. Ahead, too, were technical perfections and improvements in programming breadth and sophistication. Nevertheless, as the nation entered peacetime, it also entered the long-awaited television age. After 1945, TV was becoming available and increasingly affordable. The FCC issued new licenses, private companies erected transmitters. With repeated exposure in such public locations as bars, hotels, restaurants, and the windows of department stores, millions of Americans viewed television for the first time.

For all practical purposes, TV came of age in 1948. That year Ed Sullivan and Milton Berle brought scores of celebrities and overwhelming popular interest to the new medium. That year television entered the homes of average people as manufacturers produced 975,000 sets, an increase of 689 percent over the output for 1946 and 1947 combined. On the four networks in 1948—NBC, CBS, ABC, and Dumont —viewers found more programming and in a wider variety. Importantly, with this mass acceptance of video the broadcasting of news events could no longer be left to the sightless aural world of radio. Television demanded pictures, and television news meant reportage that offered visual images as well as spoken words. With such a mandate, in the late 1940s the Cold War quickly became the nation's first "television war."

That the Cold War and television emerged simultaneously was the result of converging historical trends. That video would soon be consumed by the East-West struggle and become a willing conduit for imagery and rhetoric uncritically supportive of partisan Cold War policies, was the result of still another historical coincidence—the politicization of American broadcasting.

In the decades before World War II, the radio industry developed as a balance between private business and federal regulation. The emphasis, however, was upon broadcasting as free enterprise. Unlike the heavily controlled state systems created in Europe and elsewhere, broadcasting in the United States was primarily self-regulating. There were government rules that stations respected, but for the most part the standards and practices of American radio were products of broadcasters themselves.

In theory government acted as an honest broker. It created and administered standards intended to benefit both industry and citizenry. Federal regulations concerned such matters as the licensing of stations, the strength of broadcast signals, the number of stations allowed in a single geographic area, the hours during which stations were permitted to broadcast, and the community standards that stations were expected to respect. In this way, the federal role was to ensure that commercial rivalries between stations did not harm the industry, and that listener sensitivities were not offended by rude, immoral, or illegal programming.

The federal government was also involved as a producer of programs. As early as December 1920—only one month after the first regular radio broadcast—the Department of Agriculture began airing market reports for farmers. Within four years there were 1,000 stations carrying such government-issued information. Throughout the 1920s federal agencies—including the Children's Bureau of the Department of Labor and the Office of Information of the Agriculture Department —produced radio series. On such programs as "Your Child's Health," "Housekeepers' Chats," and "The Farm and Home Hour" listeners received helpful information, entertainment, and the image of an active and caring government.

During the years of the New Deal, government exploitation of commercial radio increased markedly. Informational programs flowed from the National Park Service, the Department of Commerce, the Social Security Board, and the Works Project Administration. In most instances such programming consisted of useful hints on home maintenance, personal health, government regulations, and the like. In the series produced by the Interior Department's Office of Education, however, the themes were patently political. In shows with titles such as "Gallant American Women," "Democracy in Action," "Let Freedom Ring," and "Americans All-Immigrants All" the Roosevelt administration used radio to popularize its liberal political values.

Federal broadcasting was popular. In 1936 there were 27 agencies regularly producing programs. By 1940 there were 42 such government producers. Further, if the success of the Federal Housing Administration was any indication—82 network hours and 28,160 hours on independent stations in the fiscal year ending June 1937—federal programming on commercial radio was massive.[1] All such broadcasts, moreover, were carried by stations and networks as no-fee, public service programs.

Government officials also made ample use of radio to communicate directly with the public. For example, CBS reported that in addition to paid speeches at election time and guest appearances on discussion shows, between 1929 and 1940 senators and congressmen spoke to its network audiences free of charge on more than 1,200 occasions.[2] Added to this should be the utilization of radio by presidents—Herbert Hoover appeared 139 times on network programs in the period 1930-32, and Franklin D. Roosevelt exploited the medium even more.[3] This reality prompted Carl J. Friedrich and Evelyn Sternberg to conclude in 1943 that politicians "have in radio a potent molder of public opinion—a powerful instrument which can help them to victory or defeat in the next election—and they have used it and will continue to use it to serve their personal fortunes, their parties, and their platforms."[4]

There were no Communists regularly on American radio, although Communist Party candidates purchased air time during election campaigns. Except for WEVD, a local New York City outlet named for Eugene V. Debs, socialists were not heard regularly on capitalistic American radio. Even the Cooperative League, representative of the nation's rural cooperative movement, was barred from advertising on network radio until congressional pressure forced CBS and NBC to compromise. By late 1942 those networks agreed to accept advertisements from cooperatives "as long as their commercial copy advertises a specific product and does not attack other business systems."[5]

Nonetheless, within the spectrum of mainstream, capitalistic politics, American commercial radio did present divergent opinions. In his dinner speeches, addresses to Congress, and fireside chats, President Roosevelt presented the controversial views of his New Deal. Cabinet officers and other administration officials were heard frequently. Roosevelt's political enemies were also on radio. Apostates such as General Hugh S. Johnson and Raymond Moley broadcast their views. Republican critics were heard, as were Democratic nonconformists such as Senator Huey P. Long of Louisiana. Throughout the 1930s Father Charles E. Coughlin railed on CBS, and then on his own ad hoc network, against international bankers, Jews, Franklin D. Roosevelt, and other matters troubling this proto-Fascist priest and political force.

In their varying political viewpoints, network news commentators presented a range of interpretations. On the conservative side, listeners encountered Boake Carter, who in the 1930s attacked the War Department, the U.S. Navy, organized labor, and President Roosevelt. Another prominent conservative was Fulton Lewis, Jr., a thorough isolationist and critic of the New Deal. But radio also featured liberal commentators such as H. V. Kaltenborn, who assailed such matters as Alabama racial injustice and the Francoist side in the Spanish Civil War, a side that enjoyed widespread support in the United States. Similarly, Dorothy Thompson spoke in favor of American involvement in European political and military affairs long before events at Pearl Harbor brought the United States into World War II.

The networks were careful, however, to limit broadcasts of opinion to those news personnel specifically rated as commentators. Newscasters simply reporting events of the day were not allowed to editorialize. And entertainment shows scrupulously avoided politics. The great radio comedians of the 1930s, for instance, seldom told political jokes. With the exception of Will Rogers—whose reputation as a political jester had been established long before he came to radio—the radio clowns who helped listeners escape the doldrums of Depression life did so without joking about American or foreign government leaders, without humorous topical material, and without partisanship.

Network radio eschewed partisan politics in other forms of programming. Drama shows avoided stories involving war, domestic subversion, international intrigue, and governmental maneuvering. Discussion programs were careful to present balanced opinion on controversial matters. Although children's serials may have placed their young heroes abroad, these champions were studiosly uninvolved with the world economic crisis and the rise of Fascism, Communism, and dictatorship in other countries.

Especially in matters of foreign policy, broadcasters sought a balance of acceptable ideas. Even the influence of President Roosevelt did not alter the balance in radio. By the late 1930s, Roosevelt spoke for a more active role for the United States in deteriorating world politics. He floated the idea of quarantining aggressor nations in the Far East. He challenged the Neutrality Act, which required an embargo on arms shipments to belligerent states. In the Atlantic Charter in 1941, he formally aligned the neutral United States with Great Britain, even though the British had been fighting a world war for two years.

Still, while public opinion by the early 1940s gradually moved into agreement with the president, broadcasters maintained their objectivity. Additionally, there were many interest groups to make certain radio remained neutral. Members of the isolationist America First movement monitored news and entertainment programs, and complained to authorities whenever they detected bias. The Republican party also protested when it felt the Roosevelt administration received too much air time for its interventionist ideas.

To guard against criticism, network and local executives reiterated station neutrality even though there was war in Europe, North Africa, and Asia. Importantly, the FCC took a hands-off position, allowing individual broadcasters to solve their own problems regarding news coverage and other programming.

After December 7, 1941, American broadcasting abandoned its careful neutrality, quickly becoming an instrument of support for administration policy. In many ways, too, it became a manipulative medium for government propaganda. This was a crucial development in a nation where the boundary between federal regulation and federal manipulation of broadcasting had been strongly delineated. While this may be understood in terms of wartime exigencies, the politicization of broadcasting that occurred in the early 1940s established a precedent that endured well beyond the end of World War II.

In a certain sense, all radio before Pearl Harbor had been filled with material supportive of the American way of life. In part this resulted from the tendency of broadcasters themselves to support the general values, directions, and institutions of society. Second, because of the commercial nature of mass culture in the United States, it was always necessary for the competitive capitalist media to appeal to customers by reflecting, espousing, and defining attitudes that were popularly shared. In this way the contents of American radio propagated interpretations helpful to bourgeois American society with its liberal-democratic political and social system and its capitalistic economic arrangement. Whether in a formulaic situation comedy or in the interpretation of world news, listeners could anticipate the appearance of themes such as the sanctity of private property, the importance of individualism, the rectitude of the national cause, and the prevailing of justice.

Government involvement in wartime broadcasting took distinct directions: the airing of vital information, the boosting of home-front morale, and the selling of the war itself. Whether through its own productions or by influencing private broadcasters, the government used radio to inform the citizenry about wartime problems. This might entail 30-second announcements regarding the conservation of fuel or rubber, or a request on a network entertainment show for the planting of victory gardens or the saving of scrap metal, old newspapers, magazines, and cooking fats. The Office of War Information was most active in this area. Three times monthly it provided government fact sheets to radio writers. These gave the latest information regarding federal policy on the domestic and international fronts. Thus, a writer wishing to relate his show to wartime realities had the most current positions on such matters as manpower shortages, the need for women to undertake factory work, the course of fighting in the Far East, and monetary fluctuation at home.[6]

Government propagandists also used commercial radio to convince listeners that the United States was right in fighting World War II. The sting of Pearl Harbor did not ensure a lengthy popular commitment to wage a two-front war. The patriotism evidenced on regular network programming was also insufficient to ensure popular acceptance of the war. Instead, the federal government became a producer of propagandistic shows whose intent was to keep domestic morale committed to the national war policies.

Dozens of programs carried out this mission. "The Army Hour" was a music and drama feature program that stirred listeners' emotions throughout the war. "Soldiers with Wings" was a Mutual network presentation that emanated from military installations and featured music, comedy, guest celebrities, a GI audience, and a positive image of the Army Air Corps. "Music for Millions" was a Treasury Department show on which renowned singers and musicians performed to raise money for War Bonds. The most flamboyant of government propaganda pieces, however, was "Treasury Star Parade." This series consisted of more than 300 15-minute programs produced for the Treasury Department and heard in 1942 and 1943 on more than 90 percent of American radio stations. In the hyperbolic rhetoric of propaganda, this show sold War Bonds and American involvement in World War II. The programs were produced in Hollywood and distributed free to all stations willing to air them—whenever and as often as the recipient station desired.

This was radio in the service of government. "Treasury Star Parade" manipulated traditional social values, appealed for domestic unity, painted the enemy as demonic and the Allies as noble. It also intimidated listeners into buying War Bonds and supporting the war—all within a format that was well produced and highly entertaining.[7]

Listeners were told that they, the noble common people, were indispensable, because this was a "little guys' war." As one show explained it, "Hitler ain't fightin' kings and queens, no more. We're the only ones who can win it. . . the little people, all dressed up in our haloes and gas masks." Deep-voiced announcers projected the horrors of Nazi-occupied Chicago, and they spoke of the savagery of the Japanese attack upon Hong Kong. Nazis were associated with arrogance, the enslavement of women and children, and the barbarization of European culture. The Japanese were mentioned in racially disparaging terms that depicted them as monkeylike and subhuman. Consider the words spoken by Fredric March in a program called "A Lesson in Japanese":

> Have you ever watched a well-trained monkey at a zoo? Have you seen how carefully he imitates his trainer? The monkey goes through so many human movements so well that he actually seems to be human. But under his fur, he's still a savage little beast. Now, consider the imitative little Japanese who for seventy-five years has built himself up into something so closely resembling a civilized human being that he actually believes he is just that.

These were emotional times. In many ways World War II threatened the American republic. But the war had begun in 1939 without the United States. For two years, while the official policy in Washington was neutrality, the brutal Nazis and Japanese had been ravaging the British, French, Chinese, Dutch, Polish, Russian, and other peoples. Yet, until the Americans joined the battle, commercial radio reported, but did not dramatize, the inhumanity of the German and Japanese conquests. Thus, rather than an accurate picture of Axis militarism that transcended government policy and public opinion to report the truth, accuracy seemingly had to wait until the United States entered the war. Then, it was rhetorically distorted, charged with emotion, and turned into propaganda supportive of the new government policy.

There were those in government and the military who argued that wartime radio should be placed totally under federal control. They pointed to examples among European and Asian allies where, even before hostilities began, government-owned radio was a reality. By the terms of Article 606 of the Communications Act of 1934, moreover, the president had the legal right to confiscate all broadcasting facilities in time of national calamity. Yet, American radio was not confiscated. Government policy makers opted for an approach offering the best of both situations, maintaining the structure of broadcasting as a privately owned commercial business but inundating the air with propagandistic information and entertainment often produced under the auspices of federal agencies.

Further, while private ownership of stations and networks continued, many broadcasting executives entered government service during the war. The head of the government's principal propaganda agency, the Office of War Information, was Elmer Davis, a respected radio newsman who resigned his position with CBS to direct the OWI. William B. Lewis, a CBS vice-president, also left the corporate world to work in Washington. William S. Paley took a leave of absence as president of CBS to become a radio expert on General Eisenhower's staff as deputy chief of the Office of Psychological Warfare. He left the service a full colonel. David Sarnoff of NBC, for years an officer in the U.S. Army Signal Corps Reserves, entered wartime service and emerged a brigadier general. In this manner the federal government gained experienced and influential broadcasting personnel, and commercial broadcasting was assured sympathetic government "insiders" who respected private ownership and operation of the nation's radio stations and networks.

Government also enlisted the political services of most well-known entertainers. Celebrities from radio, film, popular music, and the stage patriotically lent their energies to the government. Personalities such as Al Jolson, Bob Hope, and Jack Benny visited American troops at home and overseas under the auspices of the USO. Kate Smith, Eddie Cantor, and Ralph Edwards were among the most successful campaigners for War Bonds. Special projects, such as the "Committee of 25," utilized the talents of Nelson Eddy, Kay Kyser, Jean Hersholt, George Burns and Gracie Allen, and others in morale- and fund-raising ventures.

This politicization of American entertainment was most pronounced in broadcasting. Here the federal government overstepped the boundary between regulation and manipulation, and became a prolific programmer throughout the war. Less than six months after Pearl Harbor, listeners were being bombarded with messages from the Departments of War, Treasury, Labor, and Justice—as well as from the Office of Emergency Management, the Office of Civilian Defense, and the Office of the Coordinator of Inter-American Affairs. During the period May through July 1942, for example, radio stations carried 1,541,640 spot announcements and 186,075 live and transcribed programs, all supporting the national war effort. This represented a total of 35,995 free hours of air time given to the government.[8]

The government also was concerned about programming it did not oversee. Although no harsh censorship laws were enforced, Washington depended upon an admixture of federal guidelines for broadcasters and self-censorship by the industry. In January 1942 the Office of Censorship issued the Code of Wartime Practice for American Broadcasters. It urged stations to censor news reports, ad-lib talk or audience participation shows, and foreign language programs—especially those in German and Italian. Broadcasters avoided references to the weather, fortifications, troop and matériel movements, casualty lists, war-related experiences, and the like. This censorship—in part self-imposed by American journalists and in part a required reaction to the Code of Wartime Practice—was justified as a precautionary measure. Its purpose was to frustrate domestic spies and saboteurs, as well as enemy military and naval commanders wishing to use commercial radio to communicate secret messages.

Radio cooperated fully with government during World War II. In a speech in 1950 at the FBI National Academy, Niles Trammell, chairman of the board of NBC, reflected on the closeness of commercial broadcasting to the war effort:

> Radio in the United States shouldered arms and, together with the American people and American industry, geared itself for total war. Throughout the long years until victory was won, it carried the responsibility of broadcasting for the United States government. The story of its contribution is too large ever to be recorded in its entirety. Every wartime effort found its support in radio . . . . in every area of the war effort . . . American radio proved itself a mighty weapon in the nation's service. . . .[9]

The relationship between commercial broadcasting and government was altered by the experiences of World War II. While propagandistic excesses might have been rationalized as aberrations of those dire war years, the lessons of that era were applied to postwar American politics. Government would rely on radio, and soon television, to create consensus and support for its policies. Networks and stations would offer politicized programming in harmony with government policies. This was particularly true of federal efforts at thwarting the perceived threat from Communism and its political henchmen in the Soviet Union, China, Eastern Europe, and elsewhere.

In this Cold War era, government would consistently use the air to persuade the nation. From the development of public relations images to the enlistment of mass support for specific decisions, national leaders relied increasingly on broadcasting to reach the widest audience in the shortest time. Broadcasters, in turn, eager to demonstrate their loyalty and to continue the struggle against those they felt would destroy the American way of life, offered their facilities and energies in the crusade.

Interestingly, the first great postwar test of this new cooperativeness occurred at exactly the time television was emerging as a popular medium, and the wartime alliance of the United States and the Soviet Union was disintegrating into an East-West struggle. Now the politicized broadcasting industry quietly stepped back while government purged the entertainment world of liberal and leftist personalities it felt to be subversive. Liberal-thinking entertainers had been warmly hailed when the national enemy was rightist Fascism. But in the postwar period, the new enemy was leftist Communism.

The impetus for national purification in this "Red scare" came from the House Committee on Un-American Activities (HUAC), which went immediately for highly visible and newsworthy targets—celebrities in the motion picture and broadcasting industries. Some bona fide Communists were uncovered. Some ex-Communists confessed their prior politics and named other party members. There were also those who had never been Communists, but who felt they knew colleagues who were party members—and also named names. No bomb throwers or spies or sellers of military secrets were discovered. But HUAC did find a few idealistic actors, directors, and screenwriters who felt the Democrats and Republicans were impotent during the Depression and, wanting to stop the rise of Fascism, joined the only outspokenly anti-Fascist party in the United States, the Communist Party of the United States (CPUSA).

The broadcast industry readily fell in with the government purgists. Entertainers adversely touched by the hearings found themselves blacklisted from radio and, more important, the burgeoning new medium, television. It made little difference to broadcasters if, in the jargon of the day, these political deviates were "card-carrying members" (actual dues-paying members of the CPUSA), "dupes" (those fooled into supporting Red goals without realizing the error of their ways), "Pinkos" (those who were leftists, but not Red enough), or "Comsymps" or "fellow travelers" (those who sympathized with Communist ends without joining the party). The CPUSA was considered to be an arm of the Soviet Union, not a legitimate political party springing from the fabric of American society. Those said to be associated with Communism, then, were considered anti-American conspirators. They were unwelcome in broadcasting. In this way the entertainment business became a political arena in which Cold War fears and ignorance became the basis for exclusionary professional policy. This was to be expected in a business that had been heavily politicized during the war.

Beginning in the late 1940s, television amalgamated these several historical developments. As the United States entered the Cold War and the age of video, it did so in an atmosphere of anti-Communist fear that gained persuasive popular expression in TV. Now a politicized industry, broadcasting quickly espoused the anti-Communism of the times. As the following chapters will demonstrate, in news and entertainment programming television presented Americans a picture of world affairs in which the honest, selfless United States was forced to defend the Free World against the barbarous onslaught of Communism—with its godless ideologues and automaton commissars intent upon conquering the planet. Those not wholeheartedly in favor of the national crusade were often suspected of being at least tolerant of the evil enemy. It was an oversimplified picture. But in the context of the United States at midcentury, it was widely perceived as genuine.

2

COLD WAR POLITICS IN NEWS
AND INFORMATION PROGRAMMING

Television was apolitical at birth. It was the product of scientists and engineers establishing new technological boundaries, and businessmen seeking a profit-making utility. To a degree TV was American, but throughout the 1930s British research often was more advanced than that in the United States. In Europe government financial support assisted technology. In the United States the fiscal foundations of video rested in the world of free enterprise.

The programs on television in the United States, however, were of great political significance. These were Americanized products. Whether it was a detective show, romantic play, newscast, Western, children's show, or even a commercial, the content of TV programming reflected the environment in which it was created. This meant that TV mirrored the mentality of most of the nation. And given the commercial nature of the medium—programs were meant to attract the largest possible audiences and sell sponsors' products—television sought to present materials with which a majority of viewers would be comfortable.

Every time a policeman or private eye captured, reformed, or killed a criminal in a detective story, TV communicated the message that crime does not pay. Every time a boy met a girl, lost her, then regained her, the program promoted the importance of personal fulfillment in romantic love. Inherent in every religious broadcast was endorsement of freedom of religion. Whenever a child on TV followed the command of an adult, that show communicated to youngsters the validity of obedience. Even news programs had an American slant, focusing primarily upon what transpired at home—be it the local town, the state, or the nation—or upon external matters impacting upon the United States.

As surely as a child's fairy tale—whether spoken, read, on film, or in a radio dramatization—TV shows communicated educative moral lessons and imparted values strategic to the viability of American society. Since the smooth operation of society was the goal of politics, TV was necessarily political.

For the most part these programs were authentic cultural phenomena, created by and for people generally sharing a perspective on social life. There were censors, however, at network and production levels to ensure that program content adhered to such a perspective. There were community tastes, network standards and practices, and industry codes that had to be met by creative personnel. In most cases such censorship involved matters of vulgarity or graphic violence. But the history of American television is not without instances of political censorship touching upon matters as diverse as racial politics, foreign policy, and the sensitivities of military and government leaders.

Whether news-related or entertainment, American TV programming from its inception was political. This was especially the case in the former, where in a multiplicity of ways viewers were shown the world through politicized cameras. Since one of the dreams of the developers of television had been to bring news and information into the homes of all Americans, it was inevitable that this communication would reflect the values of those airing it and those viewing it. A study of the nonfiction programming from the late 1940s and into the 1960s clearly illustrates that the video road to the Vietnam War was paved in part by the distorted understanding of the nation and world transmitted by nonfiction television.

TELEVISION IN POLITICAL CONTEXT

There was much about which to be excited in those first years of television. After decades of anticipation, the promise had become real and available. Now the world would be seen in the average American living room. Now there would be information and entertainment in this home theater. Most agreed that the United States—the entire planet, for that matter—would be a better place for having television.

Industry spokesman were quick to trumpet the significance of their achievements. For M. H. Aylesworth, former president of RCA, the new medium was the greatest single phenomemon to emerge in the past century—superior to the automobile, airplane, or any other technological invention.[1] Allen B. Dumont, one of the developers of the industry, envisioned television strengthening the bridge between nations and complementing international linkages such as trade, transportation, and other forms of communication. With TV as the catalyst, Dumont wrote in 1950, "These links will be so tightly welded that the economic, cultural, educational, linguistic, entertainment, and technological interdependence between the nations of the world may well solve problems that have resisted the bonds of pacts and treaties."[2]

Another proud parent was Niles Trammell of NBC. For him, TV was "a scientific marvel which, like the harnessing of the atom, is unparalleled in history." He proclaimed in 1950 that television was a great business venture, for "Already American private enterprise is building television stations in South America and is furnishing equipment to European nations." Above all, Trammell praised TV as a "mighty weapon for understanding between nations and races" because, through its programs, TV would show the commonality of mankind, "that essential human understanding that all people share."[3]

These were statements of pride as much as of salesmanship made by men who had nurtured the medium. Yet, inherent in many such analyses was a strong political message: television had great potential for influencing the nation and the world, and in the Cold War it would play a strategic role in enhancing the American position.

This was a notion well comprehended at NBC. Of all the networks, executives of NBC were outspoken in their political perspectives on the medium. As early as 1946, network vice-president John F. Royal, who anticipated TV becoming "the most important public relations medium in our history," called for "typical red-blooded American programs of a clean and wholesome and cultural nature."[4] Five years later Frank M. Folsom, president of the parent company, RCA, wrote that TV was "in the forefront as a vital service to the nation." He argued that during this time of war in Korea, television was crucial as an information source "when swiftly changing events may otherwise cause confusion and alarm to the detriment of unity of purpose in safeguarding the democratic insitutions of our land and our determination to assist other freedom-loving people against aggression."[5]

In August 1951, NBC joined CBS in setting up large color TV screens in West Berlin, hoping to counter Communist influence during the World Festival of Youth being held in East Berlin. With 2 million people from throughout the world attending, the American networks acceded to the wishes of the State Department by providing the latest in color video as a "secret weapon" to thwart propagandistic claims of Communist technological superiority.[6]

Sylvester L. (Pat) Weaver wrote in 1953 on the importance of television as a molder of domestic ideology. The president of NBC noted that because "our shows can serve purposes beyond diversion" and because of "the tremendous influence we know we have on viewers," producers at NBC were "constantly vigilant to choose those subjects and those characters which will serve to illuminate the problems of our times, and the character of our fundamental beliefs." According to Weaver this meant programming " 'within the area of American agreement,' with all the implications of that statement, including however some acknowledgement in our programming of the American heritage of dissent."[7]

No one in the fledgling industry better understood the anti-Communist potential of TV than Brigadier General David Sarnoff, chairman of the board of RCA. Broadcast pioneer, business giant, and patriot, Sarnoff strongly bound television to national political goals. As head of the Armed Forces Communications Association, he told Army officers and engineers in 1948 that video would play a major role in any future war. By employing TV in guided missiles, remote-controlled explosives, and pilotless bombers—in mapmaking, reconnaissance, and observing dangerous operations from protected positions—Sarnoff felt "We will make a worthwhile contribution to military preparedness and to national security."[8]

Certainly, Sarnoff comprehended television as a nonpolitical business venture. Yet in the fall of 1948, on an NBC radio program, "Living—1948," he declared that television had a political dimension, for "Through its proper use, America will rise to new heights as a nation of free people and high ideals." By 1950 Sarnoff was calling for the employment of television as part of a network of anti-Communist propaganda media communicating a "Marshall Plan of Ideas" around the world. "The Communists smother the truth with their falsehoods," Sarnoff told an audience in the summer of 1950. "Through radio and television, the motion picture and the printed word, we have a great opportunity to reveal the truth to the rest of the world. We must expose [their] lies and spike [their] false propaganda."[9]

Sarnoff's political expectations for TV were most fully delineated in April 1955, when he presented President Dwight D. Eisenhower with a 42-page memorandum entitled "Program for a Political Offensive Against World Communism." It was a guidebook for the spread of American propaganda to the world via TV and other media of communication. It was conceived primarily as a counterattack against global Communist propaganda.

In Sarnoff's view, the West and the other non-Communist areas of the world were being swamped with Red propaganda. It came in literature, sports contests, United Nations activities, and myriad other forms. The head of RCA was also upset by Communist agents—"thousands of Kremlin-oriented individual writers, commentators, editors, and trained propagandists"—who were being smuggled into strategic social positions where they supported Soviet policies. Further, Sarnoff lashed out against fellow travelers, those "newspapers, magazines, radio and TV stations, either overtly under pro-Communist control or in 'liberal' disguises."

Sarnoff called for a massive counterthrust against the Red menace. He advocated the use of TV, film, radio, leaflets, balloons, secret presses, even "scrawls on the wall" to spread the American message. He wanted fixed and mobile broadcasting stations surrounding the Soviet Union. He wanted cheap, lightweight radios distributed free of charge behind the Iron Curtain and in other critical areas. He asked for large-screen TV—color or black and white—in Asia and elsewhere to show American propaganda to impressionable natives. Sarnoff also called for free phonographs to be smuggled to people living under the domination of Russia and Communist China. Pro-American propaganda would then be placed on unbreakable cardboard phonograph records, flown behind the Iron Curtain and the Bamboo Curtain, and dropped from the skies like leaflets.[10]

While statements by network officials illustrate clearly that industry leaders understood the Cold War potential of television, such assessments were not confined to TV executives. American government leaders also welcomed TV as a political utility. Their early comments ranged from predictions that TV would change politics—no more long-winded speeches, the eventual merchandising of candidates through TV advertising, greater voter participation because of exposure of candidates and their views—to more practical suggestions, such as one senator's plan for members of Congress to disperse throughout the country in case of atomic attack but still vote on legislation via TV.[11] Most, however, would have agreed with the general point made in 1949 by J. Edgar Hoover, director of the Federal Bureau of Investigation, that "The advent of television offers a new adjunct to law and order, and I see in this new medium an instrumentality of great aid and assistance in the future protection of society."[12]

Government leaders also appreciated the propagandistic importance of TV. When the "Kraft Television Theater" in 1948 aired a play in which a senator took bribes and conspired with a private power company to defeat a public power project, a congressman publicly warned that television needed self-censorship because such a program was "excellent Communist propaganda."[13] Thus, early in the history of the medium, government pressure was exerted to assure the "loyalty" of the imagery offered on TV.

With a broader perspective, Senator Karl Mundt in 1950 proposed the creation of an agency for televising government propaganda abroad. This "Vision of America," according to the senator, would complement the Voice of America radio agency. It would be a "see bomb" producing anti-Communist values by televising Americanism around the world. In Mundt's words, "If we could supplement our know-how with some concentrative, repetitive, understandable, sympathetic and practical show-how, we could improve the lot of mankind and at the same time we might well arouse mass sympathetic desire to embrace the philosophy of freedom and democracy which has made all this possible."[14]

For Paul G. Hoffman—former president of the Studebaker Corporation, and after 1948 director of the Economic Cooperative Administration, which coordinated Marshall Plan aid for postwar European recovery—broadcasting was crucial in the Cold War. "On the international front of the struggle between the free world and the Kremlin slave world we are outmanned 50 to 1," he declared in 1950. Further, he asserted, in each country there existed a "hard core of Communists" seeking "to capture the minds of people by the well-known Goebbels method. They use the big lie—they make glittering promises—but above all they seek to instill fear and hatred." Hoffman called upon American broadcasters to counter the threat of world Communism: "As I see it, your responsibility is to develop the techniques by which an understanding of intangible truths can be brought home to all the people. It is your responsibility to find the words that will not only inform but will, to quote Kipling, walk up and down in the hearts of men."[15]

Interpretations such as those expressed by industry and government leaders in the first years of video were not the musings of conspirators anxious to manipulate the medium for personal aggrandizement. Instead, they were ideas reflecting the era in which TV was maturing. TV emerged at the time of the Berlin blockade and airlift. Only weeks before that confrontation, the Communists had usurped power in Czechoslovakia. Without the firing of a shot, that country became a Communist state solidly within the Soviet sphere of influence.

Resolution of the Berlin crisis effectively ended Communist expansion in Europe. When unrestricted contact with West Berlin was finally restored in May 1949, the political condition of Europe was stalemated. The German nation would remain divided between East and West. As inconvenient and expensive as it was to maintain, West Berlin would continue to be a democratic half-city deep inside the Communist empire. The Free World would no longer "lose" territory in Europe.

But there were other crises. From Chile and Algeria to Iran and Indochina, there were confrontations between Communists and anti-Communists. Not minding that anti-Communist forces might be brutally undemocratic or antinationalistic, American policy makers often found themselves uncritically supporting right-wing dictatorships rather than accept leftist solutions. In some cases even captured Nazi officials were exonerated and employed by the American government in anti-Communist operations. Senator Mundt explained this policy on the public affairs show "American Forum of the Air," televised August 19, 1950. Speaking of foreign aid recently voted for the authoritarian government of Generalissimo Francisco Franco, the senator told viewers:

> The reason the loan to Spain was essential is because in a worldwide warfare against Communism, we have to work with people who are on our side, people that control the beachheads so essential if we're going to land troops in Europe. We have to work with people who will stand up and fight against Communism, just as in the war against Hitler we had to make an alliance with Russia in order to defeat Hitler. This time we have to work with types of government which we do not approve in order to be sure we can defeat this menace of world Communism.

Western imperialism was dying in the postwar world. The upshot of two world wars was the destruction of British, French, Dutch, Spanish, Belgian, and Portuguese colonial empires. Moreover, the process of disintegration often was accelerated by native rebellions in Asia and Africa.

Ironically, the chief American allies against Communism were those nations rapidly losing imperial power. Although itself born of armed revolution and committed to the notion of self-determination of nations, the United States found itself pitted against colonial rebels and supporting European imperialists. Every blow against colonialism was a blow against American power. Every embarrassment of an imperial nation weakened the U.S.-European alignment against Communism.

The Soviet Union had no difficulty identifying with anticolonial revolutionaries. In many cases the leadership of native movements was Communist. The Cold War was a struggle for leverage in an unstable postwar world. With Western Europe and the United States arrayed against it, the Soviet Union found it both politically advantageous and ideologically fulfilling to champion the liberation movements in the Third World.

Besides being tied to imperialistic allies, U.S. policy generally was hostile to social change precipitated by the political left. It did not matter that radicals had legitimate reasons for revolting, or that native nationalism was not necessarily Communistic. While they might favor orderly democratization under selected pro-Western native leaders, American policy makers did not require social freedom as a prerequisite for political or military support. A strong anti-Communist was preferred by Washington over a liberal, socialistic or even neutralist leader. Any movement toward democracy coming from the radical left was almost automatically opposed.

Innocently and often ineptly, American foreign policy emerged from centuries of noninvolvement in great-power international politics. Now the linchpin of the anti-Communist bloc, the United States quickly asserted itself around the globe. Presidents found bipartisan support for their foreign policies as Democrats and Republicans sought to show the world that the United States was solidly committed to a nonisolationist course of action. Indeed, George Washington's venerated dictum about avoiding entangling alliances was abandoned. By the end of the 1950s, the Americans had organized bilateral and multilateral anti-Communist alliances throughout the world—among them the North Atlantic Treaty Organization (NATO), the Organization of American States (OAS), the Central Treaty Organization (CENTO), and the Southeast Asia Treaty Organization (SEATO).

The men who early defined the political nature of television were solidly a part of the American system. As such they were committed to a conservative understanding of the need for process. In the corporate world view, social change had to be orderly, evolutionary. With vested interests in a world arrangement that were moral and psychological, as well as economic and political, these men felt especially threatened by the course of events following World War II.

The Cold War was a threatening development. Regardless of which side "caused" the confrontation, the fact remained that a polarized planet of mutually distrustful ideologies created a situation of general anxiety. At home this meant real fears of invasion or nuclear sneak attack. Afraid of subversion by a rival ideology, Americans lashed out at suspected Communist influences. In some of its more ludicrous forms, this translated into attacks against the fluoridation of drinking water, which was seen as a Red plot to weaken the health of Americans. Books such as *Robin Hood* were banned from public libraries. In New York a divorce could be granted if one spouse charged that the other was a Communist.

But there were more ominous manifestations of domestic public fear. Dissent was effectively stifled. Police spies abounded, as did neighbors eager to inform on "suspicious" neighbors. Governments at all levels demanded loyalty oaths from millions. For purposes of employment, businesses had blacklists of suspected political deviates, and "whitelists" of the politically reliable. The careers of teachers, librarians, singers, actors, journalists, scientists, writers, and other professionals were interruped or destroyed in this era of social purge.

Contrary to what J. Edgar Hoover in 1949 had wished from TV, this time of fearfulness compromised law and order. Guilt by association or innuendo frequently replaced due process of law. Men and women were persecuted and even prosecuted, not for crimes but for ideas. As David Caute has argued so effectively in *The Great Fear*, his study of the period, the true target of this social rage was

> the Enemy—the Alien, the Nonconformist, the Critical Force. Here then was a palpable lack of trust in the Other, who he was, where he came from, what dark gods he might worship in his strange language, and whether he was qualified as a good American or a dangerous "un-American."[16]

Anxieties of the Cold War—plus residual distrust from the New Deal years and World War II—compromised American social freedoms at exactly the moment the nation appealed to the non-Communist world in terms of the preferability of liberty. The nation that had carved civil freedom into its legal foundations now failed to abide by its own ethics. This led Joseph L. Mankiewicz, president of the Screen Directors Guild, to decry in September 1950 the attack upon liberalism. "As much as the Negro or the Jew, as much as any other minority in the U.S.," he claimed, the American liberal is being "slandered, libeled, persecuted, and threatened with extinction." He continued, "The American liberal is being hounded, persecuted, and annihilated today—deliberately destroyed by an organized enemy as evil in practice and purpose—and indistinguishable from—the Communist menace that fosters and encourages that destruction."[17] This philosophical and professional destruction was most evident in the blacklisting of TV entertainers whose names became associated with Communism.

Following the lead of the House Committee on Un-American Activities, anti-Communist privateers had focused their energies on "exposing" the Red-tainted backgrounds of people associated with the motion picture industry. Their earliest medium of revelation was a weekly four-page tabloid, *Counterattack: The Newsletter of Facts to Combat Communism*. Founded in 1947 by three former FBI agents, this publication attacked "Commies," "quislings," and "dupes" in Hollywood. It named "Communist front" organizations, many of which the U.S. attorney general did not consider subversive. It called for the blacklisting of "traitorous" actors, producers, directors, announcers, writers, and others in the entertainment world. In this time of Cold War fear, it mattered little that *Counterattack* charges were unsubstantiated, distorted, out of context, based on rumor, or culled from questionable newspaper citations.

Soon, however, the purgists were looking for Red influence specifically in broadcasting. On August 10, 1950, on a WOR-TV panel discussion about Communist traitors in American society, the managing editor of *Counterattack*, Ted Kirkpatrick, spoke bluntly to his audience. He warned that a few Reds could influence thousands of innocent citizens. He revealed that Communists were infiltrating American life—from trade unions to PTA organizations. Kirkpatrick added that this infiltration "extends into radio and television. Yes, to a great extent in radio and television."

Network executives, local stations, advertisers and advertising agencies, even theatrical professionals cooperated in creating blacklists for television. The main instrument for ascertaining an employee's adherence to "the American way of life" was the loyalty oath. Since the mid-1940s, for example, NBC had required loyalty statements from all new workers. CBS went on step further. In December 1950 that network required all its paid personnel to answer the following questions:

(1) Are you now, or have you ever been, a member of the Communist Party, U.S.A., or any Communist organization?
(2) Are you now, or have you ever been, a member of a Fascist organization?

(3) Are you now, or have you ever been, a member of any organization, association, movement, group or combination of persons which has adopted a policy of advocacy or approving the commission of acts of force or violence to deny other persons their rights under the Constitution of the United States, or seeking to alter the form of government of the United States by unconstitutional means?[18]

Those answering any of the queries affirmatively were instructed to "make any explanation you desire regarding your membership or activities therein."

Most employees signed the oaths. A few refused for various reasons. Those not cooperating, however, resigned or were discharged. Fred Freed, a leading documentary producer at NBC in the 1960s, worked for CBS during the "Red scare." He explained the fear that compelled men and women to violate their rights and consciences by signing the oaths: "I suppose finally we were afraid. If you made a stand on principle and got fired for it, you'd be out of the business. That would be the end of your career. It wasn't just a job you were concerned about, it was your life's work. But I'm not sure that was any excuse."[19]

To assist employers in identifying "subversives" in their midst, in June 1950 a new publication—a 213-page booklet, *Red Channels: The Report of Communist Influence in Radio and Television*—named 151 celebrities from the popular arts and culture as being involved in pro-Communist activities. As *Red Channels* explained, "The Cominform and the Communist Party USA now rely more on radio and TV than on the press and motion pictures as 'belts' to transmit pro-Sovietism to the American public."[20]

Jean Muir had been hired to play the mother in a video version of the hit radio series "The Aldrich Family." But she was listed in *Red Channels*. One week before the show was to premiere in September 1950, Muir was dropped from the program because General Foods, the sponsor, did not want controversial actresses associated with Jello. Ireene Wicker—17 years on radio and 2 years on TV as hostess of the popular children's show "The Singing Lady"—was also named in *Red Channels*. Although she pleaded her innocence of all charges, she was abruptly dropped by Kellogg's, her long-time sponsor. And after two years on TV, in the fall of 1951 General Foods demanded and received the termination of Philip Loeb from his role as Jake Goldberg in "The Goldbergs." Loeb, too, had been named in *Red Channels*.[21]

Two entertainers said to be "pro-Communist in sympathy"—Paul Draper, a tap dancer, and Larry Adler, a harmonica player—appeared on Ed Sullivan's "Toast of the Town" in January 1950. Sullivan quickly offered a public apology to the Ford Motor Company and its ad agency, Kenyon & Eckhardt. From that experience, Sullivan learned to clear controversial performers through Ted Kirkpatrick. By 1954 Sullivan was calling for the entertainment industry to establish a board to review the political loyalty of accused entertainers, so that "If they can't clear themselves, the industry can blacklist them with a clear conscience."[22]

Adler and Draper were banned from television. Wicker had another sponsored children's show in the 1953-54 season, but when it was canceled, she left TV. Jean Muir did not work on television until December 1960.[23] Philip Loeb, despondent over his failed career, committed suicide in 1955.

Hundreds of creative personalities were proscribed from TV in the 1950s and into the following decade. A few, such as Lucille Ball and Gypsy Rose Lee, were powerful enough to fight the charges, prove them baseless, and continue their careers. Others, including Canada Lee, Lee Grant, Paul Robeson, Hazel Scott, Louis Untermeyer, Joseph Papp, and the folk group The Weavers, lacked the mass popularity with which to counteract and overcome their blacklisting.

Interestingly, no crimes were committed by those who were banned from TV. None ever went to trial or was found guilty of breaking a law. None went to prison or was deported. But in this time of loyalty oaths and distorted reactions to Communism, these blacklisted celebrities had histories of support for liberal causes. That was their crime. Erik Barnouw has written understandingly of these "crimes" of human concern:

> They had opposed Franco, Hitler, and Mussolini, tried to help war refugees, combatted race discrimination, campaigned against poll taxes and other voting barriers, opposed censorship, criticized the House committee on un-American activities, hoped for peace, and favored efforts toward better U.S. Soviet relations. Most had been New Deal supporters. Some had favored Henry Wallace. They had backed lost causes. They had used the neglected right of petition. Many had perhaps been naive.[24]

Blacklisting and the hunt for subversives in prominent places continued throughout the 1950s. As late as March 1957, a Senate committee headed by James O. Eastland of Mississippi issued a report titled "Communists in Mass Communications and in Political Activities." Into the early 1960s, moreover, the House Committee on Un-American Activities held contentious public hearings in its search for Communists and their sympathizers.

Few broadcast journalists seemed willing or able—or courageous enough—to report on the personal injustices created by blacklisting and related censorial activities. The TV networks that maintained lists certainly did not favor such reportage. Not until the late 1950s—on Edward R. Murrow's "Small World" program of March 8, 1959, when Murrow involved Ingrid Bergman, Darryl F. Zanuck, and critic Bosley Crowther in a discussion of the phenomenon—was blacklisting broached with candor by CBS.[25]

More forthrightly, however, ABC received a special Peabody Award in 1951 for its resistance to outside political pressure. Presented to network president Robert Kintner and his associates Robert Saudek and Joseph McDonald, this prestigous award from the School of Journalism of the University of Georgia praised the network and its officials, according to *Broadcasting*, "for a firm stand at a time when stations and networks were firing or refusing to hire writers and actors on the basis of 'unsupported inneundoes' in the publication *Red Channels*."[26]

Two years later, in accepting a Peabody Award for his reporting, ABC newsman Martin Agronsky spoke frankly of journalistic silence and the blacklists. He recalled the words of Robert Kintner, spoken upon receiving the Peabody Award in 1951, that "Where there is smoke, there need not necessarily be a fire, but just a smoke machine, or perhaps a vote machine." Agronsky continued:

> The irrational fears and emotions that psychiatrists tell us are the usual product of the tensions under which we all live these days, do not make easy the job of those reporters who conceive it their duty to keep looking through the smoke to see whether it comes from a fire, or whether it is just spewed out by the smoke machine operators, burning their trash and rubbish. And if there are those who think this an inconsequential duty, they might usefully remember the one freedom which the great Chief Justice Holmes denied to even the most passionate libertarians when he wrote this—"No one has the right to yell fire in a crowded theater." Reporters who try to make people aware of those who would arrogate themselves this dangerous kind of right—which Justice Holmes decried—are more often criticized than rewarded. For that reason, I sincerely hope this honor from my fellow fire wardens of the Peabody Board will constitute an encouragement to reporters everywhere to report what they see exactly as they see it. I can think of no more useful service a reporter can perform.[27]

TV NEWS AND THE KOREAN WAR

As a medium of popular enlightenment and in-depth explanation of actualities, early television was unspectacular. Newscasts in the late

1940s were primitive affairs, usually consisting of a man reading copy at his desk, a series of still pictures, charts, and maps, plus film footage of recent events. The networks had no experience at blending aural and visual material. There were early problems with obtaining, processing, and distributing current film. In many instances networks incurred the displeasure of theatrical newsreel companies. For years the latter had filmed national and international events, and edited compilation newsreels for theaters throughout the nation. Television was a threat. Should it ever develop its photographic potential, TV could render newsreel companies obsolete.

TV news seems to have had little importance for early audiences. A survey in 1948 showed that more than 46 percent of set owners preferred comedy-variety programs. The rate for TV news was 2.3 percent. When asked what they would like to see on television that was not then available, 22.7 percent named new and better movies, while those wanting more of the latest news totaled 1.2 percent.[28]

TV news improved at a slow pace. In mid-1948, CBS newsman Robert Trout admitted that "There is a lot of experimenting to do before the perfect television news technique is evolved."[29] Five years later *Variety* reported industry criticism that claimed "Television, in the news field, is not providing enough variety or depth of understanding in its coverage of world events."[30] By late 1957 that trade journal contended that while "methods for gathering the news and putting it on the air are improving all the time, the actual visualization process is, if not deteriorating, at a standstill."[31]

Despite early audience indifference, TV news developed a following that relied increasingly on television as a source of its news. Although network newscasts continued until 1963 to be only 15 minutes nightly, in 1948 news-related broadcasts accounted for 15.3 percent of the NBC program schedule.[32] By the middle of the following year, "The Camel News Caravan" with John Cameron Swayze—on NBC until replaced in 1956 by "The Huntley-Brinkley Report"—was the highest-rated multiweekly evening show on TV. By the end of 1957 "Douglas Edwards and the News" on CBS reached more than 14.1 million viewers daily and almost 34 million people at least once a week, while NBC news with Chet Huntley and David Brinkley reached more than 7.6 million homes nightly. Interestingly, comparative figures placed *Time* magazine at 8.1 million weekly readers, and *Life* reached 30.4 million each week.[33]

If network news was slow to develop thorough reportage, local news programming was even more stunted in its growth. This was especially the case in telecasting news film. Even in the mid-1950s local advertisers were reluctant to spend the large sums needed to produce first-rate news shows. Few local outlets could afford mobile units to gather and transmit from the site of a news story, and video-tape was not in wide use until the end of the decade. Local stations usually purchased film from CBS or NBC, or from commercial news-reel producers such as Telenews Productions or United Press-Fox Movietone.

What television news could do well, almost from the beginning, was broadcast well-contained historic events, panel discussions, and documentaries. The presidential nominating conventions of the Democratic and Republican parties were televised in 1948. In 1949 CBS telecast live debates from the United Nations meeting in Lake Success, New York. One of the early highlights of live coverage was the signing of a peace treaty with Japan. Aired live from San Francisco in September 1951 to 94 of the 108 stations in the United States, this television event inaugurated the coaxial-microwave link making possible live nationwide transmission.

Early TV also demonstrated its potential to inform the public about government activities. The most significant event of these first years was live coverage of the Senate investigation of organized crime. Chaired by Senator Estes Kefauver of Tennessee, the Senate Crime Investigating Committee held hearings in February and March of 1951 that involved the top figures in the underworld. TV brought the spectacle to the nation. Not only did the networks preempt morning and afternoon programs for this coverage, they illustrated the power of the new medium to inform. Importantly, audiences responded. One audience survey in March found every set in New York City tuned in to the hearings. Chicago television realized its largest audiences. Factories and businesses in Minneapolis blamed the hearings for increased employee absenteeism. When Kefauver focused the questioning on organized crime in the automobile industry, TV in Detroit experienced a record number of viewers.[34]

Another news-related format that TV handled well was the panel discussion program. This genre, involving newsmakers and journalists, evolved in radio in the 1920s and thrived in video from the beginning. By the early 1950s several mainstays, such as "Meet the Press" and "American Forum of the Air" on NBC, and "America's Town Meeting of the Air" on ABC, were broadcast simultaneously on radio and television. Some were aired in prime time. The panel discussion was inexpensive to produce, timely to watch, and frequently made news.

As might be expected, TV also generated its own discussion programs, among them "Chronoscope" and "Face the Nation" on CBS; "On Trial," "Answers for Americans," "Open Hearing," and "Press Conference" on ABC; and "The Big Issue" and "Court of Current Issues" on Dumont.

The nascent medium also developed the documentary. On radio this format was not fully realized until the postwar years, when wire-recording and tape-recording facilitated the gathering and editing of the sounds of actuality. Filmed documentaries appeared on TV as early as June 1949, when ABC aired a "telementary" concerning the Marshall Plan and the economic redevelopment of postwar Europe. A year later the producers of "Studio One" on CBS began regularly including filmed documentaries among their weekly live dramas.

Many involved with the TV documentary shared with CBS producer Fred W. Friendly an optimistic outlook for the genre. Speaking in July 1951, Friendly said the documentary "gives promise not only of being part of the television anatomy but its very backbone." He alleged that, because this format changed with the events it covered, it would never grow stale. Most important, however, Friendly reiterated the great expectations for TV as a news medium when he said of the documentary:

> Television will command the biggest audiences in the history of communications. It will enable the American people to be the best informed people in the world, or the worst, depending upon how well we make use of it. . . . For if we are to hold up a mirror to the world with one hand, and a microphone with the other, we must be worthy of conducting the greatest mass information gazette in the history of man. To use it simply as another method of peddling soup and peanut butter will be to destroy a reporting, and therefore selling, opportunity never handed to any race of men.[35]

The Korean War began at 4 A.M. on June 25, 1950 (2 P.M., June 24 in Washington, D.C.), when troops of the Communist government of the Democratic People's Republic of [North] Korea invaded the Republic of [South] Korea. From a nationalistic perspective, this was a civil war between rival regimes intent upon reuniting the Korean peninsula. Korea had been a divided nation since 1945, when the industrial North was occupied and politically restructured by the Soviet Union, and the agricultural South was occupied and reorganized by the United States. By 1948 the two superpowers had withdrawn and both Korean governments operated autonomously. Interestingly, the dream of reunification upon which North Korea acted was also the outspoken goal of the nationalistic, anti-Communist president of South Korea, Syngman Rhee.

There were other factors explaining the Korea War. With the victory of Communism in China eight months earlier, creation of a fully Communized Korea, in North Korean eyes, seemed consistent with the "march of history." And with geopolitical stalemate in Europe, from the Russian point of view the Far East was a propitious place in which to test further the resolve of the West. In addition, the Americans seemed to encourage the invasion when, on January 12, 1950, Secretary of State Dean Acheson in a major policy speech defined the American line of defense in Asia as excluding Korea. While the United States would defend Japan and the Philippines, Acheson explained, should Korea be attacked, it would be a matter for the United Nations.

Twenty-four hours after the invasion, the U.N. Security Council issued a resolution demanding a cessation of hostilities and the withdrawal by the invaders above the thirty-eighth parallel—the border between North and South Korea. The resolution also asked U.N. members to assist in the execution of this order. With the Soviet Union boycotting Security Council meetings since January because of an unrelated matter, there was no Russian veto of U.N. action. However, the failure of North Korea to meet the conditions of this edict led two days later, on June 27, to a second Security Council resolution, this one recommending that U.N. member nations "furnish such assistance to the Republic of Korea as may be necessary to repel the armed attack and to restore international peace and security in the area." This second decree was tantamount to a declaration of war by the United Nations.

Although the United States was instrumental in the actions of the Security Council, President Harry S. Truman carefully followed the lead of the United Nations. He ordered American sea and air support for South Korea only after the first resolution was clearly ignored by the invaders. Not until June 30—after General Douglas MacArthur witnessed the fall of Seoul, the South Korean capital, and was convinced that the North Koreans would soon hold all the peninsula—did Truman order U.S. troops into the battle.

While the Korean War was officially a U.N. undertaking, the military commitment came overwhelmingly from South Korea and the United States. Further, American involvement was never formalized with a congressional declaration of war. Legally, this was a "police action" ordered by the commander in chief of the armed forces, President Truman, as a function of American membership in the United Nations and American belief in the ideals of that world body. U.S. action was at once a blend of the new and the old—the collective security mentality of the United Nations and the resolve not to appease Communism, as had been done with Nazism in the 1930s. The Korean War was also the first great test of the American strategy of containment—a Cold War policy that understood Communism as an aggressive, monolithic political dictatorship to be contained within its postwar borders until it was eventually overthrown by its oppressed subjects. President Truman melded these themes on July 19, when he appeared on national television and radio to explain his actions:

> These actions by the United Nations and its members are of great importance. The free nations have now made it clear that lawless aggression will be met with force. The free nations have learned the fateful lesson of the 1930s. That lesson is that aggression must be met firmly. Appeasement leads only to further aggression and ultimate war.

The American Congress and public opinion supported Truman's early anti-Communist resolve. But issues within the war grew controversial, especially when U.N. troops under General MacArthur's command drove the invaders out of the South and deep into their own country. Under MacArthur, the United Nations seemed no longer to be fighting only to oust the North Koreans—the general seemed intent upon reunifying the peninsula under South Korean auspices. With American and South Korean troops nearing Manchuria and threatening air raids on enemy "sanctuaries" in that Chinese-controlled territory, by the end of 1950 the People's Republic of China entered the war. MacArthur's troops were quickly driven out of the North, and the war was stalemated for the next two years near the thirty-eighth parallel.

Importantly, public support for the war rapidly evaporated. Whereas 65 percent of the American people approved of the war after its first seven weeks, by February 1951 only 39 percent still approved, and 50 percent now did not favor it. By October 1951 the figures were only 33 percent in favor and 56 percent disapproving.

The American people, who had resisted involvement in World War II until Pearl Harbor, clearly had not abandoned their isolationist heritage in less than a decade. With patriotic fervor now dissipating and quick, decisive victory impossible, popular backing for the conflict rapidly eroded. It is interesting to note that in the Vietnam War—coming as it did after years of political conditioning primarily by television—public opinion supported the American commitment significantly longer. As late as May 1970 a Gallup poll showed 36 percent in favor, a figure reached with Korea in less than a year. Also in May 1970, some 56 percent of the public disapproved of the war, a figure reached with Korea after only 16 months of conflict.[36]

The Korean War was the first great international test for fledgling TV news operations. Until an armistice agreement became effective on July 27, 1953, video coverage of the war steadily improved. But, unlike the conflict in Southeast Asia in the next decade, the Korean War was not a television war. TV was neither technically nor professionally sophisticated enough to report the Korean hostilities thoroughly.

Network news bureaus were not prepared for the conflict in Korea. CBS and NBC, the leading TV news operations, were well equipped to report the war only on radio. Less than five years earlier, network radio journalists had kept Americans apprised of the latest developments in World War II. But television demanded the synchronization of words and pictures. It was one thing for a newsman to summarize government battle reports, or even to fly over the battlefront and broadcast his impressions, but video demanded fresh supplies of battle films. TV needed front-line action reported and filmed by a breed of journalist not yet developed by the networks.

TV relied on newsreel companies. Since it took time and money to assemble a first-rate video crew to cover the Korean War, it was easier to buy film from organizations with a history of producing compilation films of weekly news. To build their wartime TV crews, moreover, the networks often hired photographers away from newsreel companies and even newspapers.

Another plentiful source for Korean War footage was the U.S. Army Signal Corps. The military had its own motion picture photographers, many enlisted or drafted from employment in Hollywood movie studios. These soldiers had access to front-line action as well as to lighter feature material. The film they produced was offered free of charge to network and local TV. While this footage undoubtedly enlivened nightly newscasts, it was not gathered according to journalistic standards. It was the product of the American military, screened by the armed forces before being released. In essence, this film presented what the military wanted Americans to see of the conflict. In this way domestic video became a willing conduit for preselected images flattering to the military and its commitment.

There were other instances in which the military influenced what was shown on home-front television. Broadcasting had little experience

covering front-line action. At best, during World War II radio correspondents were confined to impressions gleaned from shuttling to
battle areas, or to interviews with servicemen returned from the front.
To get to the front, whether for radio or television, journalists depended upon the armed forces for transportation and protection. Reporters also relied frequently on the military for housing and even
food, especially when away from urban areas. Such amenities undermined the objectivity journalists preferred to have when gathering
material for a story.

For its part, the military was aware of the importance of TV as a
propaganda medium. Within two weeks of assuming command of
the U.N. forces in Korea, General MacArthur issued orders to provide free film to newsreel firms and television networks. When he
undertook a flying visit to the war front, MacArthur was careful to
take along a Signal Corps photographer to record the event for viewers
in the United States.[37]

What Americans saw in those first months of the Korean War was
a highly sensational interpretation of the conflict, complete with anti-
Communist rhetoric and exciting government-supplied film. Typical
of the programming was "Telenews Weekly," a half-hour review of
the news produced by Telenews Productions, International News Service, and International News Photos. The installment aired as "Front
Line Camera" on July 25, 1950, on the NBC station in Chicago, was
a showcase for the war as an anti-Communist effort.

President Truman spoke of how "free nations" had to be on guard
against invasion, aggression, and—linking the North Korean invasion
to events at Pearl Harbor a decade earlier—"against this kind of sneak
attack." Other than saying that Americans were "united in their belief in democratic freedom," he did not justify American involvement
in the hostilities. Instead, he offered clichés. "We are united in de-
testing Communist slavery," he said. While "the cost of freedom is
high," he continued, Americans "are determined to preserve our
freedom no matter what the cost." In a few short, unquestioned
sentences from the president of the United States a civil war between
two strong-willed Korean governments had become a crusade to protect the freedom of all Americans.

Even without Truman's logic, this installment of "Telenews Weekly" uncritically aired Cold War propaganda. Here, early in the history
of video, were themes destined to become familiar: the overriding
importance of air power; the invincibility of U.S. aviation; the military,
man, and technology in synchronized excellence and dedicated to the

protection of freedom. With bold music in the background and film of various American aircraft, the announcer spoke of leaflets being dropped in Korea: "As Communist forces lower an Iron Curtain over conquered areas, instituting Marxist reforms and bringing their brand of democracy to once-free Korea, from the air comes word that the Red triumph is only temporary. United Nations answers Communism's programs of lies and promises."

In Korea, television news, like that of radio and newspapers, was subject to military censorship. In December 1950, General MacArthur imposed complete censorship on information coming from journalists at the Korean front. While most of American journalism exercised self-imposed control over the type of information it made public, government concern was with curbing the disclosure of vital production information through domestic media, restricting the announcement of troop movements at home and abroad, and maintaining public morale at an optimistic level. Interestingly, *Broadcasting* reported that many journalists in Korea hailed censorship as "long-awaited and much needed." According to this influential trade journal, "Many reportedly had requested formal censorship, not only to provide real security but to equalize breaks on important stories. This was understood to have been true of many radio newsmen."[38]

Censorship existed throughout the war. As late as December 1952, the U.S. government was exercising field censorship—now through public information officers of the armed forces rather than through intelligence officials of the various branches. Nonetheless, by the end of 1952 government restrictions were liberalized to the point that while news continued to be censored "for security reasons," the government announced that news controls "will not be used to prevent the transmission of news upon the grounds of anticipated adverse reaction by the American people."[39]

Hampered by its technical immaturity in delivering pictures and sound from a foreign war front, and inhibited for security and policy reasons in what it could communicate, TV responded to the Korean War to the best of its ability. The CBS and NBC stations in New York City occasionally carried live coverage of the sessions of the U.N. Security Council. Films and kinescopes of these proceedings appeared on network and local newscasts, sometimes as quickly as two hours after they occurred. Within six weeks of the commencement of hostilities, NBC-TV had three cameramen in Korea providing as much as half the footage aired by that network. Early results were usually disappointing. When NBC-TV aired "Battle Report" on August 13, 1950,

Variety attacked this "weekly official briefing of the people of the United States" as "boring" and "anything but adept." The trade journal was especially upset by the failure of the program to exploit the visual potential of video. "But this is television," the reviewer noted, "and TV is video as well as audio. . . . Instill a visual interest."[40]

Similarly unexploitive of the visual potential of television were network gestures on December 19, 1951. Beginning in the evening and extending into the early morning hours, the four networks televised moving tapes on which were written the names of 3,198 American prisoners being held in North Korea. On network radio, announcers read the complete list of names, which the Pentagon had released that day.

Nonetheless, by the spring of 1951 improved TV coverage of the Korean War was evidenced in the four-part CBS series "Crisis in Korea." This was a filmed documentary hosted by Douglas Edwards and culled from network news film, newsreel companies, and U.S. Army sources. *Variety* applauded the "interesting and informative" nature of the series, and was impressed that CBS avoided editorial comment, preferring to let "the documented film speak for itself."[41]

Nevertheless, "Crisis in Korea" was recapitulation, not reportorial invention, a filmed history of the war that was technically, if not journalistically, impressive. However, if any single reporter did improve TV coverage of the Korean conflict, it was Edward R. Murrow. The maturation of Murrow as a video journalist occurred during that war. He had emerged as a prominent radio newsman while covering Great Britain for CBS during World War II. He came to the visual medium in late 1951 with "See It Now," a news documentary series focusing each week on major national and world developments as well as relevant feature stories.

Even before "See It Now," however, Murrow discussed the Korean War with his radio audience. He well understood that the conflict had several levels. He saw it as a battle for popular allegiance in a changing world. "The Communists have captured and channeled the surging desire for change, the resentment of foreign domination," he maintained on his broadcast of September 6, 1950. He continued, "Communism means both peace and plenty. The fact that Communism hasn't meant any of these things in practice in Asia is beside the point."

Murrow also saw the Korean conflict as a struggle between the Soviet Union and the United States for leverage in world politics. The American nation, he remarked on December 5, 1950, was committed "to the proposition that our foreign policy must be based on strength, ours and that of our allies." The United States, he said, "concluded that the Russians would not negotiate realistically until we had created sufficient 'situations of strength.' "

But Murrow was realistic. He dispassionately noted that, as for creating "situations of strength," it was clear "that we do not have sufficient strength as of now to deal with the Communist threat in a situation where the Russians have not committed a single soldier." As for the American salvation of Asia from Communism, Murrow wryly noted:

> We must accept the proposition that the *people* of Asia will decide their future, that we will not attempt to dictate it and that we will use armed strength, as we are in Korea, to prevent Russia from dominating them. If we accept that proposition, then it seems to me an urgent obligation rests upon us to provide them with the information, and the example, upon which decision can be based.[42]

In addition, Murrow understood the Korean conflict as a war of the technologically advanced upon social backwardness. He wondered about the plight of Korean peasants caught up in the war. "When we start moving up through dead valleys, through villages to which we have put the torch by retreating," he mused on August 14, 1950, "what then of the people who live there?" This report was recorded but never aired. Executives at CBS censored it. They felt that parts of it contravened orders from General MacArthur forbidding news personnel to criticize command decisions. Still, it was a sobering broadcast that asked a question whose poignancy was perhaps not fully appreciated only seven weeks after the war had begun. Speaking of the abused villagers, Murrow continued, "They have lived on the knife-edge of despair and disaster for centuries. Their pitiful possessions have been consumed in the flames of war. Will our reoccupation of that fleabitten land lessen, or increase, the attraction of Communism?"[43]

In such broadcasts and in his television activities in Korea, Murrow demonstrated a particular sensitivity for average people caught up in war. Whether it involved a Korean noncombatant or an American GI, Murrow's awareness of the human condition emerged on "See It Now." Half the premiere broadcast on November 18, 1951, was a filmed report on a day in the life of Fox Company, Second Platoon, 19th Infantry. Well photographed and edited, it drew viewers into the actions and feelings of a combat unit about to assault enemy installations on high ground. On February 24, 1952, "See It Now" offered Robert Pierpoint reporting on case histories of three wounded GIs, tracing their ordeal from evacuation in Korea through assignment to base hospitals near their homes. On September 7, 1952, it was a view of the war through the eyes of a Marine division at Beetle Gulch trying to oust the enemy from another strategic hill. On April 19, 1953, "See It Now" offered the first reports of Americans being released from North Korean prisoner-of-war camps.

Still another familiar Murrow theme was the need for home-front support of American soldiers, particularly in terms of donating blood to aid the wounded. As early as December 2, 1951, he took up this issue on "See It Now" with a dramatic filmed sequence telling what happened to a pint of blood donated in the United States by an average citizen. Murrow followed it to a Korean military hospital, where it and eight other pints of blood were used to save the life of a badly injured GI.

Murrow's most acclaimed achievements in wartime coverage were "Christmas in Korea," on "See It Now" on December 29, 1952, and its follow-up, "Christmas in Korea—1953," aired one year later. The human focus of Murrow's reportorial style was fully developed in these programs. Together with 16 photographers and reporters—including CBS newsmen Robert Pierpoint, Ed Scott, Lou Cioffi, Larry Leseur, Bill Downs, and Joseph Wershba—Murrow went into the daily lives of the foot soldiers.

Most GIs expressed greetings for the Christmas season or light-hearted jokes about the routine of fighting a war. Murrow's cameras settled on Americans—whites and blacks, men and women—as well as British, French, Irish, and Ethiopians. Among the Americans, opinions of the conflict were wide-ranging. One soldier felt it was "a good cause," that "We must either stop Communism here or it is going to come closer to the United States," and "this is the place to stop the progressiveness of the Communists." Another defined his participation more fatalistically. "I am just over here firing, that's all," he told Ed Scott, and "When they holler 'Fire Mission,' I fire a lot." Still another GI concluded of the war, "I think it's a bunch of nonsense."[44]

The journalistic legacy created early by Murrow and his long-time producer, Fred W. Friendly, was singular. More responsibly than most, Murrow and Friendly avoided overblown patriotism, fear-mongering, and empty rhetoric. During the Korean War their journalism relied on a balance of opinions from those involved. It was patriotic without being uncritical, and it skillfully blended pictures and words to communicate a human perspective. From Murrow and Friendly came a sensitivity generally absent from nonfiction Cold War programming. In praise of such reportage, *Variety* editor Abel Green in late 1952 credited Murrow and Friendly with having created "an historic chapter in the new American journalism."[45]

TV AND THE POPULARIZATION OF FEAR

"See It Now" was distinctive because it was relatively balanced, critical, and penetrating. In contrast were the panel-discussion and newsmaker-interview programs of the Cold War. Ostensibly an opportunity to clarify current issues by quizzing those in government, these programs frequently were narrow adventures into the simplified emotionalism of the anti-Communist era. Whether in a press conference format, a roundtable discussion, or a debate between viewpoints, such programs seldom gave viewers a wide variety of opinions. Aside from foreign officials, guests were almost never outside the Democratic-Republican centrality of American politics. These forums usually gave politicians the chance to air well-rehearsed opinions without profound questioning.

Discussion programs treated Cold War issues such as the American military buildup, a possible World War III, domestic Communist subversion, and the numerical preponderance of Chinese and Russian troops over American forces. Such discussions often were more terrifying than educative. Unsubstantiated charges and half-truths were uncritically accepted when mouthed by important politicans. For example, on "American Forum of the Air" on January 21, 1951, Senator Robert A. Taft described "the great threat to liberty and to peace" that was "Soviet Russia which threatens the domination of the world through propaganda, infiltration, and military aggression." No one challenged Taft's charges. No one sifted fact from rhetoric in the words of the man who seemed certain to get the Republican presidential nomination the next year.

On "The Big Issue" on September 14, 1953, a former staff director of Senator Joseph McCarthy's investigating committee charged that "The largest single group supporting the Communist apparatus in the United States today is composed of Protestant clergymen." While others on the show felt this claim "wildly exaggerated," they eased their criticism by agreeing that domestic subversion was a pressing problem and Communism should be liquidated in the United States.[46]

On "Chronoscope" on January 36, 1953, Harold Velde, chairman of the House Committee on Un-American Activities, announced his plans for 1953. "Our first duty is to weed out the Communists and fellow travelers and Pinkos, as they are popularly known, from the executive branch of government," Congressman Velde matter-of-factly declared. He continued, "After, of course, we are able to do that, I think the next important thing is to act as a watchdog committee to see that no Commies or other subversives of any kind infiltrate the new Eisenhower administration." Again, no one challenged this government spokesman regarding the validity of his presumptions.

The most strident example of such politicized programming was "American Forum of the Air," an NBC series that came to TV after 21 years on radio, and then appeared simultaneously on both media until canceled in 1957. It usually presented two politicians, one Republican and one Democrat, debating an important issue. As such, it became a platform for the mainstream parties to engage in partisan politics. This seldom resulted in constructive dialogue that questioned basic Cold War values or in reevaluation of general foreign policy goals.

Furthermore, no matter how heated the senators and representatives became on the program, they consistently blurred the edges of controversy by expressing great respect and friendship for one another. What to some may have been accepted as feigned politeness, sounded to others like real cordiality and a sense of community. With phrases such as "my dear friend," "the able senator," and "my friend from . . .," it was difficult to believe the discussants had serious differences. Typically, when the liberal Senator Paul H. Douglas clashed with his fellow senator from Illinois, Everett M. Dirksen, on January 14, 1951, Douglas glossed over their differences and stressed admiration for his colleague:

> Well, first may I say that it is a happy indication of the fundamental decency of American politics that while Mr. Dirksen and I are representatives of opposing political parties, we are nevertheless close friends. And that while I did not exactly dance in the streets with joy when he was elected, now that he is a Senator I am very glad indeed to welcome him.

Although politicians on "American Forum of the Air" disputed matters such as domestic economic policies and administration attitudes toward organized labor, they were in agreement on the issue of world Communism. On the telecast of September 16, 1950, Senator John J. Sparkman asserted full agreement with his Republican colleague when Senator William F. Knowland denounced "aggressive Communism" and declared:

> If we are going to have a system of international law and order, so that the peace of the world will be secure for ourselves and our children, I

think we must stop yielding to international blackmail. Now the Soviet Union and China have been carrying on that type of international blackmail for a long time.

On the discussion of domestic Communism telecast on August 19, 1950, the conservative Senator Karl Mundt spoke of sabotage, and blowing up factories and railroad yards, as he described Communists in the United States. His opponent, Senator Hubert H. Humphrey, was quick to add his own description of American Communists. "I think that it can be honestly stated that all patriotic and freedom-loving, decent Americans are anti-Communist," noted the senator from Minnesota. Later Humphrey added that "Communists are under the control of a foreign government. I believe that the Communist Party in this country is not an independent free party. I think it's a stooge of Joe Stalin."

One of the more interesting telecasts of "American Forum of the Air" occurred January 21, 1951, when senators Dirksen and Blair Moody treated the question "Can We Prevent World War III?" In many respects it was typical of other programs. Moody claimed that Communists intended "to destroy our freedom and enslave the world if they can." Dirksen expressed agreement, and then added a partisan slap at the Truman administration, calling the Korean conflict "World War II½" and chiding Democrats for having "a penchant for getting us into war."

Although the Republican party openly criticized Truman for stumbling into the Korean War—and almost two years later Dwight Eisenhower was elected president partly because he pledged to go to Korea and negotiate an end to the hostilities—Dirksen was not ready at this early date to offer rational compromise as a way to stop the war. Dirksen wanted military victory. He called for a blockade of China, interdiction of supply shipments to the North Koreans and Chinese, "hot pursuit" bombardment of enemy sanctuaries in Manchuria, and the use of "atomic shells" in order to "prove that we mean business over there."

Moody differed with Dirksen only on the means of achieving the victory. Still, in the last moments of the program the senator from Michigan raised an issue seldom broached on American TV. Moody suggested that there were reasons of economic self-interest to fight world Communism. Assuming that Communists were by definition anti-American, Moody alleged that the United States could become isolated by Communist victories throughout the decolonizing world. In such isolation, he argued, the United States might be cut off from raw materials vital to its industries. American politicians were never frank about ulterior economic motives in the world crusade against Communism. But Moody was forthright when he concluded:

> We would be cut off from our uranium. We might be cut off from our manganese, and so on. . . . We import no less than 167 critical raw materials that are necessary for the operation of our great industrial system, including manganese, which is needed for the manufacture of steel. This isolationist stuff won't go.

In contrast with the narrow perspective offered by NBC's "American Forum of the Air" was the ABC public affairs program "America's Town Meeting of the Air." Since its inception on radio in 1935, this series had consistently sought a wide spectrum of opinion. It also solicited uncensored questions from the studio audience. On the premier program of "Town Meeting" on May 30, 1935, four discussants considered "Which Way for America—Fascism, Communism, Socialism, or Democracy?" Even in its short tenure as a television-radio simulcast—October 1948 to June 1949, and January-July 1952—"Town Meeting" continued its tradition of presenting divergent opinions. In addition to a steady stream of senators, congressmen, administration spokesmen, and others from the conservative-to-liberal political mainstream, representatives from the non-Communist left appeared often during the television career of "Town Meeting," among them Louis Fischer, James P. Warburg, and Roger Baldwin. One of the more frequent guests was Norman Thomas, the six-time Socialist party candidate for President of the United States. During the 1948-49 season, Thomas debated "How Is Peace with Russia Possible?" (October 5) and "Can Modern Capitalism Meet the Needs of Modern Man?" (January 18). In 1952 this spokesman for American socialism discussed "What Should Our Program Be Toward Asia?" (March 4) and "How Do We Fare in the Cold War?" (June 15).

"America's Town Meeting of the Air" was the product of an earlier era in broadcasting, when divergent thought was tolerated as fostering public debate. In Cold War television, however, such controversy appeared discordant, even unpatriotic, because it clashed with the consensus aired on other public discussion programs. Still, "Town Meeting" did not compromise its decades-old policy of seeking all sides on an issue. Although the program continued on radio for several more years, it left TV quickly and definitely in 1952.

Television was strategic in popularizing social and political fear in the early 1950s. This was particularly the case with public affairs programming that uncritically blended the myths and substance of the Cold War and delivered the mixture in the isolated, underinformed privacy of millions of American homes. It occurred in something as subtle as a CBS documentary about the nation's natural resources, telecast on January 10, 1954, under the politicized title "Resources for Freedom." It was there, too, in the "Crusade for Freedom" telethons broadcast nationally on CBS and ABC during the first years of the 1950s. In them celebrities from the worlds of entertainment, business, politics, and the military used donated network time to raise millions of dollars for the strongly anti-Communist broadcasts of Radio Free Europe and Radio Free Asia.

It also appeared in civil defense programs that focused on a potential nuclear World War III. Importantly, most such productions were made in close cooperation with the federal government. "The Facts We Face" was a CBS series in early 1951 that utilized officials from the Atomic Energy Commission to explain atomic warfare and ways to survive it. The Federal Civil Defense Administration (FCDA) assisted in making "Prepare to Survive," a monthly program in 1951 seen on WDTV in Pittsburgh. "Survival," an NBC series in the summer of 1951, was so successful the FCDA ordered kinescopes of the programs to be used in the training of civil defense volunteers.

Certainly, such informational programming was produced also for network and local radio. And such shows probably reached a larger audience, since in early 1951 only 58 percent of the nation's homes had television receivers. Nonetheless, the visual dimension of video increased the urgency of the message. Pictures of bombed-out cities, threatening aircraft, and atomic explosions enhanced the frightening nature of the aural message. Such was seen, for instance, on WHAS-TV in Louisville in "Survival Under Atomic Attack." Broadcast in December 1950, this series dealt with steps to be taken if and when the Russians dropped atomic weapons on Kentucky. The visual imagery of this series intensified the frightening theme pronounced so effectively on the premier show: "This is just a program, but there could be a bomber carrying the equivalent of 20,000 tons of TNT on its way to Louisville right now."[47]

Rather than criticize government policy, which was already generating a spirited East-West arms race, television rationalized, even justified, such militarism. The enemy clearly was totalitarian Russia with its aggressive, immoral Communism. America's militaristic gestures were only reasonable reactions to the global challenge emanating from Moscow. And if nuclear war and domestic devastation were the result of the noble American crusade, that price was not so horrible, because such destruction was survivable. This was the message of "You and the Atom Bomb," aired September 21, 1951, on WOR-TV. This local production gave New York City viewers a half-hour lesson in fission and the types of atomic blast to anticipate—water, land, and air. Then those watching were asked to send a dime to receive an informational pamphlet, "so you'll know what to do in the event of an atomic attack." The announcer left viewers with the strong impression that by taking a few easy precautions, nuclear attack upon the United States could be survived:

> I hope that we have been able to remove some of the fears and misconceptions that have surrounded the atomic bomb. I hope that you realize now that there's nothing mysterious about radiation, and that the atomic bomb will not create a race of monsters. And that terrible as the atomic bomb is, it does not mean the end of our large cities or country or of our population. You are not helpless if you know your atom.

This mixture of government involvement in production and distribution of misleading films, and overly simplified messages stressing nuclear survival was evident in a package of free motion pictures offered by the FCDA to every American TV station in late 1951.[48] These were ten-minute films that treated the possibility of attack upon the United States from a variety of perspectives. "Survival Under Atomic Attack" was a straightforward documentary illustrating what citizens should do in case the United States was bombed. It showed makeshift bomb shelters in basements, and it urged Americans to stockpile food and water. The fact that it was narrated by Edward R. Murrow—the respected CBS journalist who had reported warfare waged on common people in Europe and Korea—increased the credibility of the film.

In "What You Should Know About Biological Warfare" Americans encountered another dastardly potential of the Communist enemy. This frightening movie noted that despite American defenses against hostile airplanes and missiles, germ warfare could be devastating. Yet, it proffered a simple prescription for survival: keep clean in order not to spread germs, enroll in a Red Cross home nursing course, report all sicknesses promptly, and if the enemy did attack with biological weapons, remain calm, for "scientists would already be working to control the outbreak."

While most of these films were aimed at an adult audience, "Duck and Cover" directed its ten-minute message at grade school children.

Complete with a cartoon turtle named Bert, this movie showed youngsters ducking and covering their heads in many different circumstances. Children dived for their lives in classrooms, on a school bus, and while riding a bicycle. They ducked and covered while walking to school. A picnicking family sought protection from a nuclear blast by diving under a blanket spread on the grass. Here was a terrifying message: anytime, anyplace, and without warning, innocent American youngsters might be bombed. Simplistically, "Duck and Cover" ended with the animated Bert reminding youthful viewers that they would survive if only they learned "what we all must learn to do, you, and you, and you, and you—duck and cover!"

In contrast with the protective measures urged by most civil defense productions, one offering in the film package distributed by the FCDA approached nuclear war in a defiant manner. "Our Cities Must Fight" was addressed to those who might flee the cities following an enemy attack. Derided as members of "the take-to-the-hills fraternity," such self-interested citizens were informed that deserting bombed-out American cities was "something pretty close to treason." The film reminded viewers of their responsibility to remain in their cities and to keep the factories operating—a responsibility to family, friends, and country. Whereas civil defense productions usually avoided the grim potentials of thermonuclear war, "Our Cities Must Fight" was confrontive in noting that "a hell of an enemy attack could come smashing out of the sky at any time." It concluded with a brave statement about atomic warfare:

> There'll be plenty of suffering, plenty of misery, broken homes, death—dangers that used to belong only to soldiers. But we've got to be able to take it and come back fighting. Everything we hoped for, everything we believe in—everything America has fought for will depend on us and what we do. You know, a lot of people behind the Iron Curtain are wondering whether we can take it if we're attacked. They're carefully measuring our courage, our capacity to fight, our capacity for sacrifice. They think that they have the answers. Well, you and I and every American has to examine their [*sic*] hearts and come up with a few answers of their own. The question is: Have Americans got the guts? [Turning directly toward the viewer] Have *you* got the guts?

In dealing with atomic energy, and particularly the possibility of nuclear war, television in the 1950s seldom failed to exploit the dramatic and propagandistic aspects of the issue. Nowhere was this better realized than in the NBC documentary "Three, Two, One—Zero!" Produced by the network's fledgling "Project XX" staff, this hour-long program was televised September 13, 1954. Artistically scripted and photographed, and lushly embellished with an original musical score, "Three, Two, One—Zero!" interpreted the atomic age in partisan political terms. With quasi-Biblical lyricism the audience learned of the genesis of man-controlled atomic power, the creation of American science. Atomic energy was hailed as the "maximum expression" of "a free society." Viewers were told that this energy "belongs to the citizens of the United States," and that this development was nothing less than the "industrial genius of America," which now had "come into full potential." As for military use of such power, narrator Alexander Scourby praised atomic weaponry because "it guards the freedom of the West today."

This was classic Cold War propaganda delivered into unsuspecting American homes via NBC—with consultative input from the Atomic Energy Commission. Russian industrial growth from nil in 1917 to its contemporary magnitude was rationalized as the product of "generations of slave labor . . . sacrificed to this end. The means are of no consequence. The end is all important." Quoting American airmen, Scourby warned, "If the Russians go to war, they won't have a country to come back to."

As with most TV shows treating nuclear war and survival, "Three, Two, One—Zero!" offered frightful images and urged viewers to accept increasing militarism in the United States. "How many bombs do the Russions have?" asked Scourby sardonically. "The exact number is not known, does not matter," he answered, but "they have enough, if delivered on target, to inflict incredible damage on the United States, on the West." Proper response to the Russian challenge was "defense against aggression." This was demonstrated with footage of Air Force jets and bombers. Scourby continued:

> On the airfields of North America the intercontinental bombers are constantly fueled, constantly tuned, constantly ready—twenty-four hours a day, day in and day out. The planes and their crews are always on the alert, their targets picked, their courses long since set. Somebody might blow the whistle tomorrow morning.

While documentaries about atomic energy and public service shows treating civil defense preparedness were an important part of Cold War TV, for dramatic intensity they could not match the mock nuclear attack upon the United States. In both entertainment and nonfiction programming, many times in the 1950s viewers saw what would happen if enemy atomic and/or hydrogen bombs were dropped on American cities. Civil defense experts collaborated with TV production personnel in the "Motorola TV Hour" drama "Atomic Attack." Aired May 18, 1954, on ABC, this intense telecast followed the reactions of the suburban Mitchell family as it coped with an atomic attack on the New York City area. More than a ghastly foretaste of what might lie ahead, *Broadcasting* lauded the production for communicating

> . . . clearly and emphatically, the basic elements of the proper behavior following an atomic attack. If these instructions are remembered and if any watcher is stimulated to join some branch of his local Civil Defense setup, the program will be good proof of the commercial broadcasters' educational theory of teaching through entertainment.[49]

CBS was particularly fond of this genre. As early as June 29, 1952, Edward R. Murrow on "See It Now" covered a mock attack upon New York City. The premiere of "Air Power" in November 1956 simulated a Russian bombardment of Los Angeles, Chicago, New York City, and other American metropolitan centers. The network returned to the theme on December 8, 1957, when "The Day Called 'X' " surveyed Portland, Oregon, under thermonuclear attack. On its radio network, moreover, CBS presented at least two such programs. "Bomb Target, U.S.A." on March 20, 1953, featured anchorman Arthur Godfrey with three respected CBS correspondents aboard B-20 bombers making simulated atomic attacks on American cities as part of a U.S. Air Force training exercise. "The Day Called 'X' " was also the title of a radio documentary—narrated by Edward R. Murrow and aired March 18, 1959—tracing an enemy attack on the United States and probable reactions in Princeton, New Jersey.

Even when narrated by celebrated network newsmen, these programs were "fictionalized documentaries," carefully presented as such. There was nothing artificial, however, about the exploding atomic weapons seen so often on Cold War TV. The Pentagon made available to local and network television free film of its atomic and hydrogen bomb tests, beginning with the first drops in 1946 at Eniwetok-Bikini in the South Pacific. Video coverage of domestic testing from the proving grounds at Yucca Flat, Nevada, began on February 6, 1951. Two local stations in Los Angeles, KTLA and KTTV, televised and kineoscoped the bomb test. Live national coverage began the following year. On April 22, 1952, millions of Americans watched the bomb explode. With cameras as close as 11 miles to ground zero, television brought the nation the flashing blast and familiar mushroom cloud drifting up from the Nevada desert.

The second nationally televised atomic blast occurred on March 17, 1953. Network newsmen Walter Cronkite of CBS, Morgan Beatty of NBC, and Chet Huntley of ABC offered Americans a before-and-after assessment of "Operation Doorstep," the thirty-third nuclear device exploded since testing began at Yucca Flat. In two half-hour telecasts, network TV showed the early-morning detonation of the bomb, then returned eight hours later for a live report on the aftermath of the test. While the Atomic Energy Commission used the firing to assess the effect of the blast on two mock houses in the target area, and on a group of U.S. Army soldiers placed within 3,500 yards of the point of explosion, television coverage drove home the necessity for civil defense preparation. The "sponsor" of the telecasts was the Advertising Council, Inc. *Broadcasting* recognized the "commercial" message offered by the sponsor: "The 'sales message' was preparedness. It is a vast understatement to say that a more effective means could not have been found to 'move' this particular product."[50]

Apparently video coverage of nuclear tests was valuable to the public relations efforts of the military. For the test in 1952, for example, Marine Corps helicopters were used to place commercial TV relay equipment on strategic mountaintops between Los Angeles and the test site in Nevada. During "Operation Smokey" five years later, the U.S. Army ordered 1,140 soldiers into a blast area two hours after a nuclear detonation. The Army filmed the operation and produced a half-hour motion picture. It distributed the film to several hundred commercial TV stations as part of its regular propaganda series, "The Big Picture." The Army admitted it exposed servicemen to such risks of radiation in part "to portray to the public the Army at its best employing [its new Pentomic] organization in operations under atomic warfare conditions . . . ."[51]

There were financial risks associated with live coverage of nuclear tests. Since detonations were dependent upon weather conditions, poor visibility, winds blowing in the wrong direction, or similar disturbances could force short postponements of the explosion. In the spring of 1955, CBS and NBC sent a pool of 95 technicians, announcers, engineers, and photographers to Yucca Flat. Among those intending to make the nuclear blast a part of their programs were Dave Garroway of NBC's "Today," Charles Collingwood of the CBS "Morning Show," Walter Cronkite, John Cameron Swayze, John Daly, Morgan Beatty, and Sarah Churchill. The daytime "Home" program on NBC justified covering the explosion in terms of the effects of the bomb on food and construction.

This was to have been a major TV event, *TV Guide* reported, complete with "not only the blast, but the split-second reaction of people hunched in a trench less than two miles from the 500-foot steel tower that held the bomb." Nonetheless, after seven postponements because of the weather, most of the TV plans were canceled. After more than a week of live reports on weather conditions and stand-up descriptions of the mounting excitement at Yucca Flat, the networks left Nevada because of mounting expenses.[52]

In its role as showcase for American nuclear testing, network television played an important public relations role. There was reassurance in the atomic clouds televised live from the Yucca Flat. As the nation that invented the atomic bomb, it had been a disturbing psychological blow for the United States in September 1949 when the Soviet Union detonated its own A-bomb. Four years later, national fears were compounded when Soviet Premier Georgi Malenkov announced that "the United States no longer possesses a monopoly of the hydrogen bomb." Having lost its monopoly, the United States sought nuclear superiority. Those live TV pictures from the Nevada desert—as well as filmed coverage of testing in the South Pacific—reassured the nation that it would not fall behind the Communists. Each test seemed another advancement, another step beyond the Russians. The televised tests also showed that the Americans would not settle for equality with the enemy in something as vital to security as nuclear weaponry.

The military also realized the public relations potential of televising such testing. By the end of the decade, it was inviting video to cover test firings of other weapons. On August 17, 1958, TV audiences saw an ill-fated Air Force lunar probe from Cape Canaveral. Because the Defense Department would not allow live transmission until smoke appeared in the tail of the missile, the test of this moon rocket was taped and played back eight minutes after ignition. Before the end of the year, however, matters improved for viewers. On December 16, Los Angeles station KTLA covered the test firing of a Thor missile from Vandenburg Air Force Base. The Air Force this time required only a ten-second delay in airing the live TV picture. But the military forbade KTLA to make prior announcements about the test firing. As *TV Guide* explained, "The Air Force . . . didn't cotton to the idea of the TV audience seeing a Thor topple ignominiously to the ground in the event the shot should fail."[53]

If the lack of public protest against nuclear testing was an indication of the effectiveness of TV as the disseminator of enervating anti-

Communism, then television performed well. Throughout the 1950s there were practically no popular demonstrations against such weapons experimentation. If local spokespersons occasionally voiced fears of being contaminated by test fallout, Atomic Energy Commission experts were quick to appear on TV to assure doubters that atomic detonations were safe. Those more demonstrative in their opposition were treated with incredulity and dismay. On August 6, 1957, for example, 11 activists from a group called Non-Violent Action Against Nuclear Weapons were the first people to be arrested for illegally entering the AEC's proving grounds in Nevada. Here, on the twelfth anniversary of the atomic bombing of Hiroshima, Gladwin Hill reported in the *New York Times* that the protest "marked the unusual employment in this country of the 'civil disobedience' tactics made famous by M. K. Gandhi." Hill felt it also newsworthy that everyone in this "pacifist" band of farmers, ministers, artists, Quakers, and conscientious objectors "denied that their movement has any connection with Communism."[54]

Live coverage of weapons tests, documentaries, and discussions about nuclear explosions and the Cold War all helped spread a fear and loathing of Communism. In the American popular mind, moreover, such developments permanently linked Communism with Soviet imperialism, thermonuclear weaponry, and sneak attacks on the United States. This association was most poignantly demonstrated in "Operation Alert 1955."

"Operation Alert 1955" was a two-day (June 15-16, 1955) national test of the effectiveness of civil defense in the United States. It was a federally produced, simulated war in which residents of 55 American cities—and six cities in American territories—were expected to react as if the Soviet Union had launched a nuclear attack against the country. While most localities were preparing for months to carry out this exercise, several target cities, including San Francisco, were given no warning until civil defense officials announced Russian bombers were on the way.

To underscore the seriousness of this mock invasion, President Dwight Eisenhower, together with key government leaders and 15,000 Washington bureaucrats, evacuated the nation's capital. They retreated to secret emergency sites located within 300 miles of Washington, as they presumably would in an authentic H-bomb attack. Eisenhower's "evacuation" of the capital—the first since President James Madison fled the city for three days as British troops burned the White House and Capitol building during the War of 1812—was further dramatized by a hastily arranged national address carried live by the NBC and Dumont networks. "We are here," the president told an afternoon TV audience, "to determine whether or not the government is prepared in time of emergency to continue the function of government so that there will be no interruption in the business that must be carried on."

While popular reaction ranged from cooperativeness in New York City and Houston to indifference in Los Angeles and San Francisco, statistics issued by the Federal Civil Defense Administration were ominous. Assuming the Russians had struck the 61 target cities with atomic weapons of 20,000 to 60,000 tons, and with hydrogen bombs from 1 million to 5 million tons, there would have been horrendous carnage. Philadelphia counted 760,340 "dead," 363,860 "injured," and 763,329 "homeless." Chicago had 513,225 "dead" and 422,270 "wounded" in the hypothetical attack. In populous New England, there were 3,909,000 "dead," 2,579,000 "injured," and 6,733,000 "homeless."[55]

But Americans always respond more energetically to personality than to abstract issues. In a culture that places a premium on the individual, the celebrity or colorful character espousing a heartfelt political position is more attractive than a voluntary national bomb drill or a balanced intellectual inquiry forcing viewers to draw their own conclusions. On television, stars make things happen. This, of course, was the motive for using sports and film celebrities to sell commercial products. It was also the case with Senator Joseph R. McCarthy and the cause of anti-Communism. Flamboyant, self-assured, fearless, charismatic—this politician took the abstract word "anti-Communism" and made it flesh. And through video, he brought the nation together in a communion of apprehension and distrust.

THE BOUNDARIES OF TV AND ANTI-COMMUNISM: THE CASE OF SENATOR JOSEPH R. McCARTHY

McCarthy was the chief catalyst of mass anti-Communism. More than the House Committee on Un-American Activities, or President Truman's loyalty oaths, or Russian actions, McCarthy sparked this frightening era and became the principal prophet of anti-Communism as an irrational fear consuming logical analysis and orderly process. If one personality best captured the essence of hating Reds and Communism, it was McCarthy. If one individual exploited popular ignorance and apprehension, it was the junior senator from Wisconsin. If one politician was most responsible for the course of national life in the United States in the 1950s and 1960s, it too was Senator

McCarthy. As David Caute has explained McCarthy and his appeal to mass America, "His pugilistic flamboyance, blatant love of money, women, and horseflesh, his Falstaff-like war service and mythical *machismo*, caught a cowboy nation by the gut."[56] McCarthy accomplished all this in great part because of the exposure he gained from the broadcasting industry.

As early as April 3, 1947, he was on national radio as a spokesman for anti-Communist values. On "America's Town Meeting of the Air" he explained why the Communist Party should be outlawed in the United States. He called for the legal banning of the CPUSA, wiping its name from the ballot. According to McCarthy, "The Communist Party is an. agency of a foreign power." Therefore, he said, the Justice Department and the FBI should take appropriate steps.

With a broader perspective on the Communist threat, the senator returned to "America's Town Meeting of the Air" on March 30, 1948. Here he spoke of a possible World War III against the Reds. "As of now we are at war," he declared. "I repeat, as of now we are at war— a war we are rapidly losing." Should this rhetorical war become "a shooting war tomorrow," McCarthy foresaw a Russian takeover of Iceland and Alaska, vantage points from which Communist bombers could hit "practically every American city."

To protect the United States, he called for military preparedness. He lauded U.S. air power, and urged "the necessity of keeping abreast or ahead of the time, technically and scientifically, of being prepared to wage or defend ourselves in bacteriological and atomic warfare."

But television was also important to the dissemination of the senator's message. Alone before a TV camera, McCarthy skillfully manipulated half-truths and misrepresented facts. He distorted history by ignoring political context and careful analysis. He pounded his lectern authoritatively, cited documents and specific events, and sounded certain of what he was saying. With little or no convincing rebuttal to his opinions, viewers were ill-equipped to doubt McCarthy. Furthermore, his slightly disheveled appearance on live TV, or on the evening news, gave him the air of a sincere man under siege by enemies. This lent credibility to his amazing accusations.

In Wheeling, West Virginia, in February 1950, McCarthy announced that he had the names of 205 Communists who were working for the State Department. The fact that he never revealed those names—and some doubt he ever had that many—was unimportant. As McCarthy remarked on "Meet the Press" on March 19, 1950, "When you talk about being a member of the Communist Party, I'm not so much concerned about whether they have a card in their pocket saying, 'I am a member of the party.' I'm concerned about those men who are doing the job that the Communists want them to do."

In newspapers, on radio, and especially on television, Senator McCarthy seemed so confident, so convincing. And he had that air of selflessness so important to the character of American heroes. When journalist May Craig asked McCarthy on that "Meet the Press" program in March 1950 why he was chasing Communists, and if the Republican party had put him up to it, the senator's reply was classical American self-sacrifice: "It's just one of those tasks, May, that someone has to do."

McCarthy was a master of the quick phrase and the attack on reputation. On August 15, 1950, he appeared again on the ABC radio series "America's Town Meeting of the Air." He spoke of "the sellout to Communism in both East and West." He claimed China "was lost" by the State Department, and that Poland was lost to Communism because of the sins of Secretary of State Dean Acheson. American policy in general, he declared, was being made by "stooges and dupes of the Kremlin." With the customary angry growl in his voice, McCarthy complained that under the Truman administration, the United States would never win the Cold War. America, he concluded, could not "fight world Communism with planners who are either traitors or who are hip-deep in their own failure."

McCarthy could be flowery. No matter that TV exploited pictures more than words; the senator knew how to paint verbal images in the minds of his audiences. On the evening news on July 25, 1950, for example, McCarthy attacked one of his chief critics, Senator Joseph Tydings of Maryland. Speaking of Tydings' Senate committee, which had accused him of fraud, McCarthy flamboyantly told a national TV audience:

> If they are allowed to succeed, they will keep in power those individuals who are in the State Department today, and those who are responsible for American boys lying face down in the Korean mud with their hands tied behind their backs and their faces shot off. If this fraud is allowed to succeed, it will mean that the trail of blood for which those men are responsible will extend across the sands of Iran right over into the very streets of Berlin. Now if we can prevent it, that fraud will not succeed. This fight isn't over. It's only started.

Senator McCarthy appeared on many TV discussion programs in the early 1950s. He was on "Chronoscope," "Meet the Press," and "American Forum of the Air." Always, McCarthy demonstrated his peculiar argumentative style: making broad charges certain to garner headlines the next day; dropping names, dates, and specifics even if they were inaccurate; and dominating any opposing views by undermining the credibility of rival speakers on the show. On "American Forum of the Air" on June 21, 1953, for example, McCarthy employed accusations, oversimplifications, and interruptions to dominate a discussion about the meaning of McCarthyism in international affairs. To one reviewer, the senator's debating "acrobatics" were "by turn bland and savagely harsh for vocal effects," and marked by "the solemn, intense, momentous pose of a court prosecuting attorney."[5 7]

McCarthy was a good television performer. TV critic Jack Gould described him as "a master of effective understatement (he seldom telegraphs his punch lines), but skillfully exploits an elementary rule of showmanship—a sensation or two never fails to hold an audience." And his message was believed. McCarthy continued to enjoy great popularity among the American people despite the fact that his enemies used the term "McCarthyism" to mean "the use of indiscriminate, often unfounded, accusations, sensationalism, inquisitorial investigative methods, etc., ostensibly in the suppression of Communism."[5 8]

McCarthy was not alone in his crusade against a perceived Red menace. Among his closest allies was the literate, telegenic William F. Buckley, Jr., who wrote frequently in defense of McCarthy and appeared on TV to cajole critics and boost the anti-Communist movement. In addition to Buckley, close McCarthy loyalists included a host of senators, representatives, patriotic groups, and personal aides such as Roy Cohn and G. David Schine.

For anyone grown weary of the reformism of the New Deal and Truman's Fair Deal, anti-Communism was a useful weapon with which to pound the administration or any liberal Democrat who might wish to succeed the incumbent chief executive. Anti-Communism was also a tool of those Southern Democrats fearful of more civil rights progress from Truman. But the fear of Communism at home and abroad was most profitably exploited by the Republican party—20 years out of the White House—during the 1952 presidential election.

Candidate Dwight D. Eisenhower did not have to be a vociferous anti-Communist. There were others in his party willing to speak for him on this subject. Vice-presidential nominee Richard M. Nixon was on the Republican ticket primarily because of his highly publicized anti-Communist activities while in the House of Representatives and Senate. The Republican National Committee prepared strong doses of anti-Communism for the campaign. One advertisement on radio accused the Democrats of saving Communism from collapse by establishing diplomatic relations with the USSR in 1933. "Then the Communists' Trojan Horse program began in earnest in the United States," declared a deep-voiced narrator, for now "Communists, fellow travelers, and front agents promptly flooded Washington and began to worm their way into the government of the United States." In another such radio announcement, General Eisenhower lent his weight to the cause as he explained American involvement in the Korean War. "We are in that war," said Ike, "because this administration abandoned China to the Communists."

As might be expected, the most polished demolisher of the Democrats was Senator McCarthy. By the fall of 1952 he had abandoned innuendo and directly denounced his critics. In a televised speech he explained that it was the Republicans' job "to dislodge the traitors from every place where they've been sent to do their traitorous work." Moreover, he remarked:

> One Communist in the defense plant is one Communist too many. One Communist on the faculty of one university is one Communist too many. One Communist among the American advisers at Yalta was one Communist too many. And even if there were only one Communist in the State Department, that would be still one Communist too many.

McCarthy's most biting TV appearance was reserved for October 27, 1952, only one week before the election. He declared that "we are at war tonight" against international atheistic Communism, and the result would be either "victory or death." He called American foreign policy "suicidal, Kremlin-directed," and a "deliberate, planned retreat from victory." McCarthy warned that "the millions of loyal Democrats no longer have a loyal party in Washington."

McCarthy saved his most devastating accusations for Adlai E. Stevenson, the Democratic nominee running against Eisenhower. The senator pummeled Stevenson's advisers for having Communist connections. He linked the Democratic nominee to Red organizations and to Alger Hiss, a former State Department employee popularly believed to have been a Communist, and convicted of committing perjury during a congressional investigation. Because Stevenson had verbally defended Hiss—a man McCarthy casually termed "the arch-traitor of our times"—the senator slashed at the Democratic nominee's reputation. Having earlier referred to him as "Alger, I mean Adlai," McCarthy attacked:

> Here we have a man who says, "I want to be your President," claiming that Hiss's reputation was good but not very good. . . . There are no

degrees of loyalty in the United States. A man is either loyal or he's disloyal. There is no such thing as being a little bit disloyal, or partly a
traitor.

McCarthy and his "ism" represented such a powerful force that
even President Eisenhower was intimidated by its potential. Congressmen and senators feared McCarthy's wrath. When 25 Senate votes
were cast against Robert E. Lee, a right-wing nominee to the FCC
whom McCarthy backed, *Variety* in early 1954 saw the vote as a
"surprising show of strength" against the senator's formidable reputation.[59]

Several months earlier McCarthy was at his best on national television, delivering a ringing condemnation of the ousted Truman administration as one that "crawled with Communists." On November
16, 1953, Truman had delivered a televised speech in which he assailed McCarthyism. Eight days later the senator from Wisconsin was
given equal time by the networks to defend his reputation by questioning the loyalty of the former president.

McCarthy's power was based on his ability to communicate convincingly a simplistic understanding of the Cold War. Television was
a strategic medium in this process. Ironically, however, TV would
plant the seeds of McCarthy's destruction as a political force. As long
as he appeared to be the struggling champion, the underdog battling
stupidity and disloyalty in government, McCarthy was perfect for the
medium. On discussion shows, in press conferences, and in short filmed
segments on the evening news, he stood resolutely in defense of the
nation. McCarthy's undoing began, however, when TV was used to
show his investigatory style in action.

The first important blow against McCarthy occurred on "See It
Now" on March 9, 1954. Edward R. Murrow and Fred W. Friendly
launched a subtle attack upon the senator by showing him quizzing
witnesses before his Senate Permanent Subcommittee on Investigation.
The witnesses were nervous and vulnerable. Some were confused in
answering questions about actions they had taken two decades earlier.
On TV the witnesses became the underdogs as McCarthy harangued,
impugned, and defamed. In that revelatory forthrightness of which
video is capable, he appeared to be a bully. He distorted personal
histories, accused witnesses of being traitors, and generally abused
frightened people. Clearly, too, the rude senator was relying on congressional immunity to protect him from possible lawsuits for criminal slander.

Murrow did not castigate the senator for abuse of his power. Instead, he turned his verdict upon American society. However much

some would wish to deny it, Murrow said, McCarthy was a product of Cold War America, the champion of millions. Murrow's closing remarks amounted to a subtle scolding of the nation for having created and honored a mountebank:

> We will not walk in fear, one of another. We will not be driven by fear into an age of unreason if we dig deep in our history and our doctrine, and remember that we are not descended from fearful men, not from men who feared to write, to speak, to associate, and to defend causes that were for the moment unpopular. This is no time for men who oppose Senator McCarthy's methods to keep silent, or for those who approve. We can deny our heritage and our history, but we cannot escape responsibility for the result. There is no way for a citizen of a republic to abdicate his responsibilities. As a nation we have come into our full inheritance at a tender age. We proclaim ourselves—as indeed we are—the defenders of freedom, wherever it continues to exist in the world. But we cannot defend freedom abroad by deserting it at home. The actions of the junior senator from Wisconsin have caused alarm and dismay amongst our allies abroad and given considerable comfort to our enemies. And whose fault is that? Not really his, he didn't create this situation of fear, he merely exploited it—and rather successfully. Cassius was right: "The fault, dear Brutus, is not in our stars but in ourselves."

There were immediate reactions to the "See It Now" broadcast. McCarthy and his allies denounced the program and demanded rebuttal time. The result was a half-hour prepared by the McCarthy staff that defended the senator and questioned the loyalty of Murrow. It was aired on "See It Now" on April 6.

More important, two weeks after the original program, McCarthy's Senate committee voted to permit TV coverage of its most controversial investigation to date: a probe into possible Communist infiltration in the U.S. Army. The Army-McCarthy hearings, as the inquiry was popularly called, began on April 22, 1953, and continued for 18 sessions. After a week-long recess, the hearings were resumed on May 24 for another 18 meetings. Before they ended on June 24, the Army-McCarthy hearings had produced 32 witnesses, 2 million words on 7,424 pages of transcript—and 187 hours of television time. Further, the hearings proved to be a crushing experience for McCarthy. The White House would not cooperate with him. With elections in the fall, Republicans tried to end the hearings as soon as possible, as McCarthy's sullen attitude toward the Army quickly became a debilitating revelation of his own pettiness and ambition.

Clearly, the senator had exceeded the boundaries of permissibility in his attack upon the Army. His attempt to humiliate the Secretary of the Army, military officers, and Defense Department officials was capricious and unfair. McCarthy had no solid evidence to warrant impugning reputations with charges of disloyalty. It was most apparent on TV. McCarthy's failure in the Army investigation prompted his colleagues in the Senate to gather courage to repudiate his actions. By the end of the year the Senate voted 67 to 22 to censure McCarthy for abusive, contemptuous conduct toward his fellow senators.

Following the censure, McCarthy openly attacked President Eisenhower. He criticized the chief executive for showing "tolerance" toward Communist China, and for congratulating the senators who voted for his censure. McCarthy also apologized to the nation for having supported Eisenhower in 1952. The action by the Senate, however, effectively stifled his official power. Democratic control of the Senate after the elections of 1954 stripped McCarthy of his committee chairmanship. Two years later, in political eclipse, Senator McCarthy died.

Television is rightly credited with having been important in the popular discrediting of Senator McCarthy and McCarthyism. As Eric Sevareid of CBS phrased it on "Years of Crisis: 1954," "McCarthyism is changing from an 'ism' to a 'wasm.'" But it was not a clean victory. Years later, in rejecting the notion that TV had caused McCarthy's collapse, Edward R. Murrow assailed the feeble response of TV to the senator. "The timidity of television in dealing with this man when he was spreading fear throughout the land," Murrow told the British Association for the Advancement of Science in October 1959, "is not something to which this art of communication can point with pride, nor should it be allowed to forget it."[60]

Video coverage of the Army-McCarthy hearings also was no ringing victory for public affairs television. The two networks that carried the hearings live, ABC and Dumont, did so because they had virtually no morning or afternoon programming. With a roster of sponsored soap operas and game shows, CBS rejected the hearings, preferring to air a 45-minute daily summation at 11:30 P.M. NBC offered the hearings live for two days. But since those two days cost $125,000 in lost advertising revenue, that network also opted for a late-evening summary.

There were also local problems. Viewers in Seattle-Tacoma saw only the morning sessions because CBS needed the area's only TV cable to air its afternoon shows. The afternoon hearings were canceled in Cleveland because of major league baseball. Baltimore also had live coverage dropped because of professional baseball games. In Los Angeles the hearings were canceled after one week because "little interest in coverage was seen."

When the hearings resumed in May, TV interest was further diminished. Ten stations carried the Dumont coverage, the same number as in April. But the ABC video feed was accepted by only 54 outlets, compared with 71 stations originally. The May hearings were shown live in only 49 markets, a national coverage of only 60 percent. Viewer interest also lagged. After an estimated 30 million viewers saw the opening session, ratings dropped precipitously. *Variety* cynically concluded, "The Army-McCarthy hearings appear to have settled into a groove as television's latest soap opera—long run, low-rated, and sexless . . . but they take your mind off the H-bomb for an hour or so."[61]

Senator McCarthy had been useful to his Republican colleagues. He had helped the party trounce Stevenson and the Democrats in 1952, sweeping a Republican Congress and Dwight D. Eisenhower into power. With Ike came such outspoken anti-Communists as Nixon, John Foster Dulles, and Allen B. Dulles. McCarthy, however, had clearly moved beyond this category of politician. He had approached demagogic proportions, threatening even the command structure of the U.S. Army. A victory in that contest would have brought him face to face with the White House—occupied now by a retired general. In the Army-McCarthy hearings, the senator from Wisconsin had become not only a divisive embarrassment to the Republicans but also a dangerous threat to the republic.

Although McCarthy's fall meant the discrediting of McCarthyism, it did not signify the end of anti-Communism as an alluring mind-set. McCarthyism was only one of the more virulent strands of this popular hatred of the political left. Thriving on fear and ignorance, McCarthyism represented oppressive power emanating from unsubstantiated accusation. It pursued enemies of the state where there were no enemies. It was aggressive and egotistical, colorful and falsely reassuring. The Army-McCarthy hearings only demonstrated that McCarthyism had overstepped the boundaries of permissibility in American politics as well as television. They did not demonstrate popular determination to reappraise anti-Communism or to approach the East-West struggle in more realistic terms. Anti-Communism continued to thrive in politics and video.

THE BOUNDARIES OF TELEVISION POLITICS: PRESIDENTIAL USE OF TV

Politics and television formed a natural alliance between ends and means, a magnetic marriage of intention and facilitation. Where Franklin D. Roosevelt exploited radio to rally public opinion to his policies,

TV afforded politicians even greater potential for shaping public thought. Enhanced by the communication extras afforded by the ability to be seen as well as heard, government leaders now entered the homes and the privacy of millions in order to persuade. It was an irresistible one-way experience: the politician presented and the viewer accepted. The word was now visible. The argument became palpable.

Still, video had its limitations that had to be respected. Television not only could reveal inaccuracy or a slip of the tongue, it could also illustrate the errant glance, the smug expression, the exposed fang. The boundaries of TV behavior had been violated by the pugnacious Senator McCarthy, and TV nationally projected his arrogant, intimidating, ignorant reality. Television demanded the appearance of honesty and credibility. It flattered the cordial, those who seemed friendly and approachable. This was not a medium for the harangue. The long-winded boast was boring and self-defeating on TV. This was an instrument for verisimilitude. Its persuasive potential worked best for the leader who delivered ideas with apparent surety tempered by apparent human warmth. Although thespian skills could assist the politician employing video, he need not have experience as an actor. The best television politician used the medium for its emotional impact. He used it as an audiovisual conduit showing himself as a trustworthy leader and a fair, genuinely concerned authority figure.

Even before he became president, Dwight David Eisenhower found television important in keeping his name and reputation before the American public. It was no coincidence that Henry R. Luce—the publisher of *Time, Life,* and *Fortune* magazines—approved a "March of Time" TV series based upon Ike's memoirs of World War II. "Crusade in Europe" premiered on ABC in the spring of 1949. Each of its 26 episodes opened with a sketch of General Eisenhower. Then a page of text with a sentence or two spotlighted announced the theme for the individual program. The series was so successful that it was rerun immediately. As the United States entered a new war in Korea where old generals like Douglas MacArthur renewed their public careers, and fresh military leaders like Matthew Ridgeway would soon emerge as national heroes, "Crusade in Europe" kept before the American people the accomplishments of the triumphant general whose greatness as a leader was demonstrated in World War II.

If the historic Ike was impressive on television, the contemporary Ike was also memorable. One of Eisenhower's most significant uses of video occurred on February 2, 1951, when he delivered a televised report to the nation concerning the state of military preparedness within NATO. As NATO supreme commander, Ike had toured Allied facilities and now reassured Americans that peace was secure in Europe and Communism was being held in check in that most sensitive area. Coming at a time when party leaders were assessing possible candidates for the presidency the following year, this speech by the general did much to enhance his credibility with Republicans, who were seeking the White House after two decades of Democratic domination.

From the beginning of his campaign for the presidency, Eisenhower's TV persona emerged as one of warmth and dedication. He might flounder occasionally on a word or wander sometimes in his response, but he always maintained a simple air of honesty. At a news conference televised live from his hometown of Abilene, Kansas, Eisenhower on June 5, 1952, formally announced his intention to seek the Republican nomination. Here a national television audience encountered the video image that would be familiar for the next eight and a half years. Ike seemed genuine as he confessed, "When I put my hand to any plow, I know only one rule—to work as hard as you possibly can. I am certainly going to try to work honestly, honorably, and in keeping with what I really believe the American people would like me to do."

Ike also evidenced the mistakes of language that were less embarrassments than signs of his approachability. In denying any political connection with the Democratic presidents under whom he had became a military success, only warm laughter and soft applause greeted Ike's malaprop response that "As far as any possible connection between me and a political administration of any kind, it's absolutely shibboleth—there's no such thing. A shibboleth, it's just false. It's not true." And there was demonstrated this early the human, emotional quality that endeared him to American viewers. When asked if, as a boy leaving home, he ever dreamed he would someday return to Abilene to lauch a presidential campaign, there was a touch of democratic commonness when Ike replied, "Well, I don't know what dreams crowd the head of a young boy. But, I think, that before I left my real problem was whether to try to be a Hans [Honus] Wagner or a railroad conductor."

For Eisenhower and the Republicans, this was a television campaign for the White House. No whistle-stop railroad tours such as Harry S. Truman had undertaken four years earlier; there were now 19 million TV sets with 58 million viewers being serviced by TV stations in 64 markets of the United States. In one TV appearance or advertisement, Ike could speak to the electorate more efficiently than any of his predecessors. Under the tutelage of the advertising agency Batten, Barton, Durstine & Osborn, the Republican candidate concentrated on a series of short spot announcements for which TV time was purchased in the final weeks of the campaign. Ike was the first presidential aspirant to be sold in TV commercials. A typical spot offered Ike and the common man:

> ANNOUNCER: Eisenhower answers the nation!
> CITIZEN: What about the high cost of living, General?
> EISENHOWER: My wife, Mamie, worries about the same thing. I tell her it's our job to change that on November 4th.[62]

Another commercial proclaimed the humble roots of "The Man from Abilene," and the impressive accomplishments of the former 5-star General of the Army. As a picture of Ike's childhood home and then his contemporary photograph were superimposed on a silhouetted map of the United States—and as film from World War II was merged with contemporary footage—an announcer proclaimed,

> The Man from Abilene! Out of the heartland of America, out of this small frame house in Abilene, Kansas, came a man: Dwight D. Eisenhower. Through the crucial hour of historic D-Day, he brought us to the triumph and peace of V-E Day. Now another crucial hour in our history. The nation—haunted by the stalemate in Korea—looks to Eisenhower. . . . for the number one job of our time. . . . Vote for Eisenhower.

The Republican National Committee and BBD&O also purchased large chunks of national television time to demonstrate the candidate, not in the stilted oratory at which the Democratic nominee, Adlai Stevenson, was so accomplished, but in a more comfortable manner. Typical was Ike's televised discussion of issues with Earl Warren, the former governor of California and Republican candidate for vice-president in 1948. On October 31, 1952, Ike and Earl engaged in a half-hour of chitchat on NBC West Coast stations. They spoke about national security, veterans' benefits, conservation, farm policies, and the like. In this atmosphere of well-rehearsed informality, the general and the governor also treated Eisenhower's recent pledge regarding the Korean War.

> WARREN: You know, everybody out West, as they are in every part of the country, is interested in that Korean War—not interested as much as they are concerned. And they got a tremendous uplift the other day when you said if you were elected you would go out there

personally and see conditions in the field. Now I know there was some criticism about that, General. It might be that some people couldn't learn any thing about going over to Korea, but I'll bet my money that you'd learn something about going to Korea.

EISENHOWER: Well, I know this. I know that during the war I never failed to learn something every time I went forward. By the way, you know that both prime ministers and presidents came to visit my theater of war. They thought they learned something. Now I want to point out that there is no patent-medicine way of winning the Korean War. It's a difficult situation. To my mind, therefore, all the more reason for someone bearing very heavy responsibilities with respect to that should go out and see. I cannot imagine any problem today that's of more interest to the American people. Therefore, my feeling was and is, I want to learn, I want to know.

Still another pattern that would mark President Eisenhower's use of national television emerged in the 1952 campaign. This involved the use of other prominent Republicans to make nationally televised statements regarding policy matters. During his presidency this task would be most effectively carried out by John Foster Dulles. But in the campaign the role was admirably accomplished by Clare Booth Luce on two occasions in late October. The author, former congress-woman, and wife of Henry R. Luce was at her anti-Communist best in a telecast of October 26. Here she employed the hostile slogans and oversimplifications candidate Eisenhower generally avoided. She alleged that the United States could never know security or continuing prosperity—nor could the world have continuing peace—until the problem of Communism was solved. Luce referred to the way "Communism's vicious conspiracy had taken 12 countries behind the Iron Curtain, how more than 100 million people a year had been enslaved by Soviet Russia since the close of World War II seven years ago." She praised the FBI and HUAC for their fight against Red treachery, but noted that the Communists were active in Canada and even in the United States. Luce also assailed Stevenson, Dean Acheson, and Truman for "an administration which did not vigorously prosecute spies." This, she continued, "has cost us China and for that loss the American people are paying in blood and in treasure. We are paying for it in Korea." Predictably, Luce concluded with hosannahs for Dwight D. Eisenhower—"a man of courage and wisdom and wide experience, above all a man of honor."

Once elected, Ike made the president a familiar video personage. In addition to the countless filmed pieces on news and documentary shows, he made use of his access to free live television. Unlike Truman, who experimented with TV as early as 1946 but preferred to use it only in crises or on special occasions, the new president appeared on TV in traditional situations (inaugurations, State of the Union addresses), but also in contexts ranging from periodic reports to Christmas tree-lighting ceremonies. Ike even employed a popular movie actor, Robert Montgomery, to advise him on television techniques.

The networks covered Eisenhower when he spoke to conventions, university audiences, and civic organizations. There were periodic reports on topics such as his first year in office (January 4, 1954), his veto of a farm bill (April 16, 1956), and the dispatch of federal troops to racially embattled Little Rock (September 24, 1957). After six months in office he appeared on June 3, 1953, with four members of his cabinet, in a well-prepared "spontaneous" discussion of administration accomplishments. American TV covered his speech to the Canadian Parliament (July 9, 1958). And he appeared with an all-star Hollywood cast on "Dinner with the President" (November 23, 1953), the fortieth anniversary celebration of the Anti-Defamation League of B'nai B'rith. Here he spoke extemporaneously for ten minutes about his personal dedication to maintaining civil liberties and civil rights.[63]

Eisenhower also opened the presidential news conference to television. On January 19, 1955, the White House agreed to let TV networks film or tape Ike's press gatherings. In case Ike made an inadvertent statement, press secretary James C. Hagerty retained the right to review and edit all network recordings.[64]

Because of his use of free television time, the president established a powerful relationship with the American people. On the one hand it was a private tie, the concerned chief executive reporting to his constituents on matters of state or personal affairs. Following his heart attack in September 1955, for example, Ike appeared on TV to reassure the public that he could continue in office. In February 1956 he held a press conference and then spoke to the nation about his readiness to run for reelection. Following abdominal surgery in the spring of 1956, he again used TV to show the nation he was fully recovered. In no small way television was responsible for the overwhelming reelection of Eisenhower—by a larger plurality, and with more popular and electoral votes, than in 1952.

But there was another dimension to this television relationship between president and citizen. Eisenhower was forging a pattern of presidential manipulation of TV. When the chief executive requested free air time, the networks almost always gave him unfettered access to the nation. When he announced an upcoming important speech, the networks usually asked permission to televise it. Long before radio, and certainly television, Theodore Roosevelt had called the presidency a "bully pulpit" because it gave the incumbent a powerfully persuasive vantage from which to preach his political values to the public. Roosevelt, of course, was referring to a world of speeches and statements that print media would spread to a wider audience. Television increased prodigiously the ability of a modern chief executive to reach his constituents.

Eisenhower recognized the potency of video in shaping popular political viewpoints. In a speech televised nationally on May 24, 1955, the president told the National Association of Radio and Television Broadcasters that TV and radio had surpassed print and now exerted a powerful influence upon public opinion. Ike recognized the emotional force of broadcasting, telling the NARTB and the nation, "You put an appealing voice or an engaging personality in the living room of the home where there are impressionable people from the age of understanding on up." He further maintained, "In many ways therefore the effect of your industry in swaying public opinion, and I think particularly about burning questions of the moment, may even be greater than the press. . . . "

Throughout his presidency, Ike used his appealing, engaging TV persona to sway public opinion. From this electronic "bully pulpit," he preached to the impressionable people. And he found them ready to believe, willing to trust, even eager to follow. Through television, Eisenhower's strongly held political premises became the consensus values of the nation.

Eisenhower preached a cosmology of the world locked in an all-consuming struggle between Good and Evil. In his first inaugural address he called the Cold War "no argument between slightly differing philosophies. This conflict strikes directly at the faith of our fathers and the lives of our sons. . . . Freedom is pitted against slavery; lightness against the dark." Throughout the remainder of his terms in office, Ike held to this premise. In a televised speech at Baylor University on May 25, 1956, the president attacked Communism as a gigantic failure. "According to that doctrine, there is no God; there is no soul in man; there is no reward beyond the satisfaction of daily needs," he told the nation. "Consequently, toward the human being, Communism is cruel, intolerant, materialistic," he declared.

By the time of his State of the Union address in 1958, Eisenhower saw the world struggle intensified. "The threat to our safety, and to the hope of a peaceful world, can be simply stated," suggested Ike, "It is Communist imperialism." But, he added, Soviet expansion was being reinforced "by an advancing industrial, military and scientific establishment." He continued:

> But what makes the Soviet threat unique in history is its all-inclusiveness. Every human activity is pressed into service as a weapon of expansion. Trade, economic development, military powers, arts, science, education, the whole world of ideas—all harnessed to the same chariot of expansion. The Soviets are, in short, waging total Cold War.

Even in the waning months of his second term, Eisenhower delineated the same American enemy. Following his tour of the Far East, he spoke to the public on June 27, 1960, arguing that "any policy against Communist imperialism requires that we never be bluffed, cajoled, blinded, or frightened." And still, through the millions of TV sets in the nation, came the image of the honorable strength of the United States pitted against the sinister expansionism of the Red empire.

> We cannot win out against the Communist purpose to dominate the world by being timid, passive, or apologetic when we are acting in our own and the Free World's interests. We must accept the risks of bold action with coolness and courage. We must be strong but we must never forget that peace can never be won by arms alone; we will be firm but never truculent; we will be fair but never fearful; we will always extend friendship wherever friendship is offered honestly to us.

Eisenhower also saw the world in a fragile balance where stability and the security of nations were interrelated. Even before he became president, he described such a situation as it related to Europe. In his NATO speech of February 2, 1951, General Eisenhower pondered the fate of the world should Western Europe be overrun by Communism. Should this occur, he said, "many economically dependent areas in Africa and the Middle East would be affected by the debacle. Southeast Asia would probably soon be lost." He continued, "Thus, we could be cut off from the raw materials of all these regions—materials that we need for existence." His conclusion was an ominous one: "World destiny would then be dictated by imperialistic powers whose avowed purpose is the destruction of freedom."[65]

Three years later, President Eisenhower used the same political dynamic to describe what he termed "the 'falling domino' principle." In his press conference of April 7, 1954, Ike set forth the notion that, as the "domino theory," shaped the political thinking of all his successors in the White House: "You have a row of dominoes set up, you knock over the first one, and what will happen to the last one is the certainty that it will go over very quickly. So you have a beginning of a disintegration that would have the most profound influences." Specifically, the president was suggesting that if Indochina fell to the Communists, all of East Asia inexorably would fall to the Reds.

> . . . the loss of Indochina, of Burma, of Thailand, of the Peninsula, and Indonesia following, now you begin to talk about areas that not only multiply the disadvantages that you would suffer through loss of materials, sources of materials, but now you are talking really about millions and millions and millions of people . . . . It turns the so-called island defensive chain of Japan, Formosa, and the Philippines and to the southward; it moves in to threaten Australia and New Zealand. It takes away, in its economic aspects, that region that Japan must have as a trading area or Japan, in turn, will have only one place in the world to go—that is, toward Communist areas in order to live. So, the possible consequences of the loss are just incalculable to the Free World.

As important as his imagery of a world wracked by moral struggle and fragile geopolitical existence, was the president's interpretation of the United States as approaching perfection. In one of his most paternal speeches, on April 5, 1954, Ike sought to allay popular fears by emphasizing the good aspects of America. He recognized this trepidation as emanating from Communist threats abroad and at home. But he called forth nationalistic pride when he assured the TV audience, "I know that this is the most productive nation on earth, that we are richer by any standard of comparison, than is any other nation in the world." He spoke also of strength. "We know that we have a great military strength—economic—intellectual," he said "But I want to call your particular attention to spiritual strength."

The president reminded viewers of other virtues: "the American belief in decency and justice and progress, and the value of individual liberty . . . . " He described, too, a consensus national goal—"a free and prosperous world"—and he reassuringly stated, "There is a growing understanding in the world of the decency and justice of the American position in opposing the slavery of any nation." For a people gripped by Cold War anxieties, Ike concluded his calming discourse with the suggestion that America now had an international mission whose origins seemingly rested with Providence:

> Of course there are risks if we are not vigilant. But we do not have to be hysterical. We can be vigilant. We can be Americans. We can stand up

and hold up our heads and say: America is the greatest force that God has ever allowed to exist on His footstool. As such it is up to us to lead this world to a peaceful and secure existence.

Within his administration, Eisenhower was not alone in manipulating television for political ends. The United States Information Agency (USIA), a principal source for American propaganda overseas, recognized the critical role TV played in the struggle for political allegiance. Between fiscal 1955 and 1957, USIA funds for production and placement of video programs on foreign stations skyrocketed from $376,000 to $5.9 million. This latter figure represented one-quarter of the USIA budget for radio-TV operations.[66]

At home, Vice-President Richard M. Nixon certainly knew the persuasive power of television. It was a TV performance—his famous "Checkers" speech on September 23, 1952—that convinced voters he was no crook, kept him on the Republican national ticket, and saved his political career. Nixon also understood the importance of video in creating popular support for administration programs. He made this abundantly evident on January 13, 1958, when he spoke to the annual convention of CBS Television affiliates, telling the station owners it was important for them to support the administration's defense and foreign aid programs with on-air editorials. "People with your power," Nixon remarked, "have a priviledge and duty to bring the situation home to the people that we must be strong militarily, but that at the same time, we've got to do what must be done in a nonmilitary way."[67]

Excepting the president, however, no government official more fully exploited video than Secretary of State John Foster Dulles. With the approval of the White House, Dulles appeared regularly in a variety of contexts. He was interviewed on programs such as "Meet the Press" and Martin Agronsky's "Look Here!" He was televised live and/or on film when he spoke to organizations as diverse as the United Nations (June 24, 1955), the American Legion (October 10, 1955), and the 4-H Clubs (November 29, 1954), and twice he was televised in dialogue with the president (May 17, 1955, and December 23, 1957). On June 27, 1956, his press conference was broadcast live.

Dulles was most familiar on TV for his public reports on matters of urgency. During his tenure as head of the State Department, Dulles traveled 559,988 miles to conferences and meetings with foreign ministers and heads of state. Upon returning home, the secretary frequently delivered short televised reports on his accomplishments. Between 1953 and 1957, when ill health slowed him down, Dulles made 18

TV reports on his travels and related matters of national concern. Fittingly, when he died in May 1959, CBS and NBC interrupted their daytime programming to televise his funeral.

But Dulles was much more than a video personality. Until his resignation a month before his death, he was the most important creator of American foreign policy under Eisenhower. His values became administration values. His outlook on life and the world became that of the U.S. government. And long after he was gone, the legacy of Dulles endured in American foreign relations. Importantly, those values and interpretations, so often shared with the TV audience, were unalterably anti-Communist.

Dulles brought to his anti-Communism the indignation of an aggrieved moralist. He was at once the puritanical theologian of detestation and the policy maker turning Cold War fear and prejudice into national action. Communism, not Russia; ideology, not power politics, were the true enemies, in Dulles' view. The British ambassador to the United States, Sir Oliver Franks, knew well that the likes of Dulles were not new to history, for in earlier times of international tension and disorder, when levelheaded leadership was needed, other oversimplifying moralists had appeared. As Franks described it:

> Three or four centuries ago, when Reformation and Counter-Reformation divided Europe into armed camps, in an age of wars of religion, it was not so rare to encounter men of the type of Dulles. Like them ... he came to unshakeable convictions of a religious and theological order. Like them, he saw the world as an arena in which the forces of good and evil were continuously at war.[68]

Under Dulles the policy of containment was enhanced, even transcended, in a series of treaties and militant pronouncements. He forged the Southeast Asia Treaty Organization, which linked the United States with other nations—Great Britian, France, Thailand, the Philippines, Pakistan, Australia, and New Zealand—in a military alliance intended to check the spread of Communism in Asia. Dulles offered embellishments of the containment policy. He spoke now of instant and massive retaliation—and the will to use it—in meeting Red aggression. He called for a "rollback" of Communism in Asia. He spoke often, giving only unclear definitions, of the "liberation" of Asians and East Europeans living under Communism. He also boasted of "brinkmanship," his diplomatic method of taking chances for peace—"The ability to get to the verge without getting into war is a necessary art. . . . if you are scared to go to the brink you are lost."[69]

But the secretary's indignant brand of morality was tempered on occasion by a sense of political pragmatism. After all, he had come from the world of New York state politics, and in 1949-51 he had represented New York in the U.S. Senate. He understood, for example, that economic conditions in the decolonizing nations were critical in the battle for ideological adherents. He told a TV audience on December 23, 1957, "It is essential that the Free World nations which have amassed capital should increasingly put this to work in the capital-hungry Free World nations. Otherwise, they may be forced to turn to the Communist bloc for aid at a price which may be their freedom."[70]

Dulles also knew the importance of protecting the private foreign investments of influential Americans, especially when reformist governments of the left threatened expropriation. Nowhere was he more blatant in this regard than in Guatemala in the spring of 1954.[71] Here the duly elected, nationalistic president, Jacobo Arbenz Guzman, took power in March 1951 and expropriated unused land owned by the powerful United Fruit Company. But, in Dulles' view, reformers considered anti-American could not come to power in the Western Hemisphere even by democratic means; and the property of wealthy American corporations, even if not being utilized, could not be confiscated by foreign governments. What had been a legitimate Guatemalan response to the need for land and food was seen in different terms by Dulles. On television, he told a national audience that the actions of Arbenz were really part of "the evil purpose of the Kremlin to destroy the inter-American system . . . ."

With Dulles' concurrence, the Central Intelligence Agency made short work of the leftist government in Guatemala. Under its zealous director, Allen Dulles, the younger brother of the secretary of state, the CIA had already been successful in toppling foreign leftist leadership, having overthrown the Iranian Premier Mohammed Mossadegh in 1953 and returned the loyal shah to his throne. Now in Honduras and Nicaragua the CIA recruited, trained, and armed a military force to invade Guatemala. American pilots flying U.S. planes gave air cover to the invaders who in mid-June 1954 deposed President Arbenz. The CIA then installed a new president, Carlos Castillo Armas, a Guatemalan colonel who had been trained at the U.S. Army Command School at Fort Leavenworth, Kansas.

In explaining these developments, John Foster Dulles downplayed the interests of the United Fruit Company, never mentioned the role of the CIA, and instead praised the victory for freedom that was the new regime. "For several years now," Dulles told a TV audience on

June 30, "international Communism has been probing here and there for nesting places in the Americas. It finally chose Guatemala as a spot which it could turn into an official base from which to breed subversion which would extend to the other American republics." The Arbenz government, he asserted, was already getting arms from behind the Iron Curtain, already sending Guatemalan Reds into other Latin American nations to plot subversion, assassination, and strikes. Guatemala was now saved, he said, from "being used by Communist dictatorships to serve the Communists' lust for power."[72]

If the Guatemalan operation had been neat, quick, and successful, Dulles' policies in Southeast Asia were considerably less efficient. He urged the French to accept nothing less than an anti-Communist settlement in their Indochina war. After the victory of the Communist-led Viet Minh nationalist forces at Dien Bien Phu in mid-1954, and the subsequent withdrawal of France from Southeast Asia, the secretary of state continued to seek united action with France and Britain to control the destiny of the newly independent states of Cambodia, Laos, and Vietnam. At the Geneva Conference in July 1954, where the fate of Indochina was decided, Dulles snubbed the Chinese delegate, Chou En-lai, and later refused to sign the final Accords.

Dulles' policies divided Vietnam into two states, one Communist and one anti-Communist. The Geneva Accords called the division temporary and demanded elections for reunification within two years. Instead, Dulles praised the American-installed leader in Saigon, Ngo Dinh Diem, and consistently assailed the Communist leader, Ho Chi Minh, the popular favorite among all Vietnamese and the head of government in North Vietnam. Dulles and Diem opposed elections, and they were never held. When parliamentary elections in Laos gave the Communist Pathet Lao a majority, Dulles sanctioned a coup by rightist forces that imprisoned the Communist leader and led that country toward civil war.

Further, Dulles was not chary about employing U.S. troops to accomplish his ends. Throughout the late 1950s the United States abided by the terms of the Geneva Accords, which allowed it to maintain up to 685 troops—mostly CIA and Special Forces contingents—in South Vietnam. In 1959 the CIA entered Laos and organized an army of up to 40,000 Meo tribesmen to fight the Pathet Lao. When John F. Kennedy came into office, he found that 700 American troops were in Laos recruiting and training anti-Communist "mercenaries" in return for Meo control of the opium traffic in the Golden Triangle area of Southeast Asia.[73] While the Eisenhower administration did not start the Vietnam War of the Kennedy-Johnson years, Dulles' policies in the 1950s certainly laid the groundwork for that conflict.

When he spoke on television, John Foster Dulles did not explain the honest details of his politics. He used the medium to foster popular faith in his vision of an anti-Communist future for Southeast Asia. For years in news conferences, reports to the public, interviews, and airport confrontations, he assured the citizenry that national interest and belief in freedom demanded American involvement in the power vacuum that once was French Indochina.

On March 29, 1954, Dulles stated a theme familiar throughout his tenure: "The imposition on Southeast Asia of the political system of Communist Russia and its Chinese Communist ally, by whatever means, would be a grave threat to the whole free world community."[74] Five weeks later he told a national TV audience that the defense of the United States did not begin at the nation's borders. "Free people will never remain free unless they are willing to fight for their vital interests," he declared. "Furthermore, vital interests can no longer be protected merely by local defense. The key to successful defense and to the deterring of attack is association for mutual defense. That is what the United States seeks in Southeast Asia."[75]

Dulles' televised speeches never deviated from his earliest assessments. His ideas, based on his sense of moral order for the world, were frozen. On March 8, 1955, the secretary reported to the nation on his two-week tour of Southeast Asia and the western Pacific. Dulles spoke of liberty and freedom in South Vietnam, and oppression and military threats in the North. He commended Premier Diem, calling him "a true patriot, dedicated to the independence and to the enjoyment by his people of political and religious freedom," adding that "I am convinced that his Government deserves the support which the United States is giving to create an efficient, loyal military force and sounder economic conditions."[76]

What Dulles did not say in this speech was as significant as what he did say. Dulles made no reference to the repressive regime Diem was actually establishing in South Vietnam. He offered no indication that within three years popular resistance—by Communists and non-Communists—would precipitate a civil war against Diem that by January 1959 would encourage Hanoi to abandon its initial reticence and call for the violent overthrow of Diem and the unification of the two Vietnams.[77] Instead, Dulles used his TV address to state, "We have power that is great. We have a cause that is just. And I do not doubt that we have the fortitude to use that power in defense of that just cause."[78]

There were similarities between the stated policies and actions of Dulles and TV programming popular during the Cold War. He shared many of the attributes of Western heroes who raced across TV screens, saving innocents from evil men, preserving civilized society from the onslaughts of sinister, faithless criminality. Dulles embodied the morality of a Sunday-morning religious feature. Together with his brother at the CIA, Dulles had the nationalistic instincts of a television spy ready to go to the brink to save the world. His praise of American military prowess paralleled those many TV shows highlighting great performances by the armed forces in historic wars, as well as the preparedness of the military for contemporary and future challenges.

In May 1955 the secretary of state took part in a televised dialogue with President Eisenhower. The program, however, became a lecture by Dulles in which Ike only offered periodic interjections. Jack Gould in the *New York Times* reported that TV had mistakenly cast the star in a supporting role and that Eisenhower's presence only distracted from Dulles' performance.[79] What Gould overlooked, however, was that the secretary was a TV star in his own right. More than any other political personality of his time, with the exception of the president, Dulles exploited the medium to popularize his policies. Without challenge and without rebuttal, the secretary helped convince the public to accept an interpretation of the world that was dangerously self-centered and politically immature.

His biographer, Townsend Hoopes, has argued that John Foster Dulles was largely responsible for the 20-year American "pursuit of a phantom 'anti-Communist' solution" in Vietnam. He blamed Dulles for "this national self-imprisonment in an abstraction, which may have destroyed Vietnamese society and which has dragged both the Vietnamese and American peoples through oceans of blood and frightful bogs of learning." Hoopes said further of Dulles:

> His conviction, his willpower, his political maneuvering, his strident and simplistic rhetoric over a period of years made a deep imprint on the national psyche and thereby a major contribution to a national state of mind so persistent that three presidents after Eisenhower were convinced there could be no 'letting go' in Vietnam.[80]

Clearly, Dulles' "deep imprint on the national psyche" was accomplished principally by television. It seems obvious, too, that Dulles and his president showed future presidents the singular importance of television in persuading the public to accept an American military commitment in Southeast Asia.

THE FLOURISHING OF ANTI-COMMUNISM

Throughout the 1930s, as Fascism was on the rise in Europe, news broadcasters in the United States carefully avoided partisanship. Of course there were radio journalists who criticized the Nazis and their allies, but they were carefully identified as commentators, and they represented a wide spectrum of political opinions. As the industrialized nations entered a two-front World War II, Americans were well informed on pro-war and anti-war positions; they had been exposed to a variety of controversial opinions; they had information at their disposal with which to assess the world situation; and they could rely on network broadcast journalism for a relatively honest description of international developments and the American stake in them.

The objectivity and thoroughness provided by broadcasting in the 1930s was seriously debased in television by the mid-1950s. TV served a different United States by this date. This was no longer isolationist America. Instead, it was the richest and most powerful nation in the world. It was also the cornerstone of Western industrial capitalism locked in deadly struggle with Eastern Communism for political, economic, social, and intellectual control of a planet in flux.

Because it emerged in Cold War America, video reflected the popular values of the nation at the time. Because it was controlled by the same corporate and governmental institutions that directed the capitalist contest against world Communism, television became a strategic medium for preparing the American people for whatever exigencies that contest might bring.

What was created by this relationship was a context in which TV necessarily reflected anti-Communist values because audiences required, expected, even demanded them; a context in which anti-Communist values were created by television as a function of video's Cold War purpose. In a society whose capitalistic ethic made popular culture the servant of money, there should have been political diversity on television. For those who did not accept anti-Communist politics and its cultural expressions, there should have been anti-anti-Communism. But TV never accommodated diversity in the 1950s. Instead, it offered consensus politics and culture, a perspective that preached sameness and conformity. The rich multiformity of American society was never reflected in commercial TV. Just as there were few blacks, Latinos, Asians, Arabs, or native Americans honorably portrayed in network video, there was no diversity of political or cultural views. The same fearful mentality that homogenized and politicized broadcasting during World War II was now part of the fearful mentality that gripped Cold War America.

This was demonstrated, for example, in the nightly newscasts, which sought to explain the world in 15 minutes. Typical was "The Camel News Caravan" aired July 28, 1954. Hosted by John Cameron Swayze and featuring reports from some of the better NBC journalists, this telecast was marked greatly by its preoccupation with Communism and by a generalized feeling of crisis. As can be seen in Table 1, the East-West struggle was a part of virtually every segment on the nightly news except weather and sports.

Table 1 Content of "Camel News Caravan," July 28, 1954

Theme of Story or Segment	Deals Directly with Communism	Deals Indirectly with Communism	Uses Cold War Phraseology	Deals with Threat of War
1. Eisenhower and Rhee on U.S. relations with China	X		X	X
2. Suez Canal problems		X		X
3. Eisenhower's legislative program in Congress	X			
4. Congressional attack on McCarthy and McCarthyism	X		X	
5. East German military	X		X	X
6. Senator McClellan renominated	X			
7. National weather				
8. Sports scores				
9. Headlines segment:				
A. American atomic weapons plans	X		X	X
B. Niagara Falls land collapse				
C. Canada to police Vietnam armistice	X			X
D. New British cabinet appointments				
E. Ellis Island to be closed				

Anti-Communism was clearly a dominant part of American politics and culture by the mid-1950s. If this telecast from July 1954 was quantitatively preoccupied with stories about the Red menace, qualitatively the content of the evening news showed a world threatened by the spread of Communism and protected by selfless American might. In separate stories, viewers saw Red activities in China, the Soviet Union, Korea, Vietnam, and East Germany, where one of Hitler's former generals was now leading "the Red German army."

In the world projected by TV news, the United States was the only important force countering international Communist subterfuge. It was a frightening perspective in which viewers were compelled to choose sides, to opt for the evil of Communist aggression, or the good of Free World self-defense. Reassuringly, here was a tough and legalistic President Eisenhower—former leader of the American military crusade against European Fascism—defending U.S. military prerogatives in the Far East. He explained that the United States was within its rights in shooting down two Communist Chinese airplanes off the coast of China; and he demanded congressional support for his anti-Communist legislation. While viewers saw President Syngman Rhee of South Korea tell Congress that the U.S. should lead a full-scale war against Communist China, they also saw the White House righteously inform the United Nations that the U.S. would continue to arm its military with atomic weapons "as long as the Communist world continues its aggressive policy."

This anti-Communism was tough and reassuring. But it had limitations. While President Rhee was honored as a noble leader, his call for crusade was not heeded. And there was Senator Joseph R. McCarthy publicly under fire for exceeding his powers as a senator and the nation's chief anti-Communist. As can be discerned in the following transcript of that "Camel News Caravan" telecast, in both instances TV reported not only the substances of these stories but also the impracticality of both Rhee and McCarthy.

"The Camel News Caravan" as Telecast July 28, 1954[81]

ANNOUNCER: Opening.

SWAYZE: Ladies and gentlemen, a good evening to you! The Presidents of the United States and the Republic of South Korea made top news in Washington today with separate statements on the Asian problem. David Brinkley has those stories for us at NBC NEWS, WASHINGTON.

BRINKLEY: At his Wednesday news conference President Eisenhower told reporters this country will not be truculent with the Chinese Communists, but he said we will defend our rights and he said the U.S. Navy planes that shot down the two Chinese had a right to be where they were. This was taken here to be a kind of warning to the Chinese to be careful and also as a word to those of our allies who think we've been too belligerent and quick on the trigger. The President said our planes were there on legitimate business looking for the British survivors and that they would defend themselves and stay there until they have finished. Otherwise he served public notice that candidates for Congress who want his support had better vote for his program. This was a new Eisenhower policy over that of the last election when he said he supported all Republican candidates for office. Otherwise here today Syngman Rhee, President of South Korea, had the unusual honor of being invited to address a joint session of Congress in the House Chamber. His wife came with him, sat in the gallery to listen. Members of the Washington diplomatic corps were there too. He had a prepared speech but departed from it occasionally; once was when he said in an emotional way that while he is a Korean by law and by birth, by sentiment he is an American. Rhee's English is a little difficult and the members of Congress had some trouble catching all of what he said, but they got most of it like this: (Rhee in heavy accent) What he said was there ought to be what he called a counter-attack on Communist China and said it would be successful if carried out by an Asian army of more than two million men, backed up and supported by U.S. planes, guns and ships. In short, he called on this country to join in a full-scale war on China. He said he knew this would be a momentous decision for us to make but said unless the Chinese mainland is taken away from the Reds the free world ultimately will lose the war against Communism. After Rhee had spoken most members of Congress expressed admiration for him as a man and a patriotic leader but no enthusiasm for his call to arms. For example, Senator George of Georgia said it was a great fighting speech, that if all our allies had the same spirit we'd be in good shape. But as for war with China he wouldn't express any opinion. When he finished Rhee was loudly applauded but the applause was for him personally and not for his call to World War III. Now back to Camel News Headquarters in New York.

SWAYZE: In another part of the world, less than a day after Egypt and Britain settled their ancient feud about the Suez Canal, it's reported the United States played a key role in that agreement.

NARRATOR: At Kings Rest House near the pyramids final details of the agreement were worked out over a dinner that lasted five hours. Egypt's Premier, Gamal Abdel Nasser signed for his country where ratification is assured because rule is by a small military junta. British initials were affixed by War Secretary Anthony Head to an agreement providing British military withdrawal from the Suez Canal Zone in 20 months with a return permitted in case of attack on the Arab states or Turkey. The agreement was speeded up by U.S. promises to boost dollar assistance for Egypt. Winston Churchill stakes the fate of his government on its ratification tomorrow.

Commercial Announcement.

SWAYZE: Today President Eisenhower said he would be greatly disappointed if Congress failed to pass a half dozen bills in his legislative program. He named them as tax, farm, foreign aid, anti-Communist, housing and social security. Almost as he spoke the House did pass the big tax revision bill, including a cut in taxes on incomes from dividends. The measure, which reduces revenues $1,363,000 goes to the Senate tomorrow. And the House passed the foreign aid bill after cutting it a little more than 800 million dollars. Likewise in Washington senatorial critics of their colleague from Wisconsin spoke out sharply again today. And for this report we return to the nation's capital.

BRINKLEY: Today Vermont's Senator Flanders said he is determined to go ahead this Friday with his resolution to censure Senator McCarthy in spite of attacks that have been and will be made on him. Here's what he said:

FLANDERS: Let me say that I am confidently expecting attacks on myself and the supporters of my resolution, perhaps between now and July 30, certainly on July 30th. There are gumshoe tracks all around me and fingerprints on all the doorknobs. I don't have to send for an expert to trace the source of these gumshoe tracks and the fingerprints. But I'll not be diverted from my purpose of getting on Friday a vote of censure on the Junior Senator from Wisconsin. I intend to produce my own Bill of Particulars. Other senators have theirs and I hope they will state their own particulars with regard to the Senator from Wisconsin. But we should always remember that we are not merely condemning a particular action on a particular date, but that we are also dealing with an "ism." The depredations of McCarthyism launched from the perch of the chairmanship of the government's operation committee have affected the lives of all of us. McCarthyism has invaded the religious, military, educational, cultural life as well as the political affairs of our country. It is all-inclusive in its effect and must be deplored in an all-inclusive manner.

BRINKLEY: The vote will be this Friday, July 30th. Now back to New York.

SWAYZE: Senator McCarthy himself left Washington today for New York and tonight's big testimonial dinner honoring Roy Cohn. Our cameras were on hand to cover the Senator's arrival.

NARRATOR: He landed this afternoon on the way to the Hotel Astor. There, before 2,000 people tonight, Senator McCarthy will deliver the main address at a testimonial dinner for Roy Cohn, sponsored by the Joint Committee Against Communism. Accompanied by his wife and staff members Frank Carr and James Juliana the Senator faced an immediate barrage of questions that ranged from his role at tonight's dinner to his reaction to Senator Flanders.

REPORTER: Tonight's the big dinner and some of us are going on the air before the dinner. Can you tell us what words you're going to have for Mr. Cohn?

MCCARTHY: No, I don't think I can tell you now—I haven't prepared the speech yet.

REPORTER: Well, could you tell us just exactly how important you think Roy Cohn was to the committee?

MCCARTHY: Extremely important.

REPORTER: Are you gonna have a replacement soon, do you think?

MCCARTHY: It'll be impossible to replace Roy. We'll get a man to take his place, yes, but it'll be impossible to replace him.

REPORTER: Senator, how about the Flanders thing on Friday?

MCCARTHY: No reaction at all. I haven't listened to Flanders, I don't know whether I will.

REPORTER: Do you expect to be present on Friday?

MCCARTHY: I don't know if I'll take the time to listen or not. I may....

REPORTER: Senator, tonight you know for the dinner tonight some 5,000 applications have been turned back.

MCCARTHY: I understand so.

REPORTER: Do you think that's because you're speaking there or do you think it could be for Roy Cohn?

MCCARTHY: No, I think that was strictly a tribute to Roy Cohn.

SWAYZE: In Europe, where prospects for a unified defense seemed to be dwindling, the Communists are adding more men and more equipment to their growing East German military organization.

NARRATOR: And the man who heads the Red German army is the same man who surrendered to the Russians at Stalingrad. Hidden away by the Kremlin until very recently, former Field Marshall Friedrich Pollus finally emerged from obscurity at a carefully staged East Berlin news conference. American newsmen were excluded but the U.S. now sees and hears the famous marshal as he appeared at the conference on film from behind the Iron Curtain. (VOICE IN GERMAN ON FILM) His statements themselves were far from startling, mostly to the effect that Germany must not be influenced by the U.S. His appearance was headline material because it gave to the Communist-run East German forces a name famous to all Germans. Friedrich Pollus emerges to head more than 100,000 known as the People's Police, but organized as the nucleus for the rearmament of Red Germany.

SWAYZE: In Arkansas Senator John L. McClellan has apparently won renomination. However, his margin is a thin one and his chief opponent, former Governor Sid McMath, has not yet conceded. At midday

McClellan has claimed victory by 5,000 votes but what the final margin will be is a guess. McClellan blamed his thin majority on his having had a part in the Army-McCarthy hearings.

Commercial Announcement

SWAYZE: Now it's time once again for our daily reports from the Camel Weatherman. Here he is—Clint Youle at NBC in Chicago.

YOULE: Getting a little unhappy. We sure missed Chicago's forecast today. We had an unexpected shower and we cooled off, but it's only temporarily. Be hot again tomorrow from west and central Texas right diagonally clear on up, say, about as far as New York and Washington area and tomorrow there'll be some showers in the Detroit-Cleveland area, a few in through Pennsylvania and New York and to upper, oh, say interior New England. It'll also be kind of humid in with this hot area. And there'll be some heavier rains in through here and a tropical storm is coming in, not quite a hurricane, but a pretty good-sized thing. It'll give some good rains and the storm will die out as it gets in. Some showers up in through there. Quite warm with clear skies along the west coast. That's it, now back to New York and the "Camel Scoreboard."

SCORE: In the American League, it was New York 7, Chicago 5 after repeated delays. And Detroit beat Philadelphia 10-2. In the National League New York smashed St. Louis 10-0 with all other games in both leagues at night. And that's the major league picture on tonight's "Camel Scoreboard."

SWAYZE: Hopscotching the world for headlines: United Nations, New York: The United States told the United Nations today that it will continue to build its military establishment along the lines of atomic weapons as long as the Communist world continues its aggressive policy. Niagara Falls: A section of the well-known Prospect Point fell today into the chasm of the Niagara River gorge. It has long been a popular observation point on the brink of the American Falls. It was reported that no one was hurt.
Ottawa: Canada has agreed to be a member of the supervisory group for the Indochina armistice. The other two member nations are India and Poland.
London: Prime Minister Churchill has shaken up his Cabinet, making some new appointments and doing so following the resignation of Colonial Secretary Oliver Lyttleton.
Washington: They may abandon Ellis Island as an immigration station. It has been recommended.

(U.S. Savings Bonds announcement)

That's the story, folks. Glad we could get together. This is John Cameron Swayze saying good night.

Nightly newscasts reflected national concern with the East-West struggle. These were reminders of the all-pervasiveness of the Cold War and what was generally felt to be at stake in the rivalry with world Communism. But in its quarter-hour framework, the evening news had neither the time nor the intention to educate the public. There could be no deep background or historical context in what was essentially a program of news snippets and headlines.

What such shows confirmed, therefore, was the image of an evil Red force intent upon world conquest. There were no varieties of Communism, even though Communism in Yugoslavia already had given evidence of being antagonistic toward the Soviet interpretation. There were no vestiges of national history in this TV Communism, for although Chinese antipathy toward Russia dated to at least the sixteenth century, American newscasts projected only a Sino-Soviet monolith. There were no probes of domestic factors that made Communism strong in Western nations such as Italy and France, but weak in Great Britain and the Scandinavian states. There were also no consistent attempts to understand the appeal of Communism to nationalist revolutionaries in the decolonizing Third World.

Significantly, in many ways Americans understood Communism as a new variety of Nazism. All of the animus so richly directed toward Hitler and Nazi Germany was now channeled toward the Soviet Union and Marxism-Leninism. As if they were following the Fuhrer's "artichoke" policy of peeling away and conquering one country at a time, the Russians were seen as taking over the planet one nation after another. American leaders, however, consistently assured their audiences that in contrast with the attitude that allowed Hitler to violate international law and capture other nations, there would be no giving in to Communist would-be conquerors. As President Eisenhower phrased it in a nationally televised address on June 3, 1953, "In the conflict with international Communism there will be no appeasement —no new Munich."

If evening newscasts were superficial, network documentaries had the potential to offer educative analyses in the process of treating critical issues. Yet even in this type of programming, Cold War television evaded its responsibility and used the documentary to perpetuate the anti-Communist slogans of the era.

As a video format the documentary matured by the mid-1950s. Edited, written, and musically scored better than in the early days of the medium, TV documentaries in some cases became prestige programs at the networks. That was especially the situation with the

"Project XX" productions, which brought honor and many awards to NBC. Ironically, nowhere was anti-Communism more lavishly trumpeted than in this highly acclaimed series of documentaries.

"Project XX" presentations were television masterpieces. They beautifully blended historical and contemporary film, inspired writing, lush original music, and a general aura of video craftsmanship. In the eight TV seasons between the fall of 1954 and the spring of 1962, the "Project XX" unit at NBC produced 19 documentaries that, counting network reruns, accounted for more than 43 hours of national air time. Although the series ran until 1970, by 1965 it had received 50 international awards for excellence. A list of all its productions is shown in Table 2.

In his pioneering study of the television documentary, A. William Bluem distinguished two varieties of the format. The "TV news documentary" was one in which journalistic interpretation of issues and events was paramount. In the "TV theme documentary," according to Bluem, the emphasis was on the artistic totality of the production. While journalistic values were always important, they were not as crucial as artistry in the realization of the latter type. Bluem accurately described "Project XX" programs as the "peak" of the TV theme documentary.[82]

The series, however, had a political dimension not discussed by Bluem. "Project XX" played a strong role in communicating anti-Communist values in the 1950s. It was born, moreover, of the politicized and highly successful "Victory at Sea" series. This was an epic production of 26 half-hour programs tracing the record of the U.S. Navy in World War II. "Victory at Sea" won many awards after appearing in the 1951-52 TV season. At the time it was the most sophisticated documentary series in the history of the medium.

The "Project XX" team consisted of men who had put together "Victory at Sea." Until his death in 1957 Henry W. Salomon headed the production unit. He was then replaced by Donald B. Hyatt. Others included Isaac Kleinermann, Robert Russell Bennett, and Richard Hanser. Their first effort in the series was the documentary on atomic energy, "Three, Two, One—Zero!," which was written and produced by Salomon and Hanser, edited by Kleinermann, and scored by Bennett. Its success convinced NBC to keep the group producing documentaries at the rate of about two per year.

One theme dominated "Project XX" films: the historical evolution of civilization toward human freedom, with American sociopolitical achievement being a model for the rest of the world. This was

Table 2 "Project XX' Productions, 1954-70

First-Run Date	Title and Theme
September 13, 1954	Three, Two, One—Zero! (atomic energy)
December 27, 1955	Nightmare in Red (history of Communist Russia)
March 14, 1956	The Twisted Cross (rise and fall of Nazi Germany)
October 16, 1956	The Great War (World War I)
December 6, 1956	The Jazz Age (America in the 1920s)
January 7, 1957	Call to Freedom (modern Austria)
November 21, 1957	The Innocent Years (America, 1900-17)
February 11, 1959	Meet Mr. Lincoln (close-up of Abraham Lincoln)
October 16, 1959	Life in the Thirties (Depression America)
February 19, 1960	Not So Long Ago (America immediately after World War II)
April 22, 1960	Mark Twain's America (late-19th-century America)
November 22, 1960	Those Ragtime Years (popular music, 1900-17)
December 21, 1960	The Coming of Christ (the Nativity in great art)
January 21, 1961	The Circus
March 28, 1961	The Story of Will Rogers (American humorist)
March 29, 1961	The Real West (authentic American frontier life)
September 17, 1961	Laughter, U.S.A. (American humor)
March 18, 1962	Cops and Robbers (American crime from Colonial to modern times)
April 15, 1962	He Is Risen (the Resurrection in great art)
November 20, 1963	That War in Korea (ten years after the armistice)
June 9, 1964	The Red, White and Blue (nostalgia for old-time patriotism)
August 13, 1965	Smalltown, U.S.A. (three rural American towns portrayed)
January 13, 1967	The Island Called Ellis (immigrants to America)
March 16, 1967	The End of the Trail (Plains Indians in the 19th century)
April 13, 1967	The Law and the Prophets (Old Testament in great art)
December 11, 1968	Down to the Sea in Ships (man's chronic fascination with the sea)
*January 25, 1969	Down on the Farm (salute to American farmers)
April 24, 1969	Meet George Washington
May 11, 1969	Mirror of America (Washington, D.C., mirrors the American experience)
January 7, 1970	The West of Charles Russell (frontier paintings)
May 27, 1970	The Shining Mountains (romantic look at the Colorado Rockies)

*An "NBC News Special" produced by Donald B. Hyatt and scored by Robert Russell Bennett.

evident in those programs that nostalgically and proudly treated the social history of the United States. The theme was apparent in "The Jazz Age," "Life in the Thirties," and "Not so Long Ago." It was also integral to those productions with an earlier focus, including "Meet Mr. Lincoln," "Mark Twain's America," and "The Innocent Years."

Volatile issues mellowed in these documentaries. Agitators and their causes were glossed over, and viewers were left with a flattering image of the United States as a nation of independent-minded, hard-working pioneers who had fought adversity while clinging to their dreams. Furthermore, they and their dreams had emerged triumphant. The old days were "the good old days" in "Project XX" television. They tested personal mettle and created a society of free and honorable citizens.

If the series approved of the American social experiment, it abhorred authoritarianism. A collapsing, anti-democratic Old World was revealed in "The Great War." The rise and fall of Nazism was told in "The Twisted Cross." In two of its better realizations, "Project XX" focused on the despotism of Communism.

"Call to Freedom" considered the history of modern Austria as a paradigm for other nations. The documentary sketched that nation as it became an independent state following the collapse of the autocratic Hapsburg monarchy in World War I. Early hope for a free and democratic society was thwarted by a forced annexation by Nazi Germany and then partial occupation by the Soviet Union following World War II. After much negotiation and compromise, the emergence of Austria in 1955 as a democratic and internationally neutral nation was an uplifting story. Although the neutral Austrian republic was not an ally of the United States in its struggle against Communism, its liberation from Soviet influences was sufficient, as far as "Project XX" was concerned, to make the Austrian story a lesson in anti-Communism.

The most direct attack upon Communism occurred in "Nightmare in Red." The moral of this program was cited as "an ancient prophecy come true—'My father chastizes you with whips, but I will chastize you with scorpions.' " "Nightmare in Red" argued that for all its ineptitude and intolerable oppression, tsarist autocracy was preferable to Communist tyranny. Mixing actuality and theatrical footage, the program traced Russian history from the time of Nicholas II. While democratic revolution seemed justified by 1917, Communist victory was unforgivable. Russia now endured under a "shroud of evil." The secret police used terror to solicit approval. "The state, knowing no creed but blind obedience," the narrator rhythmically declared, "demands a captive mind, a captive spirit, a captive body."

In asserting a favorite theme of American Cold War rhetoric—the notion that the noble Russian people would one day rise up, overthrow their Red masters, and embrace democracy—"Nightmare in Red" ended with a poem of promise written in the nineteenth century by the nationalist poet Alexander Pushkin:

Deep in the Siberian mine,
Keep your patience proud.
The bitter toil shall not be lost,
The rebel thought unbowed,
The heavy-hanging chains will fall.
The walls will crumble at a word,
And freedom greet you in the light,
And brothers, give you back the sword.

More than entertainment or an attempt by NBC to offer a history lesson, "Nightmare in Red" was patent propaganda. This was made apparent when General Motors, specifically its Pontiac division, withdrew from sponsorship of the documentary in October 1955, shortly before it was to air. The airing was postponed two months until new advertisers were found. *Variety* offered considerable speculation about the motives behind GM's withdrawal.[83] Some suggested that General Motors did not want to offend possible Iron Curtain customers, and that the program might undermine the new cordiality in U.S.-Russian relations following the Geneva summit conference during the previous summer. There was also the fact that Secretary of Defense Charles E. Wilson was formerly the chief executive of General Motors, and even indirect association with such blatant propaganda might affect relations with Moscow adversely. Whatever the real reasons for General Motors' reaction, certainly few in commercial television could be unaware of the contemporary political relevance of this "Project XX" production.

TELEVISION JOURNALISM IN THE LATE 1950s

Led by Edward R. Murrow and Fred W. Friendly, CBS opened new professional territory for video journalism in 1956 and 1957. Particularly on "See It Now," the network televised lengthy interviews with major world leaders. Typical was the conversation between Murrow and Israeli Prime Minister David Ben-Gurion.

So long as those interviewed supported American foreign policy objectives, there was nothing controversial about the CBS strategy. In fact, as early as September 1954, "See It Now" aired interviews with French Premier Pierre Mendes-France and German Chancellor

Konrad Adenauer. But when Murrow and his colleagues began to converse in depth with statesmen opposed to American international activities, a new level of sophistication and controversy was achieved in TV. This was the case, for example, with Gamal Abdel Nasser, the prime minister of Egypt, who criticized the United States for its support of Israel in the Middle East, of France in North Africa, and in general of "the colonial countries against the countries who want to be free." In the foreign policy created by John Foster Dulles, even neutralist nations were considered unfriendly to American aspirations. Thus, when Murrow interviewed Premier U Nu of Burma, "See It Now" again demonstrated a new degree of broadcasting courage. And when "Face the Nation" offered Howard K. Smith, Alexander Kendrick, and Howard Handleman of the International News Service in an in-depth interview with neutralist Prime Minister Jawaharlal Nehru of India, TV journalism once more set precedents.

Head of State	CBS Program	Date
David Ben-Gurion/Israel	"See It Now"	March 6, 1956
Gamal Abdel Nasser/Egypt	"See It Now"	March 6, 1956
Chou En-lai/People's Republic of China	"See It Now"	December 30, 1956
U Nu/Burma	"See It Now"	February 3, 1957
Nikita Khrushchev/Soviet Union	"Face the Nation"	June 2, 1957
Tito/Yugoslavia	"See It Now"	June 30, 1957
Jawaharlal Nehru/India	"Face the Nation"	July 7, 1957

Murrow went even further. He conducted revealing conversations with prominent Communist leaders. His program with Chou En-lai allowed the Chinese Communist premier to explain the goals and conduct of Chinese international policy. Speaking with Marshal Tito of Yugoslavia, Murrow probed the thinking of an anomaly in Cold War stereotyping—a Communist leader who was nationalistic and defiant of Kremlin leadership.

Following the Chou En-lai and Tito interviews, CBS added a live panel of experts to state views opposing the Communist leaders. Carlos P. Romulo, the Philippine ambassador to the United States, and Dr. T. F. Tsiang, the Nationalist Chinese delegate to the United Nations, rebutted Chou En-lai. Tito was answered by Clare Booth Luce, the former American ambassador to Italy; Hamilton Fish, the editor of *Foreign Affairs* and director of the Council on Foreign Relations; and William H. (Bill) Lawrence, then of the *New York Times*.

The climax of this provocative journalistic trend occurred when "Face the Nation" presented a special one-hour discussion with Soviet

Premier Nikita Khrushchev. Filmed in Moscow and featuring B.J. Cutler of the *New York Herald-American* and CBS newsmen Daniel Schorr and Stuart Novins, "Face the Nation" dared to bring to American viewers for their own evaluation the views of the leader of world Communism. This time, there was no live panel of anti-Communists to challenge the ideas put forward by Khrushchev.

Reactions to the Khrushchev interview were quickly forthcoming. Even before the program aired, the commander of the Catholic War Veterans wired CBS urging its cancellation since, as he saw it, the Soviet premier would only mouth uncontested Red propaganda. The American Socialist party demanded equal time to distance itself from Communism. Similar calls for free air time came from political refugees from several nations within the Soviet empire.

In government, too, many felt the Khrushchev interview gave the Communist leader an unfair advantage. Some demanded equal time for President Eisenhower on Russian television. The Senate majority leader, Lyndon B. Johnson, suggested a weekly exchange of political views on Soviet and American TV. At his press conference three days after the interview, the president impugned the network's journalistic endeavor, referring to the interview as a stunt, the product of "a commercial firm in this country trying to improve its commercial standing." In one sentence, Eisenhower undermined those who felt the interview was effective journalism, not a money-making gimmick.

In defending the actions of CBS, *Variety* attacked those in government who were appalled because "Khrushchev came across on television as a human being instead of a monster, which has upset Washington into believing that he may have created a favorable impression among the American audience."[84] No defense, however, came from NBC or ABC. Most pointedly, Frank M. Stanton, the president of CBS, justified the program. He cited a Jeffersonian dictum that the citizenry "may be trusted to hear everything true and false and to form a correct judgment between them." Further, he added:

> We were as much aware of our responsibility as we were of our freedom. We were doing our job as journalists. Khrushchev and his views are of great importance to our world and to the world of our children. The less this man—or any man of his importance—remains a myth or a dark legend or a mystery to the American people, the more certain they are to size him up correctly.[85]

As righteously indignant as Stanton and CBS appear to have been, the interview with Khrushchev was not a turning point after which network news-related programming began to approach the Cold War

more realistically. If anything, reactions to the program only confirmed the precarious social position occupied by commercial television. Edward R. Murrow later assailed his network bosses for defer-
ring to the U.S. government following that "Face the Nation" broadcast. Speaking in October 1958 to the Radio-Television News Directors
Association, Murrow revealed:

> When my employer, CBS, through a combination of enterprise and good
> luck, did an interview with Nikita Khrushchev, the President of the United
> States uttered a few ill-chosen, uninformed words on the subject, and
> the network practically apologized. This produced a rarity. Many news-
> papers defended CBS's right to produce the program and commended
> it for initiative. But the other networks remained silent.[86]

More than any medium of communication before it, television
had the power to inform and persuade mass audiences. Where other
media required efforts of reading and concentrated listening, TV was
easy to experience. It communicated through an alluring amalgam of
pictures, words, music, personalities, body gestures, and captivating
ambiance. It entered private homes during times of relaxation, there
to spread its well-crafted messages.

Yet, even its journalists were wrapped in the clichéd mind-set
that typified American popular thought in the Cold War. Reporters
clearly identified with the United States. They spoke consistently of
"our bloc," "our side," "our power," and "our policy." This was
journalism as advocacy. Reporters spoke as partisans, and viewers
were hard pressed not to support "our position" on any given issue.
Typical of such reportage was the analysis of American foreign policy
offered by Winston Burdett on "Years of Crisis: 1957," a CBS discussion show aired on December 29, 1957. Explaining the failures of
the Eisenhower-Dulles policy in the Middle East that year, Burdett
argued:

> We went ahead on the premise that we could set up some kind of Amer-
> ican protectorate over the Middle East by military means; that we could
> make anti-Communist allies of the Arab states, and in this way exclude
> the Russians from the area. We proposed to extend the Cold War to the
> Arab world. And we ignored both the inherent weakness of the Arab
> states and the emotional backfire of Arab nationalism.

For those who might have been depressed by "our" poor performance in the Middle East, later in the program Eric Sevareid offered
more encouraging words. "This country is by no means a push-over,"
he told viewers:

We've got the greatest industrial plant in the world, the greatest industrial leaders. We've got a wonderful pool of scientists and engineers if their energies are channeled. We have unlimited money. . . . I think we have a world record of generosity and goodwill toward other parts of the world—and of nonaggression that honest men cannot really doubt. We have a President that people will still most willingly follow. . . . We have a great deal.

Of course, there were alternative media from which to obtain a broader perspective on the Cold War. But television had captured the national soul and overwhelmed its communications rivals. During the 1950s TV helped drive magazines and daily newspapers out of business. By 1952, Americans were spending more late evening hours with video than radio. A poll in 1959 indicated that in only 11 years television as a popular source of news had moved far ahead of radio and magazines, and was equal to newspapers in terms of audience trust.

As a medium of communication, however, television was often reluctant to communicate critically. Although the FCC ruled in 1949 that stations could offer editorials—if equal time were provided for opposing views—throughout the 1950s the networks wrestled with the idea, usually deciding to waive their right to state opinions. Several factors militated against regularized commentaries in news programming. There were considerations of time, since the evening news lasted only 15 minutes and, as ABC news chief John Daly suggested in 1956, editorials required about four minutes to develop satisfactorily. There were also political and economic realities. Network officials feared editorials might trigger government anger, cause viewers to change channels, or precipitate demands for equal and free time from disgruntled parties. Sponsors, moreover, were not pleased with paying the high fees demanded by TV, only to alienate viewers who disagreed with the position being taken in an editorial.[87]

Further, by the late 1950s television networks were extremely profitable operations, and TV executives were reluctant to do anything controversial for fear of adversely affecting a rising curve of financial success. By 1957, for example, CBS was the largest advertising medium in the world, its programs daily reaching 42 million American homes and its profits after taxes reaching $22.2 million. And if CBS was the top network in commercial television, NBC and ABC were right behind the leader, competing desperately to reach the summit. But success did not translate into better, quality programming; it bred the desire for even greater success. As David Halberstam has described the situation, for network executives making money "brought its own ruthless truth, and pushed aside other forces, other interests in the company."

> So it was not enough to succeed, to put on a good program that was sponsored, and make a profit, now there had to be a dominance of the ratings, a super-profit. . . . Nielsen was the new god of television; his truths were not truths, they were commandments; what was rated high was good; what was rated low was bad. There was room for nothing else, no other value systems, no sense of what was right and what was wrong. The stakes were too great, and became greater every year.[88]

During most of the 1950s there were few news commentators on national television. Elmer Davis, the former CBS newsman who headed the Office of War Information during World War II, had a short and unspectacular commentary program on ABC in 1954. Davis was hindered, no doubt, by charges of disloyalty hurled at him that year by the crusading anti-Communist group Aware, Inc. That organization assailed Davis for his civil liberties positions, and it characterized the distinguished broadcaster as an "anti-anti-Communist . . . who tries to identify anti-Communists at home with 'thought control.' "[89]

More successful as a TV commentator was Walter Winchell. With a national reputation earned from his newspaper columns and radio commentaries since the 1930s, Winchell came to ABC television in 1952 and remained with his weekly quarter-hour news and gossip commentary until 1955. Winchell was a virulent anti-Communist and supporter of Senator Joseph R. McCarthy. It seemed unimportant that he was more likely to be inaccurate than exact in his reports. *New Yorker* magazine once researched five typical Winchell newspaper columns with a total of 239 items in them. The magazine found him to be only 40.5 percent accurate in what he reported.[90] Nonetheless, Winchell's inimitable style—a forceful staccato delivery punctuated by the sound of a telegrapher's key—now made him a familiar Cold Warrior on early TV. Winchell's program was also sponsored.

There were other editorial broadcasts. In 1956 Howard K. Smith offered his unsponsored commentaries on the CBS weekend news program. ABC News on occasion aired editorials, but they were scarce and noncontroversial.

By virtue of the topics they covered on "See It Now," Murrow and Friendly often produced the effects of a controversial editorial. In a time of political fear, they challenged the U.S. Air Force, which was discharging a young lieutenant because his father was believed to have Communist sympathies ("The Case of Lieutenant Milo Radulovich," October 20, 1953). They challenged the American Legion, which refused to let a local chapter of the American Civil Liberties Union meet in the auditorium of the Legion's War Memorial ("An Argument in Indianapolis," November 24, 1953). They also challenged Cold War prejudices by airing a conversation with J. Robert Oppenheimer, one of the developers of the atomic bomb and a Princeton professor of nuclear physics, who had been widely discredited after losing his government security clearance (January 4, 1955).

When "See It Now" had a sponsor, the weekly program was aired in prime time. By the fall of 1955, however, the show had lost its sponsor and was condemned to monthly appearances on Sunday afternoons—a time derisively called the "cultural ghetto." Having no advertisers meant that many affiliate stations would drop the show in favor of a revenue-producing program. At times "See It Now" was aired on as few as 57 CBS outlets.

With production costs mounting and network executives weary of Murrow's and Friendly's embarrassing frankness and independent-mindedness on and off the air, the network scrapped "See It Now" in July 1958. Much more under CBS corporate control, a disenchanted Murrow continued on the network—on "Person to Person," "Small World," and an occasional special or "CBS Reports" documentary. Murrow resigned from CBS and broadcast journalism in January 1961.

Nevertheless, CBS was the first network to adopt a policy of editorializing on the air. This meant that in well-reasoned summations, particularly in TV documentaries, CBS news personnel would be permitted to draw their own conclusions. The first program to reflect this policy was "Where We Stand," an assessment of the relative strength of the American and Soviet military, economic, and educational programs. This 90-minute evaluation was aired January 5, 1958, less than three months after Russian scientists had placed their Sputnik satellite in orbit. The program concluded that in rocketry the United States was obviously trailing the Soviets. In military weaponry the United States still possessed ICBM superiority, and with the Titan missile the Americans had " 'the big baby'—the most terrible weapon yet devised by man." In economics, according to Howard K. Smith, "We still hold a commanding lead, but the very fact that they can challenge us affords us no room for complacency." As for preparing young people for the missile age, Alexander Kendrick left no doubts about the leader here when he spoke of the math and science fundamental to Russian education, and then interviewed three California boys who boasted of their high school class in "coed cooking."

"Where We Stand" was hailed as "precedential," "a key triumph," and "a major contribution to television journalism."[9] CBS was pleased enough with the program to do an update a year later, this time in the wake of the Soviet satellite Lunik, which had escaped the earth's gravitational field and was now in orbit around the sun. Televised on January 4, 1959, this installment of "Where We Stand" drew similarly distressing conclusions. Again in vital areas of Cold War rivalry the United States was trailing or strongly challenged by the Russians. The conclusions enunciated by narrator Walter Cronkite left no doubt that the United States was facing a crisis: "Decisions need to be made. Policies need to be set. They must be bold, imaginative, made from an open and honest estimate of danger, and a real conviction on the worth of our own goals. Or else we may forfeit the power to choose at all."

By the late 1950s the Cold War had changed. Josef Stalin was dead and the brutality of his regime loosened greatly at home and abroad. At the twentieth congress of the Communist party in 1956, Khrushchev roundly denounced Stalin's police state tactics. The orbiting of Sputnik the following year clearly shocked Western leaders and precipitated popular reappraisal, even imitation, of Communist scientific and educational practices. Diplomatically, there was slight moderation of East-West tensions following the Geneva summit conference in 1955. The Soviet premier visited the United States in late 1959, and Eisenhower was scheduled to visit the Soviet Union the next year. Plans were also made for a second summit meeting of Russian, French, British, and American heads of state to be held in Paris in mid-1960.

Change in East-West relations was even noticeable in the logistics of television journalism. In mid-1955, Irving R. Levine of NBC became the first permanent broadcast correspondent accredited by the Soviet Union. This allowed him to air the first reports from Russia since 1947. Other network newsmen soon followed Levine to Moscow.

On the other hand, there continued to be Cold War crises that reaffirmed the anti-Communist slogans of the time. In the fall of 1956, Soviet military strength crushed a social revolution in Hungary and threatened invasion of a restive Poland. The involvement of native Communists in rebellions in Africa, Latin America, and Asia led many to interpret the anticolonial revolt within the Third World as a Kremlin-directed phenomenon. And for all his apparent humanity on American TV, Khrushchev still could pound his desk with his shoe during a session of the United Nations, argue petulantly with Vice-President Nixon about the relative merits of American and Russian television, and announce that through competition in peaceful coexistence, "We will bury you."

Such developments justified the predilection of network TV to visualize Communism within a stereotyped, Cold War perspective. "The Face of Red China," a CBS documentary on December 28, 1958, spent much of its time revealing propaganda employed by the Maoist regime to brainwash its citizens. It showed those familiar hordes of antlike Chinese workers straining to erect by hand the dams, factories, and blast furnaces of industrializing Communist China. "The 20th Century" documentary series launched its 1958-59 season with "The Red Sell." This was a two-part analysis of Soviet mass persuasion techniques in action—everything from movies showing Americans as drunkards, looters, and degenerates to propagandistic exploitation of the Sputnik achievement.

In "Is Cuba Going Red?", telecast on CBS on May 3, 1959, Stuart Novins rightly concluded that Communist influence was dominant in the new regime of Fidel Castro. But only four months after Castro had captured Havana, it was premature for Novins to conclude that Cuba was already "a totalitarian dictatorship." Novins also left the impression that a Red invasion of the West Indies and Latin America was imminent when he added that Cuba was "a Communist beachhead in the Caribbean."[92]

Behind the scenes, too, there were familiar Cold War activities. When the State Department asked the networks to downplay coverage of Khrushchev's American visit, only ABC and the Mutual radio network criticized this government attempt to infringe upon press freedom. Later, Edward R. Murrow blasted NBC and CBS publicly for failing "to defend not only their limited independence, but one of the basic principles of a free society."[93]

One of the strongest critiques of television's failure to become an ideal communicator was contained in "Controversy on Radio and TV," a report issued in December 1958 by the Department of Communication of New York University. Television, said the study, "with the greatest potential of all mass media to bring to the very living rooms of our nation a basis for political enlightenment, offers nearly none." What was needed, it stated, was "sober, mature, logical commentary," for American viewers were drowning in a flood of uncritical facts issued by "statesmen, reporters, press agents, lobbyists, and other mass communicators." In arguing that "Facts alone are often meaningless since our world is inundated by an ocean of facts," the NYU report concluded that instead of promoting probative discussion, video offered only "a mass of material severely in need of ordering and interpretation by incisive minds which relate them to one of the various perspectives from which this disturbed planet can be viewed."[94]

Significantly, in these last years of the Eisenhower administration there were some documentaries and nonfiction programs that faced the East-West struggle without resort to simplistic slogans. This was the case with "John Gunther's High Road" and its consideration of "Russia's Next Rulers?", telecast on ABC on September 14, 1959. In describing Nikita Khrushchev, journalist Gunther painted a picture of a man considerably more human than the popular contemporary description of the Soviet leader as "the butcher of the Ukraine." According to Gunther, who admitted having met and drunk with him at an embassy party, Khrushchev was a fascinating character.

> He's tough. He's resilient. He's full of bounce and zip. He has quite a pronounced intellectual capacity. He's shrewd. He's obviously possessed of great energy and drive. And he's the only European dictator I ever met who has a sense of humor. He's sharp. He's indiscreet. He's sometimes rude. But it would be a serious mistake to think that he's a buffoon, as some people did 'til quite recently. Probably his dominant quality, next to spry toughness, is a kind of rough peasant's common sense. Like President Eisenhower, Mr. Khrushchev was a poor boy. His father was a coal miner. Eisenhower's father was a locomotive boiler. Khrushchev was self-educated.

Occasionally, too, it was possible to encounter criticism of the American government. "The Ruble War" was a roundtable discussion among CBS foreign correspondents on the topic of Russian-American trade rivalries. Telecast on July 21, 1958, the program ended with a stern warning to Congress to stop its annual battle over foreign aid and reciprocal trade. "They must become commonplaces—regular, natural things to do," declared Howard K. Smith, "or we may lose the Ruble War." Similarly, "The U-2 Affair," an "NBC White Paper" aired on November 29, 1960, was unfavorable to President Eisenhower for his equivocation—first denying American planes spied on the Soviet Union, then admitting U-2 aircraft regularly surveyed Russia from high altitudes, but refusing to apologize as the Russians wanted—in the wake of the Soviets', in May 1960, shooting down a piloted American reconnaissance aircraft over Russian territory and then canceling plans for the Paris summit conference.

Controversial news-related programming was the exception, not the rule, in nonfiction TV. And public affairs shows were exceptions to the norm in network video. By the end of the decade—with advertising rates skyrocketing and network profits following suit—this was no time to produce unprofitable current events programming. Apparently it was enough that the networks gave the nation 15 minutes of news nightly.

As Alexander Kendrick pointed out, during the 1960-61 TV season there were 108 scheduled series on network television. Only 6 of these were public affairs shows, compared with 23 Westerns, 22 crime dramas, and 23 situation comedies. Within those half-dozen public affairs programs, moreover, the networks had learned how to treat "controversial subjects in a noncontroversial manner."[9][5]

Nonetheless, in one case network television consistently presented a wide range of controversial viewpoints. At the close of every year CBS and NBC each brought together their foreign correspondents to discuss the events of the past 12 months. Whether it was the CBS program, "Years of Crisis," or the NBC roundtable, "Projection," for one hour annually viewers encountered provocative analyses by the leading American TV journalists.

In a medium disinclined to allow its employees to offer commentary on camera, these annual roundtables gave indication of how provocative American TV could be. They also revealed that the happy unanimity projected by network correspondents actually masked a variety of opinions, all of which could be persuasively argued, and all of which promoted viewer thinking. In these rare discussion shows, TV was truly a learning experience.

On "Projection '59" Pauline Frederick assailed the American policy of refusing recognition of Communist China and its 600 million citizens. She also predicted diminishing importance for Russian and American influence, and the rise of Third World diplomatic prowess. On "Years of Crisis: 1955" Bill Downs declared: "We've lost, or appear to be losing, the international title as the greatest revolutionary power in the world; and we seem to be losing it to a revolutionary form of totalitarianism." He wondered, "Maybe the American revolution is over."

With a bluntness never a part of regular news and documentary programming, Peter Kalisher attacked the myopia of American policy in the Third World, especially Asia. On "Years of Crisis: 1957" he maintained that "We've got to revamp our thinking entirely in regard to about half the world's population, maybe more: the semi-colonial and colonial and former colonial peoples." He continued with specific reference to the People's Republic of China. "We've also got to admit that our China policy is bankrupt. . . . I think we've got to do what our major allies in Europe and Asia have admitted and recognize the Peking regime for what it is: the unfriendly but existing government of mainland China." He called for aid to mainland China and urged the United States "to get out from behind this wall we're building around China, which is really a wall we're building around ourselves."

Most reporters were moderate, middle-of-the-road thinkers who could criticize both sides in the Cold War but still remain conspicuously pro-American. Here were men such as Eric Sevareid, Howard K. Smith, Alexander Kendrick, Wells Hangen, and Frank McGee. More willing to see the Cold War objectively were Daniel Schorr and James Robinson. And strongly anti-Communist in their opinions were Richard C. Hottelet and Cecil Brown.

Stationed in Moscow, Schorr described a dichotomy in Soviet society: the people and the regime. The young people, he argued, were bored with Communism. The Russian people, he asserted, were pressuring the government for normalcy and a mellowing in leadership tactics. He felt that world Communism would be a reality for a long time, but that through trade, tourism, and the exchange of ideas Americans might assist the softening process in the Soviet Union. Schorr's attitudes on East-West militarism also were empathic. On "Years of Crisis: 1957," he criticized those who wished to accelerate the arms race because Sputnik had demonstrated Russian supremacy in missile technology. A reactive speedup in the American arms program, said Schorr, militated against negotiating "a better and more real solution than just catching up, and then keeping pace in means of destruction."

From his position as NBC correspondent in Hong Kong, James Robinson offered a realistic understanding of Communist China and Southeast Asia. On "Projection '59" he suggested considering the Chinese point of view in world affairs. Robinson argued that leftist guerrilla activities in Laos were not controlled by China, but that the government of North Vietnam was operating on its own to fuel the Laotian insurgency. Chinese tensions with India, he noted, could be seen as emanating from sincere and historic boundary disputes. Referring to the Chinese invasion of Tibet in 1959, Robinson noted that "Tibet is and always will be China in Chinese eyes." As for the rivalry between Peking and the Nationalist Chinese government on Formosa, Robinson explained that in the opinion of Communist leaders, this was a civil war and not the business of the United States.

Robinson was also critical of American policy in the Far East. After a decade of nonrecognition of the Peking government, he scolded, "It's nonsense to talk of disarmament and world peace when you exclude this, the biggest country, from world tribunals."

If Schorr was the liberal realist at CBS, Richard C. Hottelet was that network's principal anti-Communist. Hottelet saw the Cold War as a "basic struggle between freedom and unfreedom." Stationed in West Germany and then South America and the United Nations, he described the Soviet Union as a savage colonial master, calling it "this artificial system" and an "invisible police empire." Hottelet was at his most vitriolic on "Years of Crisis: 1956," aired only two months after the Hungarian revolution had been crushed and tensions in Poland threatened revolution there. Here he announced that "This year has put an end to Communism as a world revolutionary force." He felt the uprisings in Eastern Europe had administered "perhaps fatal blows" to Communist control and now the "era of obedience is over." To Hottelet the revolutions were "an elemental force, it's the essence of man's history. It's the irrepressible striving for truth and for a better life."

Sensing the collapse of Communism, Hottelet felt the United States had a role to play in the Polish crisis, even to the point of going to war. The American government, he said, must persuade the Russians "to let freedom take its course" in Poland, for if Soviet troops invaded Poland, "it will make Hungary look like a junior prom." That Hottelet's viewpoint was not popular among the CBS correspondents is apparent in the following excerpt from "Years of Crisis: 1956."

Hottelet: What are we going to do? Are we going to give the Russians the freedom to do anything they please in Eastern Europe behind the Iron Curtain?

Schorr: What kind of warning do you have in mind, Dick?

Hottelet: A diplomatic warning. It can be discreet. It can be most secret. It need not humiliate.

Smith: It means the threat of fighting, doesn't it?

Hottelet: I think it means, gentlemen, the threat of war, yes. Because I think, we must see that our vital interests are caught up in Central Europe.

Sevareid: Great democracies cannot go to war on the basis of a discreet private diplomatic warning. We have a Constitution.

Hottelet: Fine, but if the government of the United States is not backed up by the people of the United States in a case like this, then I think this position should be clear, too, and we should abdicate the initiative to the Russians which I don't think the people are ready to do once they see the problem in that light.

Smith: I don't think one-tenth of one percent of the Western people would be willing to go to war over something behind the Curtain.

Hottelet: But I think a great deal can be done. We saw that in Berlin. During the Berlin airlift we told the Russians that if they attacked Berlin . . . .

Schorr: But Berlin we had. We've never given a warning about a place which we didn't have.

Hottelet: Well, I don't know, have we divided the world into areas really which are the Soviet's preserve and which are our own?

Schorr: Well, we've drawn lines about what we will defend, and what we are there to defend. But we can't go into Poland to defend it.

Hottelet: No, we're not going into Poland. But I wonder if we should be bound by old lines in a situation now where the whole of Eastern Europe is in flux—where things have changed. There is a Polish problem today that didn't exist two months or three months ago.

Schorr: I think we've found the mad bomber.

Murrow: Dick, are you saying if we are now in fact going to draw a line in the Middle East and say that aggression there by Russia in any form means war, that we ought also to do the same thing in Poland and say that if there is overt aggression by the Soviet Union against Poland that this would mean war? Is that the essence of what you're suggesting?

Hottelet: I think so. I think we cannot afford to abandon 26 million Poles.

Matching Hottelet in his intense distaste for Communism was Cecil Brown of NBC. An honored and experienced broadcast journalist who emerged on network radio in the 1930s, Brown was inveterate in his hatred of Communist China. On "Projection '60," when his colleague James Robinson again urged an appreciation of the Chinese point of view, Brown bristled. "I'm shocked by your remarks," he said, "it seems to me you're applying upside-down logic to every concept of what's happening in China. There's no mystery about what Red China is trying to do: it's trying to destroy every non-Communist country in Asia." Brown accused Robinson of putting "the stamp of virtue on banditry and murder."

"The Brown buzz saw," as Edwin Newman described him, was the NBC correspondent in Tokyo. A year earlier, on "Projection '59," Brown was even more explicit in explaining his detestation of the Peking government. "There is an actual war going on in Southeast Asia," he proclaimed. This, he explained, was the essence of "the massive Red Chinese drive to absorb all of Asia—from Japan to Indonesia, and from Formosa all the way across to India." But Brown offered a remedy. "There is time for us to save Asia from the Communist dragon," he declared, "but not much time."

When others were critical of American nonrecognition of the Peking government, Brown warned against changing this policy. In his view, "If we recognize Red China, Formosa disappears." Recognition, he felt, would compel other Asian states to recognize the Maoist regime. This in turn would allow the Chinese to station military, economic, and political missions in those countries, thereby giving China a fifth column with which to overthrow neighboring governments. This was classic "domino theory" applied to the Far East. "Therefore," Brown concluded, "if we recognize Communist China, we are in effect kissing off Southeast Asia, and I don't want that to happen."

While TV failed to develop an independent, interpretative posture in American society, it did bombard viewers with images and words that were strongly politicized. All those situation comedies in the 1950s that showed happy white families living in clean suburban homes, all those quiz programs giving huge sums of money to brainy waitresses, cobblers, jockeys, and schoolteachers, all those private eyes and policemen forever capturing criminals—these were all part of a mass mythology that soothed and reassured the citizenry by showing the rewards of working within the system. In shows ranging from "Leave It to Beaver" to "The $64,000 Question" to "Dragnet" there was political content. That content suggested that the American way of life was the best on the planet, that dreams could be fulfilled by average folk, that the institutions guarding American society would protect its struggling, law-abiding citizens, and that a happy ending was inevitable.

If programming preached conformity, it also insulated viewers from the real world. World news was condensed to a few headlines each evening. There was no frequency and little depth in documentary programming. The great international issues over which the nation would go to war in the 1960s were never analyzed accurately on television in the 1950s. Where were the realistic studies of international relations? Why did television never probe the Russian or Chinese perspectives in the Cold War? Why were there no profound analyses of the anticolonial movement? Why did TV find fault so easily with Communist states, but seldom with pro-American dictatorships and with the United States?

For their part, American audiences seldom expressed great interest in learning the fullness of reality from television. Never in the first

28 years of television did a public affairs program rank among the leading network shows. Americans desired television for escape and relaxation, and TV responded to that want.

For all its shortcomings, however, TV was immensely important. It was the mass communications experience most shared in the United States and, increasingly, in the world. It was so significant that Pope Pius XII in 1958 named St. Clare the patron saint of television.[96]

With the demise of the Dumont network by the mid-1950s, TV in the United States was controlled essentially by an oligopoly of networks—ABC, CBS, and NBC—that saw video principally as a business. Through their ownership of key stations, and by providing programming to most American outlets, these corporations were wealthy and powerful. They also had a vested interest in keeping the nation entertained with TV, and happy with the socioeconimic system in which they flourished. Further, because advertising costs were exorbitant, only the wealthiest American corporations could afford to advertise regularly on network TV. What emerged from the confluence of such factors was an image of the United States and rest of the world that was pleasing to viewers who wanted nonthreatening programming, and acceptable to influential political and economic interests that eschewed public controversy.

Such an arrangement was not necessarily pernicious. Despite the interlocking arrangements among government, the military, the communications industry, and the corporate capitalistic world, most Americans would probably have chosen their television arrangement over the government-controlled TV systems in most other countries. Still, without a commitment to support independent investigation and interpretation, or to allow uncomfortable truths to be widely disseminated, corporate American TV could be as manipulative as any system with direct government control.

In essence this was the thrust of President Eisenhower's admonition to the nation in his farewell address. On January 17, 1961, on live television, the outgoing chief executive warned that the Cold War had brought forth in the United States a threatening amalgamation of military and industrial interests. "In the councils of government," Ike declared, "we must guard against the acquisition of unwarranted influence, whether sought or unsought, by the military-industrial complex. The potential for the disastrous rise of misplaced power exists and will persist."

The president did not demand the abolition of this complex. Instead, he argued for its importance in a world of international crises—

as long as it was kept in harmony with the laws and freedom basic to the republic. Eisenhower said of American society and the challenge of its military-industrial establishment:

> We must never let the weight of this combination endanger our liberties or democratic processes. We should take nothing for granted. Only an alert and knowledgeable citizenry can compel the proper meshing of the huge industrial and military machinery of defense with our peaceful methods and goals, so that security and liberty may prosper together.

From within the broadcasting industry, Edward R. Murrow offered advice similar to that of President Eisenhower. As early as May 1957, Murrow admitted publicly that "The money that pays for television and radio comes from a relatively small number of corporations." This, he felt, guaranteed that "The thinking of the executives in these corporations will have a profound effect upon what happens in television and radio," to the point where these corporate officials "could possibly decide the course of our civilization." Murrow urged corporate America to face the social responsibility inherent in such power by financing public affairs programs with independent points of view, and by sustaining news-related shows, even those with low national ratings.[97]

Two years later Murrow went even further in his critique. He condemned commercial television for creating a medium of "decadence, escapism, and insulation from the realities of the world in which we live." While the country was "in mortal danger" in this age of East-West struggle, Murrow complained, TV blithely went about seeking bigger profits and avoiding the responsibility to inform fully and accurately. Instead of "this endless outpouring of tranquilizers," Murrow pleaded for video that would provoke thought and stimulate the search for answers.[98]

Significantly, Murrow did not attack the validity of the American corporate structure. When he left CBS in disillusionment, he joined the Kennedy administration as director of the nation's chief bureau of foreign propaganda, the United States Information Agency. Murrow seemed to realize that all political societies must have some type of organizational system. And the best society in which to live was the one that made life most comfortable—consistent with social justice and responsibility in foreign and domestic affairs. Yet, should Americans think that they already had the best of all possible systems, Murrow in 1958 offered a frank assessment.

> We are currently wealthy, fat, comfortable, and complacent. We have currently a built-in allergy to unpleasant or disturbing information. Our

mass media reflect this. But unless we get up off our fat surpluses and recognize that television in the main is being used to distract, delude, amuse, and insulate us, then television and those who finance it, those who look at it and those who work at it, may see a totally different picture too late.[99]

There was a legacy left Americans by more than a decade of television journalism. For the most part, viewers had grown used to seeing the world superficially, simplistically, and nationalistically. Although few might have recognized it, news and public affairs programming was shaped by military, corporate, and government influences that generally robbed TV journalism of its professional imperative to inform in depth. Relying on such a medium for so much of their understanding of world affairs, the American people were acting neither wisely nor safely.

Importantly, too, this legacy was enhanced by what viewers encountered on TV when not watching news, documentaries, and discussion programs. The entertainment shows that dominated viewing patterns were also conduits for the nourishing of a popular Cold War ideology. Perhaps more effectively than in news-related programming, the amalgamation of politicized broadcasting and the Cold War was better achieved in entertainment television.

3

THE COLD WAR AS
TV ENTERTAINMENT

Television emerged as America's prime medium of entertainment and information at exactly the moment the nation became deeply embroiled in the Cold War. The United States was forced to adapt video to its social reality at the same time it was experiencing the anxieties of the East-West confrontation, fighting a limited war in Korea, and learning to live with John Foster Dulles' diplomatic philosophy of "brinkmanship," "massive retaliation," and the "liberation of captive peoples." Within this tense atmosphere TV was assimilated and became the most important vehicle through which citizens learned the latest developments in a rivalry that, in simplified terms, matched good Democracy against evil Communism.

As a persistent aspect of its dissemination of the news, television brought the international struggle into millions of homes nightly. In news, documentary, discussion, and similar types of actuality programming, the Cold War became familiar. Yet, such nonfiction shows were limited in how they could present the Cold War. Tied to fact and the presentation of actual events, news programs could not effectively illustrate emotional ramifications, such as the nature of the enemy or the consequences of defeat.

These ambiguous qualities were best handled through literary and theatrical techniques. The more flamboyant images of the East-West battle emerged in entertainment programming. Here, throughout the 1950s TV plunged the nation into a bath of Cold War clichés and fear— a flood of propagandistic messages that urged the public to support unquestioningly the policies of the U.S. government.

THE ANTI-COMMUNIST SPY AS TV ENTERTAINER

Spies came in all guises in 1950s television. Whether they were trained government agents risking life and limb to keep the nation safe from Communist schemes, or "average guy" do-gooders who mixed espionage with their other careers, the spies who populated TV during the Cold War were powerful communicators. By their words and actions they embodied freedom, religious belief, and individuality. They were brave in standing up against Red tyranny. They were humane in their concern for the downtrodden being pressed further to the earth by the jackboots of Communist dictatorship. And they were self-sacrificing, facing imprisonment or death if they failed in their weekly contests with Communism.

Video spies were plentiful during the Cold War. As Table 3 suggests, throughout the 1950s American secret agents battled Communism in hundreds of dramatic encounters.

No entertainment series did more to champion anti-Communism than "I Led 3 Lives." The show was based on Herbert A. Philbrick's best-selling account of his nine years as an FBI agent posing as a member of the Communist Party of the United States. The producer of the program, Frederic W. Ziv, was no novice with such topical material. In 1952 his company had produced and syndicated a popular radio series, "I Was a Communist for the FBI," which was drawn from the actual exploits of another FBI counterspy, Matt Cvetic.

Although the FBI had no direct input into "I Led 3 Lives," former agent Philbrick was actively involved with the production of scripts. For two seasons the story lines came from his book. During the third season plot ideas came from the files and notes kept by Philbrick. In all cases he reviewed scripts for historical accuracy and conformity with FBI practices. "I knew of the things that the Bureau does and doesn't do, and the things that Mr. Hoover liked, and the things he didn't like," Philbrick told an interviewer in 1974. "So, that was my job," he added, "to kind of make sure that they [the FBI] didn't have to take care of this."[2]

Interestingly, for many who were creatively involved with "I Led 3 Lives," the program was intended as classic spy-genre entertainment,

Table 3 Spy Series in the 1950s[1]

Program	Years of First Run	No. of Episodes
Passport to Danger	1951-52	39
Dangerous Assignment	1951-52	39
Foreign Intrigue	1951-55	156
Biff Baker, U.S.A.	1952-53	26
The Hunter	1952-54	26
China Smith	1952-55	52
Pentagon, U.S.A. (Pentagon Confidential)	1953	8
I Led 3 Lives	1953-56	117
Secret File, U.S.A.	1954-55	26
The Adventures of the Falcon	1954-55	39
The Man Called X	1955-56	39
I Spy	1955-56	39
Soldiers of Fortune	1955-56	52
Crusader	1955-56	52
O.S.S.	1957-58	26
David Harding, Counterspy	1958	*
The Invisible Man	1958-59	26
Behind Closed Doors	1958-59	26
Counterthrust	1959-60	13

*not available

not as Cold War political propaganda. Yet for Philbrick—who wrote a weekly anti-Communist column for the *New York Herald Tribune* during the first run of the series, and who fashioned a career as a professional anti-Communist writer and lecturer—the program was clearly intended as political information as well as entertainment. For Frederic W. Ziv, too, the series was political. He remarked, two decades after the show appeared:

> It's very difficult in these times to realize what was going on then. But it was felt that there was a genuine Communist threat to undermine the United States, perhaps to take over the United States. The FBI felt that they must have surveillance, and the public was entitled to know that that type of surveillance was going on. I feel that we rendered that service to the general public. You may or may not approve of that in today's times. At that time I felt that it rendered a proper service.[3]

On TV, "I Led 3 Lives" enjoyed great success. It was released to syndication in 1953 and ran for 117 half-hour episodes. As late as the

1980s it was still being shown on local stations. Throughout the series Richard Carlson appeared as the FBI agent whose heroics seemed to be saving the United States from impending collapse. A typical show might involve Red plans to introduce a low-cost narcotic to American youngsters, an attempt by the Communists to steal top-secret information, or a plot to incite labor unrest by spreading hate-filled pamphlets among factory workers. Occasionally, Philbrick might even be ordered by the party to a foreign country—certainly outside the legal jurisdiction of the Federal Bureau of Investigation—where he invariably caused FBI ingenuity to defeat Communist goals.

The world of "I Led 3 Lives" was a threatening one in which Philbrick was balanced between subversive Reds intent upon destroying the American system, and the demands of an FBI "plant" secretly struggling to thwart and expose these diabolical goals. Each weekly victory meant "eliminating one more threat to our national security." Each Philbrick triumph was the result of American character and morality besting the deceit and general malevolence of "the Red underground." And in case viewers missed the immediacy of Philbrick's martyrdom, each week Carlson reminded viewers that this was for real:

> This is the story, the fantastically true story, of Herbert A. Philbrick, who for nine frightening years did lead three lives—average citizen, high-level member of the Communist Party, and counterspy for the Federal Bureau of Investigation. For obvious reasons the names, dates, and places have been changed. But the story is based on fact.

Like most entertainment programs with Cold War themes, "I Led 3 Lives" never discussed the East-West issues in rational terms. It offered no explanation of why adult Americans joined the Communist party. It never honestly discussed the extent or effectiveness of subversion in the United States, nor did it explain the degree to which the party was infiltrated by other FBI agents. Viewers encountered instead a traditional morality tale in which the forces of Good always won, but the forces of Evil were never fully vanquished.

Further, Communism was never presented as a legitimate economic and political arrangement of society. Instead, viewers saw it in terms of domestic subversion, brutal Russian dictators, expansionist world views in Moscow and Peking, and ruthless suppression of East European and Asian democracies. Just as it would have been invalid to interpret capitalism with Nazi Germany the only example, so Communism needed a perspective much broader than Soviet imperialism. There were, however, no discussions of the relative strengths and weaknesses of Communism, the different types of socialism, the exploitation of workers around the world, and the comparative records of capitalist and Marxist economies in newly emerging nation-states. American TV in the 1950s sought no real answers. Instead, it flooded the culture with politicized rhetoric that, rather than reason with viewers, bombarded them with anti-Communist platitudes.

The propagandistic content of "I Led 3 Lives" and its indirect connection with the actual FBI were well understood in the United States and abroad. At the request of three separate government military organizations, Ziv Television Programs, Inc., in 1954 provided copies of those episodes of "I Led 3 Lives" dealing with Red sabotage training and Communist infiltration of civil defense groups. Ziv offered the films to these government organizations at no cost, "since the films are to be used for indoctrination and enlistment purposes."[4]

Overseas, the reception of "I Led 3 Lives" was not always as appreciative as in the United States. The series was barred from distribution in Hong Kong, Australia, Argentina, Venezuela, and Colombia. When it was telecast in Mexico, the Russian embassy filed an official protest with the Mexican government. When the British Broadcasting Corporation aired several episodes in the mid-1950s, the series became a point of dispute in the House of Commons.[5]

As an FBI agent, the hero of "I Led 3 Lives" was legally confined to activities within the borders of the United States. Occasionally the writers placed Philbrick abroad—but always sent there at the behest of the party and always operating as a private citizen. There was, however, a vast array of TV undercover agents patriotically working overseas to protect American interests and entertain television audiences.

In "Passport to Danger," Cesar Romero portrayed Steve McQuinn, a diplomatic courier whose duties for the State Department took him to such cities of intrigue as Sofia, Belgrade, Berlin, and Istanbul. "The Man Called X" and "David Harding, Counterspy" had been popular radio programs concerning international espionage before coming to TV. The Cold War so affected the old radio series "The Adventures of the Falcon" that when it came to television in 1954, its hero, Mike Waring, ceased to be a private detective and was now a U.S. intelligence agent laboring against international evil. As late as 1959-60 the short-lived series "Counterthrust" introduced viewers to the exploits of American counterespionage agents battling Communists in the Far East.

Such Cold War champions were frequently military intelligence officers. Often their adventures were said to be based on actual military records. "Pentagon, U.S.A." (originally titled "Pentagon Confidential") was a brief series in 1953 that dramatized cases from the criminal investigation files of the U.S. Army. In 1958-59 "Behind Closed Doors" was purportedly based on the experiences and records of Rear Admiral Ellis M. Zacharias, deputy chief of Naval Intelligence during World War II. Although Zacharias' achievements had come in World War II, the series had a pointedly Cold War theme. Its stories concerned activities such as the attempt by American spies to plant a listening device in the Russian embassy in London, arranging the defection of a Russian Air Force lieutenant, helping the anti-Communist Czech underground, and preventing the assassination of world leaders such as King Hussein of Jordan and Marshal Tito of Yugoslavia.

Espionage was a popular theme. It was even featured in historical series such as "O.S.S.," which focused on World War II cases of the Office of Strategic Services, the forerunner of the Central Intelligence Agency. "I Spy," an anthology program hosted by Raymond Massey, offered spy stories of even greater historical depth, ranging from Biblical times to the present. But whatever the time frame in which such series told their stories, they all presented the world of the spy as a threatening one involving life-and-death struggle. This atmosphere was delineated effectively by Christopher Storm, the central character of "Foreign Intrigue":

> When one country knows something it doesn't want another country to know, a state secret is born. Then the international fight for custody begins: government official versus government official, diplomat versus diplomat, espionage agent versus counterespionage agent. And the others, the men who never wear striped pants or frock coats, and who always carry guns and grudges—those who buy and sell secrets large and small like vegetables on the open market—men loyal only to the franc, the peseta, the dollar, the mark, the shilling—men living among us as one of us, but dying among us differently.

The degree to which the fears of the Cold War had become the grist of evening TV entertainment was strikingly evidenced in a trade advertisement in *Variety* in January 1956. Here the syndicators of "The Man Called X" purchased two full pages to trumpet the relevance of their property. "Now! TV's Most Colorful Man of Mystery!" proclaimed one banner headline. "C.I.A. Vital to U.S. Policy Makers" and "Spy Stories Always Great Entertainment," suggested others. Most pointedly, the ad announced that "Secret agents have molded our destiny." To drive home the point that "The Man Called X" was pertinent to, and exploitative of, the real fears of Americans in the 1950s, the advertisement grimly accentuated the necessity of spies.

> Survival of any nation today, in the event of an attack by an enemy power, may be directly in proportion to its advance "intelligence," or knowledge of that enemy . . . disposition of land, sea, and air power, hidden targets, weak points, concentration of physical resources, defenses, stamina of its people, intentions, plans, and capacities of its government.[6]

"The Man Called X" was the quintessential Cold War spy series. Produced by Ziv, the program featured Barry Sullivan as Ken Thurston, "code name X," whose activities took him behind the Iron Curtain to aid the cause of world freedom. In a stentorian voice the narrator proclaimed: "These are the stories of America's intelligence agents, our country's first line of defense." In the opening of one show—a drama in which Thurston arranged the defection to the West of a prominent East European ballerina—the thrust of all espionage series was succinctly summarized: protect Americans, aid free people around the world, and thwart the war-threatening goals of international Communism.

> The protection of the nation's welfare is the first concern of the United States government. And to that end intelligence agents work twenty-four hours a day in every part of the world. Also of great concern is the welfare of all free people, like those of this small country in Middle Europe controlled by an international group of corrupt and ruthless men whose ultimate goals could threaten world security.

TV images of American spies were not limited to professional intelligence operatives. Supplementing the military and government agents were patriotic citizens involved overseas on the U.S. side of the Cold War. "Biff Baker, U.S.A.," a CBS presentation in the 1952-53 season, concerned a businessman whose import-export affairs took him and his wife all over the world. While closing deals for his company, Baker invariably would do a little spying for his country. In his personality he melded the ethic of capitalism and the spirit of patriotism.

Baker and his wife were convincing. When blocked by an East European official, he could be blunt—as he was when he told a Czech military officer, "I'll go over your head, all the way to Moscow!" He could be decisive. In one episode, while vacationing in Austria he had no second thoughts about destroying a secret Communist radio station that had been jamming broadcasts from the Voice of America. And that escapade was carried out "in the name of all people who seek freedom beyond the Iron Curtain." Baker could also be brave, as when he aided a French plantation owner fighting off a murderous band of Viet Minh rebels outside Saigon. "Anything's possible with these fanatics," warned the Frenchman. Baker apparently agreed as he quipped, "I'm not partial to pink."

"Biff Baker, U.S.A." was so effective in portraying the businessman as spy that its sponsor, the American Tobacco Company, received letters from business groups protesting the implication that American businessmen in Europe were spying for the government. Fenton Earnshaw, the story supervisor for the series, was quick to defend his program. He gave the complaining letters to the FBI, and explained in a trade journal that his scripts were approved by the State Department, the FBI, and the Commerce Department. Earnshaw claimed, moreover, that the series was "attempting to create [a] positive, constructive kind of propaganda to encourage the American people along the road to worldwide democracy. Therefore any attack upon the show is an attack on democracy."[7]

The spectrum of citizen-spies ranged from Steven Mitchell, the hero of "Dangerous Assignment," who worked for a private intelligence agency that always supported American foreign policy goals, to the central character of "China Smith," a vagabond Yankee drifting from Hong Kong to Kuala Lumpur, instinctively fighting Communism because it was evil. In "The Hunter" the hero was not only an international playboy but also a patriot who at a moment's notice could leave a tennis match at Wimbledon and jet to Rumania to help an anti-Communist informer, or leave an art display in Germany and sneak into Prague to help the Czech underground. A favorite type for these series was the newspaperman. In this vein was "Foreign Intrigue," syndicated from 1951 to 1955. Also important was "Crusader," a series that in 1955-56 featured Brian Keith as Matt Anders, an international journalist who fought simultaneously for scoops and world security.

If the milieu of the professional spy was intriguing, the private-citizen-as-secret-agent was downright compelling. All the fears and frustrations of the era could be transferred to the shoulders of this hero. Here was a forthright picture of a man acting out his nationalistic convictions. Moving through a shadowy Hungarian street, dodging Polish border guards, making fools out of Russian military officials, stamping out Red guerrilla movements—in activities like these the powerless average viewer could project himself or herself through the citizen-spy and into the international struggle. In this manner, characters such as Matt Anders and Biff Baker became modern-day Minutemen, temporarily laying aside professional commitments to aid in the defense of social freedom.

Because they were amateurs, these nonprofessional spies usually happened upon their weekly suspenseful involvement. In the episode of "Foreign Intrigue" aired August 27, 1953, it was while pursuing a news story in East Berlin that journalist Bob Cannon came to help a rocket scientist defect to the West. Matt Anders just happened to be a passenger on a Polish airplane when it was hijacked at gunpoint to Hamburg and freedom. Even when Biff Baker was approached by American government officials and asked to do a little espionage work, he seemed ignorant of the implications of doing such a favor.

There was nothing serendipitous, however, about the propaganda content of these series. They all strongly asserted the anti-Communist position in the Cold War. Never doubting the political and moral rightness of their activities, their heroes acted to bring American justice to the unjust world. Casual and affable, these champions stood resolutely against Communist terror—and they always emerged as winners. This message of Americanism was strongly stated in the written preamble that rolled across the TV screen at the beginning of each episode of "Crusader":

> "Crusader" records the struggle of democratic people against the enemies of freedom and justice at home and abroad. These are the stories of people who have been helped by the many great organizations which are dedicated to bringing truth to those who are fed lies, light to those who live in darkness, protection to those who live in fear.

Inherent in most of these Cold War adventure programs was a picture of the world outside the United States as wretched and unsettled. Those clinging to the notion of a postwar united world of free and equal nations found little solace in such series. Crime, espionage, poverty, and generalized dispiritedness permeated shows like "Orient Express" and "Terry and the Pirates." Scenes in such programs often showed bombed-out cities or hungry children to American viewers grown used to the middle-class, suburban happiness depicted in programs like "Father Knows Best," "The Adventures of Ozzie and Harriet," and "77 Sunset Strip." Relative to a cholera epidemic in Libya, primitive agricultural techniques in Pakistan, or a political revolution in Burma, the United States was a fat, contented place. In the words of the hero of "The Hunter," it was "a place at the end of the rainbow where even the toothpaste is green."

As well as being malnourished and on the verge of turmoil, the world beyond the United States was pictured as treacherous and terrifying. Enemy spies seemed to be everywhere, working to inhibit individual freedom and disrupt peace. The opening to "Secret File, U.S.A."—a syndicated series filmed in Europe and featuring Robert Alda as an American intelligence officer, Major Bill Morgan—epitomized the unsettling picture of international politics offered by Cold War television.

> "Secret File, U.S.A.": a warning to all enemies of America, at home and abroad, who are planning acts of aggression. This is the story of the gallant men and women who penetrated, and are still penetrating, enemy lines to get secret information necessary for the defense of the United States. This is the story of one of our nation's mightiest weapons—past, present, and future if necessary—the American intelligence services.

If the TV image of American spies was heroic, the enemy was portrayed as the embodiment of perfidy. Communists were militant, deceitful, and merciless. They fomented revolutions, schemed for power, and lived in a gray, godless world. Arrogantly, these Communists sought to refashion the rest of the planet to match their dismal world.

For Herb Philbrick on "I Led 3 Lives," Communism was "a dangerous threat to world security"; its goal was "control of everything and everybody by any means"; and it believed that "If you scream a lie loud [*sic*] and long enough, the people will start to believe it." Starker still was the image of Communists presented in "Assignment Prague," an episode of "Behind Closed Doors" telecast on NBC on April 9, 1959. Here, as a movie studio behind the Iron Curtain churned out anti-American propaganda films under the scrutiny of distrustful Communist bureaucrats, a narrator described the project.

> This is one view of America. This view that is now being filmed in motion picture capitals of Eastern Europe—distorted, perverted, untrue. Excellent propaganda for distribution throughout Russia and her satellite countries. An insidious business closely watched and controlled by the omnipotent commissars. By carefully chosen producers such as comrade Bernasek—talented, dedicated, warped—who oversee every stage of the filming. By highly trained script girls who watch carefully for un-American errors. By top-flight cameramen recording every anti-American vilification on film. And by the best available directors, such as John Carpenter, recruited from an American Communist cell.

Every time a professional or amateur spy won his battle against a Communist enemy, television applauded the active role in foreign affairs assumed by the U.S. government after World War II. Television news may have reported the Cold War as a factual reality, but dramatized series enhanced the American position by adding characterization, emotionality, and recognizable purpose to the Cold War. And backing the believability of the TV undercover agents was the enormous strength of the U.S. military. It, too, became a significant source of entertainment on television in the 1950s.

THE MILITARY AS TV ENTERTAINMENT

In the 1950s the American military was the mightiest armed force on Earth. The existence of that arsenal was fundamental to the conduct of American foreign policy. On television during that decade the armed forces were consistently a part of popular entertainment. Reassuringly, TV praised the military, involving its stories and personnel in all types of programming. From film of actual battles and fictionalized drama, to situation comedy and sports and quiz shows, television focused frequently and flatteringly upon the armed forces. Never in the history of peacetime American broadcasting has such emphasis been placed on the military.

As Table 4 indicates, in entertainment series alone, the military was strongly represented on TV.

Table 4 The Military in TV Series in the 1950s[8]

Program	Years of First-Run	No. of Episodes
Crusade in Europe	1949	26
Crusade in the Pacific	1951	26
The Big Picture	1951-71	828
Victory at Sea	1952-53	26
Navy Log	1955-58	102
The Phil Silvers Show	1955-59	138
Combat Sergeant	1956	13
The West Point Story	1956-57	39
Air Power	1956-57	26
Men of Annapolis	1957-58	39
Citizen Soldier (The Big Attack)	1957-58	39
The Silent Service	1957-58	78
Flight	1958-59	39
Steve Canyon	1958-60	39
Men into Space	1959-60	38
The Blue Angels	1960-61	39

One of the most popular entertainment formats was the military documentary series. More than historical accounts, they were laudatory epics with Cold War implications. "Crusade in Europe" was a 26-part history of action in the European theater of World War II. Based on the memoirs of General Dwight D. Eisenhower, the series was skillfully produced by the March of Time and Twentieth Century-Fox. It premiered in May 1949, and proved to be one of the most popular attractions of the summer months. In the words of one reviewer, the series was "the most notable advance for TV in the field of narrative-visual reporting."[9] As an image of the United States in war, "Crusade in Europe" was a striking presentation. Stressing as it did the skill, bravery, and rectitude of the American war effort, Eisenhower and the armed forces he commanded emerged heroically.

The success of "Crusade in Europe" led to the production of "Crusade in the Pacific," another 26-part documentary program debuting in 1951. The latter series, however, went beyond World War II. Its coverage of the battle against aggression in the Far East included the Korean War, a conflagration that had begun less than a year before the series was released. Important to both programs was the sense of crusade they conveyed, for implicit throughout them was the idea that the national struggle against dictatorship and aggression did not end just because Hitler had been vanquished and the Japanese had surrendered.

Nowhere was the blend of military splendor and moral righteousness more powerfully presented than in the prestigious NBC program "Victory at Sea." This was the Cold War documentary series par excellence, focusing on the U.S. Navy in World War II but exploiting the militarized mentality of many Americans in the 1950s. The 26-part series was a collaboration of great talent. It was directed by Henry W. Salomon; its music came from Richard Rodgers and the NBC Symphony Orchestra; it was produced by Robert Sarnoff; and it was authenticated by the distinguished historian Samuel Eliot Morison. Supplemented by masterful editing and a vast display of authentic film of naval action during the war, the series emerged as the outstanding television production to that date.

Significantly, "Victory at Sea" struck a responsive chord within American society when it premiered in 1952. It became an instant programming success and was immediately rerun once its first showing was completed. Ten years after its release, mass acceptance of "Victory at Sea" was obvious. By that date every ship, installation, and substation in the Navy had at least one episode of the program to be used as "an educational device." It had been shown in every country in the world where there was television, and theatrically in some of those without TV. Within the United States the program had appeared at least once in 206 markets. And it had been rerun frequently—14 showings in Oklahoma City, 13 in Los Angeles and New York City, and 11 in Milwaukee. The series had also been edited and released as a 90-minute feature film. By 1963 its soundtrack had grossed over $4 million as an RCA-Victor record album.

Needless to say, "Victory at Sea" won awards. These included an Emmy from the Academy of Television Arts and Sciences, and the George Washington Medal from the patriotic Freedoms Foundation, and a Peabody from the University of Georgia. Other awards came from Sylvania, *Variety, American Weekly,* the City of Boston Film Council, and the Christopher Society. Three of its key personnel— Salomon, Rodgers, and Sarnoff—were also awarded the Distinguished Service Medal by the U.S. Navy in 1953.

Critics applauded the artistic and emotional quality of "Victory at Sea." Some suggested the intent of the series was to illustrate "the preservation of freedom and the overthrow of despotism." But is possessed more than simple historical value. There were those who understood the program in light of the Cold War, those who felt that in pictures of the German and Japanese defeat there was a lesson for actual and would-be Communist aggressors. This attitude was aptly summarized by Jack O'Brian of the *New York Journal-American*, who felt that the program demonstrated that it was not "ever safe to push the U.S. too far. It might be a good idea to show *Victory at Sea* to Nikita Khrushchev. A very good idea."[10]

"Victory at Sea" presented a chauvinistic image of the United States in world affairs. Innocent America clashed dramatically with the savage self-interest of Fascist imperialism. The American cause was couched in terms of altruism, morality and international law—the enemy motive was naked aggression. There was no discussion of issues. There was no explanation of why the British Empire should be preserved while those of Germany, Japan, and Italy should be destroyed. Instead, rhetoric replaced reason and viewers had war painted in sermonizing tones. In one episode the narrator described the purpose of the battle thus: "From island to island, continent to continent, the children of free peoples move the forces of tyranny from the face of the earth. . . . It is, it will be so, until the forces of tyranny are no more." In the program about Guadalcanal audiences learned that the American mission was divine in inspiration:

Far from the dying and destruction, far from the sailors and marines who fight and pray for victory and salvation, the United States of America organizes her land, her resources, her industry, her men to answer the distant prayers. In the greatest mobilization of strength known to the world, America prepares to rescue the world. And to the rescue America marches.

As a corollary to such factual and impersonal presentations, Cold War television frequently offered series with a humane, "nice-guy" image of the military. From stories about soldiers and sailors in many anthology dramatic programs, to an Army-sponsored G.I. talent program like ABC's "Talent Patrol," which in 1953 was hosted by Steve Allen and Arlene Francis, by spotlighting the human quality of individual servicemen and servicewomen, TV personalized the armed forces, projecting the military as "a bunch of regular guys" rather than a powerful institution with its own direction and self-interest.

"Men of Annapolis" and "The West Point Story" were light dramatic series that in the late 1950s treated the collegiate problems encountered by the nation's Navy and Army officers-in-the-making. The most engaging program in this "nice guy" style, however, concerned a noncommissioned officer, Sergeant Ernest Bilko, and his merry band of motor-pool enlistees in "The Phil Silvers Show." Throughout the history of broadcasting there had never been a successful comedy series set in a military context. But for four television seasons, 1955-59, and in countless reruns on local stations, the rascally Sergeant Bilko turned the Army into a zany world of gambling, romance, get-rich-quick schemes, and general indiscipline. It was a happy demimonde where Bilko's greatest war was a weekly struggle to outwit his gullible commanding officers.

Unlike official propaganda in many authoritarian countries, the persuasive content of American TV ideology was neither dogmatic nor heavy-handed. There were superficial contradictions that often softened the political message. Sergeant Bilko seemed to outmaneuver his commanding officers with ease, but this did not demean the officer corps. In fact, after apparent success in his high jinks, Bilko usually ended up the victim of his own scheme. The shenanigans of Bilko and his motor-pool underlings were nothing more than embodiments of the chronic barrack's gripes by countless GIs about inflexible officers and the routine of military life. Bilko and his men were benign. In fact, their recognizable, human qualities increased their propagandistic subtlety, for it was well understood that at heart they were loyal to their country if not to military decorum. This was comedy akin to that of silent films where common people threw pies in the faces of men in tuxedos and women in fine gowns. These were not the antics of social discord, but the comedy of a democratic people uncomfortable with divisions of class and rank, yet powerless to change things meaningfully.

Further, the military was not always shown as invincible. Although the U.S. Navy eventually triumphed in World War II, "Victory at Sea" often showed sunken American ships and dead American sailors. It was not an indestructible Navy that emerged here. Like the country it represented, the U.S. Navy could be wounded seriously. It might even lose. But such vulnerability only underscored the patriotic call to duty contained in such series. Like the heroes of "The Phil Silvers Show," the winners in "Victory at Sea"—and in all TV shows offering a perspective on the American role in the Cold War—were regular folks, common people who, regardless of rank or class, battled together to preserve bourgeois freedom at home and the possibility of its extension abroad. And the quintessential symbol of this ideological posture in the 1950s was the serviceman.

The American military establishment did much to ensure that television portrayed the armed services in a positive fashion. As early as 1950 it spent hundreds of thousands of dollars to produce and broadcast TV commercials aimed at recruitment. Whether it was allowing Bob Hope to film and broadcast highlights of his overseas tours, or cooperating with the networks during Armed Forces Week celebrations, the Pentagon sought to display itself in a favorable light.

Typical of this latter function, on May 12, 1957, the military establishment staged a magnificent display of its arsenal on NBC's "Wide Wide World" program. Courtesy of the Pentagon, viewers for 90 minutes saw an array of live military maneuvers—precision bombing drills from Luke Air Force Base near Phoenix; simulated vertical envelopment in an amphibious assault conducted at Marine Corps installations at Quantico, Virginia; remote transmissions from a U.S. Navy submarine, an aircraft carrier, and a guided missile cruiser; and demonstrations by the U.S. Army of its latest equipment at Fort Sill, Oklahoma. Only the constraints of time prevented "Wide Wide World" from spotlighting the prowess of the U.S. Coast Guard.

Writing in 1970, Senator J. William Fulbright of Arkansas described the efforts of the Department of Defense to enhance its public image and to convince the American people of its anti-Communist interpretation of world politics. In *The Pentagon Propaganda Machine* he cited a National War College public seminar, the purpose of which was described thus by the military: "To provide guidance to military reservists and to selected civic and business leaders regarding the deceptive Communist subversive efforts being directed toward the United States. . . . To reveal areas of Communist influence upon American youth through infiltration into theater, motion picture, television, and other entertainment media."[11]

Of great importance to this Pentagon propaganda machine, according to Fulbright, was the manipulation of television. Whether by the creation of TV programs, or by assisting approved civilian producers in their treatments of military matters, the Defense Department used television to influence public opinion. While Fulbright's book focused on the Pentagon during the Vietnam War, the propagandistic activities of the military establishment were evident early and often in the history of video.

The Defense Department told its own story in a steady supply of motion pictures produced by the Pentagon and distributed free of charge to all stations willing to air them. In mid-1957, for example, outlets were able to obtain free films about the Air Force such as "Air Defense" and "Air Power," the latter narrated by Lowell Thomas. The U.S. Navy was praised in "Take 'er Down" and the three-part "History of the United States Navy."

Networks and local stations eagerly awaited films offered by the Pentagon. When the Federal Civil Defense Administration released a 28-minute Defense Department movie of the American hydrogen bomb test in November 1952 in the Pacific, CBS took pride in beating its rivals in airing portions of it. Segments of this film, "Operation Ivy," were also shown on the Dumont network, while ABC and NBC televised the movie in its entirety.[12]

The Defense Department also produced its own network and syndicated series. As early as October 1949, "The Armed Forces Hour" was a half-hour NBC-TV public service program offering vintage military training and recruitment films, discussions of topics such as amphibious warfare and defense spending, special addresses by the secretary of defense, and musical performances by the Singing Sergeants of the Air Force Band. Secretary of Defense Louis Johnson hailed NBC for presenting the series, commending the network for "undertaking to reflect these developments which are so important to our national security." Niles Trammell of NBC noted that "Every citizen wishes to know as much as possible about the services which will defend his country if it is ever again attacked. NBC's part in this informational undertaking is to provide its facilities for the Armed Forces' message."[13] "The Armed Forces Hour" ended its run as a summer series on the Dumont network in 1951.

By far the most impressive military production was "The Big Picture," a series that each week announced: "From Korea to Germany, from Alaska to Puerto Rico, all over the world the United States Army is on the alert to defend our country—you, the American people —against aggression. This is 'The Big Picture,' an official television report to the nation from the United States Army." This program debuted in 1951 and appeared until 1971. It was filmed by the Army Signal Corps. Individual shows varied greatly—from a look at aspects of the Korean War and later armistice, to a survey of rocket weaponry or a dramatic re-creation from military history, a tour of an Army base, or defenses against a possible Soviet sneak attack upon the United States.

For several years in the mid-1950s, "The Big Picture" appeared intermittently as an ABC network presentation. But it received the greatest exposure for its hundreds of films through direct distribution to individual stations. At one point in 1957, the series appeared on 377 outlets. Although telecast whenever participating outlets desired, given its breadth of distribution and length of availability, "The Big Picture" was probably the most widely viewed series in video history.

The Defense Department supplemented its own programming by cooperating with networks and independent producers. Of course there were many individual shows—an episode of "Medic" needing a Navy locale or a "Studio One" drama requiring file footage of Air Force action—where the military assisted in creating TV entertainment. Furthermore, that assistance often was crucial to the success of a program. Such was the case, for example, with "Dry Run," a live play presented on December 7, 1953, on "Studio One." The story was a submarine epic for which the U.S. Navy was asked to provide film of the atomic sub, U.S.S. *Nautilus*, then being completed by the General Dynamics Corporation. The Navy filmed the submarine expressly for the TV show. It also provided a commandant to introduce the play—plus directors, technicians, actors, photographers, and publicity men.[14]

In addition to working with individual productions, the Pentagon supplied manpower and materials for entire television series. "The Blue Angels" incorporated U.S. Navy film footage into its dramatized stories about the pilots of the Navy's precision flying team. "The Silent Service" not only borrowed submarine footage from the Navy but also received use of a real Navy sub, the U.S.S. *Sawfish*, to lend increased authenticity to the image of the nation's underwater fleet. The U.S. Army freely lent soldiers to be used as extras in producing "Citizen Soldier" (renamed "The Big Attack"), a practice that angered the Screen Actors Guild in 1958. The dramatic series "Flight," received free film from the U.S. Air Force. The Air Force also provided footage to "Steve Canyon"—including motion pictures of the Atlas ICBM missile; of zero elevation launching, in which jets were launched from flatbed trucks; and the test detonation of a hydrogen bomb.[15] All branches of the armed services cooperated with Ziv Television Productions in developing "Men into Space," a CBS science fiction series that in 1959-60 presented a realistic picture of the space race and the future of space exploration—and a series over which the Pentagon had approval rights on all scripts.

Many historical documentary series relied heavily on the Pentagon for support. This had been the case early in the decade with "Victory at Sea," and it continued in such later CBS productions as "The 20th Century," "The 21st Century," and "Air Power." The limits to which the military establishment would go for favorable publicity in entertainment TV was evident in the premiere of the "Air Power" series. That program, "The Day North America Is Attacked," was telecast on Armistice Day of 1956. With Walter Cronkite as the announcer, the network and the Defense Department enacted the probable American military response to a surprise air attack by the Soviet Union upon the United States.

This hour-long drama was filmed on actual air bases, ships, and defense installations throughout the United States and Canada. Scores of military officers, including General Nathan Twyning, played themselves in the drama. And Cronkite filmed his narration inside the top-secret Colorado headquarters of the Continental Air Defense Command.

It was exciting TV. There was tension when the generals moved the nation from Warning Yellow to Warning Red as 1,100 Russian aircraft moved on the United States from the north, west, and east. There was excitement as missiles were taken from their silos and the Strategic Air Command and the 83rd Fighter-Interceptor Squadron scrambled. Aircraft carriers were busy with jets taking off. Cameras were inside the cockpits when American airplanes launched air-to-air missiles at incoming enemy craft. The exploding of a Russian thermonuclear bomb on an American city was the climactic finale. Five times during the telecast CBS superimposed the message "AN ATTACK IS NOT TAKING PLACE. This Is a Military Exercise." Still, it was a believable, action-packed thriller, an exhilarating example of the military as entertainment.

Another noteworthy series receiving Defense Department cooperation was "Navy Log," a production of more than 100 half-hour dramas based on actual naval events. This program dealt with personalized tales of World War II, such as Lieutenant John F. Kennedy's escape from a deserted South Pacific island following the sinking of his craft, PT 109. Senator Kennedy filmed a short comment that was aired with the episode.

Occasionally, however, "Navy Log" turned its sights directly on the Cold War. In a particularly powerful installment aired December 20, 1955, and entitled "The Bishop of the Bayfield," "Navy Log" treated the naval evacuation of Vietnamese Christians from Haiphong harbor in North Vietnam. Two years after the actual event, and long before the war in Southeast Asia became well-known, American viewers saw their somber sailors "on a mission of mercy," rescuing women, old people, and defenseless children from the onslaught of atheistic Communists. Mixing studio re-creations with government-supplied film from the actual evacuation, the episode contained classic Cold War imagery: protective and paternal American military men helping frightened, wretched refugees from the Reds. The story blatantly blended Christian religious symbols and Cold War propaganda and turned the *Bayfield* into "a ship with a halo."

In addition to providing its own productions and file footage to private companies, the Pentagon lent military bases, such as the Marine Corps' Camp Pendleton and March Air Force Base, for on-location filming. It also provided experts to check on the accuracy of everything from proper military formations to Phil Silvers' comedic references on "The Phil Silvers Show." The Defense Department even offered its academic campuses. The U.S. Military Academy at West Point was used in producing the Ziv series "The West Point Story." The U.S. Naval Academy at Annapolis was the site of many scenes in another Ziv product, "Men of Annapolis." In both cases, applications for admission to the academies rose as a result of these series.[16]

Still another manner in which the Defense Department cooperated with private producers was in the lending of military officers to act as official technical advisers on and off camera. The Air Force provided an expert on the set during all filming of "Steve Canyon." A commander who had once headed the Navy's precision flying drill team was adviser, and sometime pilot for aerial shots, on "The Blue Angels." While such advisers usually remained nameless, in several instances programs acknowledged the officers on whom they were dependent. As Table 5 indicates, video entertainment enjoyed a close relationship with high-ranking military personnel during the 1950s.

The propagandistic flow was usually from the Pentagon to the networks. However, commercial TV was not averse to providing news footage to the Defense Department filmmakers. Certainly, too, episodes of NBC's "Victory at Sea" became training staples of the U.S. Navy. At least one "See It Now" program was provided to the military and was reissued by the U.S. Army Signal Corps as *Armed Forces Screen Magazine*, issue no. 522. Originally telecast on CBS on November 17, 1953, this "See It Now" installment featured Edward R. Murrow and CBS reporters Ed Scott and Bill Downs explaining the multiple strike power of the destroyers, carriers, bombers, and helicopters of the U.S. Navy's Hunter-Killer Group White. Presented now as an informational film for armed forces personnel, the film featured the Hunter-Killer Group thwarting a mock sneak attack on Boston by a Navy submarine following the path that a Russian submarine might take.

In a multiplicity of ways, then, the military ethic was an integral part of TV in the 1950s. It even found its way into televised sports.

Table 5 TV Series Crediting Military Personnel as Advisers in the 1950s[17]

Program	Officer Credited on Screen
Behind Closed Doors	Rear Admiral Ellis M. Zacharias, Ret., Deputy Chief of Naval Intelligence
Crusade in Europe	General Dwight D. Eisenhower, Ret., U.S. Army
Flight	General George C. Kenney, Ret., U.S.A.F.
The Man Called X	Ladislas Farago, former Chief of Research and Planning, Special Warfare Branch, U.S. Naval Intelligence
Navy Log	Commander Merle MacBain, U.S.N. Commander Alan Brown, U.S.N.R.
O.S.S.	Colonel William Eliscu, Ret., U.S. Army
The Silent Service	Rear Admiral Thomas M. Dykers, Ret., U.S.N.
Steve Canyon	Lieutenant Colonel Frank Ball, U.S.A.F.
Victory at Sea	Captain Walter Karig, U.S.N.
The West Point Story	Colonel Russell P. Reeder, U.S. Army

When the National Collegiate Athletic Association (NCAA) rejected live telecasts of college football games, the Defense Department cooperated with CBS in airing Saturday afternoon contests within the Armed Forces League. In the fall of 1951 and 1952, football fans could see nationally broadcast games involving such teams as San Diego Naval Training Center, Camp Lejeune, Fort Lee, Quantico Marines, and the Great Lakes Naval Training Center. The climax of these seasons was the annual Poinsettia Bowl between the Eastern and Western service team champions. Once CBS came to terms with the NCAA in 1953, military football left network television except for the annual gridiron clash between Army and Navy.

Even before it was first televised nationally in 1949, the Army-Navy football game was an American event. But TV made visual what newspapers and radio had only been able to describe in words. "If it is true that football is the sport most closely resembling military combat," wrote Harry T. Paxton in the *Saturday Evening Post* in 1955, "then it is at the Army-Navy game that football has the perfect setting."[18] Throughout the 1950s this simulated combat drew large, proud audiences.

As a Cold War spectacle, television brought the color and pageantry of this pseudomilitarism into millions of homes. Here were brave national gladiators meeting in mock combat on the football field. Years later sportscaster Lindsey Nelson described the caliber of men in the game, referring to the players as "the best product of our country, the finest young men we can produce."[19] But it was Paxton who captured the emotionalism of the game. "When those erect, disciplined ranks come swinging in turn onto the field," he remarked, "it is a scene that does something to the normal American pulse." Even when the academies had dismal season records, network TV never failed to broadcast their football confrontation while millions of citizens dutifully watched. In addition, the new Air Force Academy seemed to gain full credibility when, in the fall of 1959, its football team played Army. The final score, a tie, was appropriate for this rite of passage. The game was televised nationally by NBC.

ANTI-COMMUNISM AS ENTERTAINMENT IN CHILDREN'S PROGRAMMING

The terror and suspense of anti-Communist adult programming was an integral part of children's TV throughout the 1950s. In the late weekday afternoons and on Saturday mornings, American youngsters were treated to an array of H-bomb scares, mad Red scientists, plots to rule the world, and humble refugees seeking a better life in the Free World.

Perhaps the most memorable propagandistic image from this type of entertainment was that of Superman—arms akimbo, with the American flag flowing behind him, standing resolutely as an announcer energetically proclaimed that this flying man was a champion of "truth, justice, and the American way." Interestingly, during its lengthy career in radio, "The Adventures of Superman" was never introduced with these specific words. Further, on television the program did not often exploit espionage or similar Cold War themes. Thus, the opening scene is all the more striking as a generalized political posture, not directly related to the story lines in most "Superman" episodes.

More thoroughly Cold War in its orientation was "Captain Midnight," later syndicated as "Jet Jackson—Flying Commando." Drawn from a juvenile radio serial popular in the 1940s, this series spotlighted Captain Midnight as the commander of the Secret Squadron. This was a clandestine group dedicated to the establishment of justice around the world. It was also an organization with which boys and girls in the audience were encouraged to identify. In the weekly process of rectifying injustice, Captain Midnight occasionally would make contact with a Secret Squadron member in a foreign country. Usually that member was a youngster.

Captain Midnight was a prepossessing hero. He flew a jet plane, conducted research in a mountaintop laboratory, and was a strong and handsome man. He was the perfect model for the United States at midcentury—an amalgam of technology, scientific investigation, and physical prowess. And he was a patriot deeply involved on the American side of the Cold War.

The captain was not averse to flying directly into international political issues. Well over half the 39 episodes in the series were intimately involved with enemy agents, national defense, military technology, and despots plotting to rule the world. In the episode entitled "Isle of Mystery," for example, Captain Midnight and his sidekick investigated the queen of the island of Luana, who had suddenly changed her mind about allowing the U.S. government to use her homeland as a test site for the atomic bomb. In "Trapped Behind Bars," he was placed in a state prison to thwart an unexpected uprising—a riot instigated by foreign agents trying to create unfavorable world publicity for the United States. One of his most frustrating assignments occurred in "Operation Failure." Here Midnight jetted behind the Iron Curtain to rescue Zabor, leader of the people's underground in Balkavia. The mission was successful, but Zabor decided, while flying to freedom in the West, that he could do more for his people by staying in his own country. Midnight returned to Balkavian airspace and the selfless freedom fighter parachuted back to his true responsibility.

If children liked their national enemies vile, "The Atom Squad" in mid-1953 offered great satisfaction. This serialized weekday program presented the exploits of three government agents who thwarted plots by Communists and others. Until the Atom Squad broke up the scheme, the Russians had financed an American traitor who constructed an underground magnet to disrupt American shipping. The squad also foiled an ex-Nazi who tried to flood the United States by manipulating the weather. This heroic band of patriots even infiltrated the Kremlin to contact the only man who could stop the Russians from using a deadly secret weapon.

Less diabolical, but still stereotyped, were the Communist spies who populated the cartoon series "Rocky and His Friends." From 1959 until 1961—and then in countless reruns—children were amused by the antics of Boris Badenov, Natasha Fatale, and the militaristic Fearless Leader. Complete with East European accents, these were bomb-throwing Red provocateurs who were endearingly hilarious. Nonetheless, within the animated sinister plots the message was clear: Russian men and women were evil, and they were out to destroy the American way of life. Only the lovable flying squirrel, Rocky, and his dim-witted pal, Bullwinkle the Moose, two all-American types, could save the day.

The most consistent expression of anti-Communist, militaristic values in children's programming occurred in adventure series set in outer space. These series flourished in the first half of the 1950s, as Table 6 demonstrates. While they were in vogue, the science fiction programs plunged American youngsters directly into the political and philosophical struggles of the Cold War.

Although affiliated with futuristic intergalactic organizations like the United Planets or the Solar Alliance, the stalwarts of these shows were nothing more than Americans operating at some time in the future. On the Commonwealth of Earth in 2350, Tom Corbett was a cadet at the Space Academy, U.S.A. Here he was training to join the Solar Guard, an interplanetary police force ensuring peace within the Solar Alliance of Earth, Mars, Venus, and Jupiter. For Rocky Jones

Table 6 Children's Science Fiction Programs of the Early 1950s

Program	Years First Run
Captain Video and His Video Rangers	1949-57
Space Patrol	1950-55
Buck Rogers	1950-51
Tom Corbett, Space Cadet	1951-55
Flash Gordon	1953
Rod Brown of the Rocket Rangers	1953-54
Rocky Jones, Space Ranger	1954-55
Commando Cody—Sky Marshal of the Universe	1955

the setting was the twenty-first century but the function was equally militaristic and identifiable—to protect the solar system against interplanetary evil.

The contemporary political relevance of such programming was explicit in the oaths of allegiance associated with many shows. When a youngster became a Space Cadet of the Space Patrol, he or she pledged, among other things, to "uphold and support the articles of government of the United Planets, and that I will defend the rights of free men against all enemies; that I will bear true faith and allegiance to the principles of right, goodness, and justice." Children who joined Captain Video's club, the Video Rangers, took an oath of loyalty in similarly political terms: "We, as Official Video Rangers, hereby promise to abide by the Ranger Code and to support forever the cause of Freedom, Truth, and Justice throughout the universe."

The most comprehensive pledge, however, was that taken by youngsters joining the Junior Rocket Rangers clubs established by Rod Brown. Although Brown operated on Omega Base, protecting Earth in the twenty-second century, his oath was a secularized Ten Commandments reflecting American politics in the early 1950s.

On my Honor as a Rocket Ranger, I pledge that:
1. I shall always chart my course according to the Constitution of the United States of America.
2. I shall never cross orbits with the Rights and Beliefs of others.
3. I shall blast at full space-speed to protect the Weak and Innocent.
4. I shall stay out of collision orbit with the laws of my State and Community.

5. I shall cruise in parallel orbit with my Parents and Teachers.
6. I shall not roar my rockets unwisely, and shall be Courteous at all times.
7. I shall keep my gyros steady and reactors burning by being Industrious and Thrifty.
8. I shall keep my scanner tuned to Learning and remain coupled to my studies.
9. I shall keep my mind out of free-fall by being mentally alert.
10. I shall blast the meteors from the paths of other people by being Kind and Considerate.[20]

Within the plots of these space series, youngsters were introduced to the moral legitimacy of battling against aggression and tyranny wherever they were encountered. Typically, for Commando Cody—Sky Marshal of the Universe, it was a battle, in August 1955, against the diabolical dictator who had found on Saturn a new element that enabled him to drop germ capsules onto Earth through the cosmic dust blanket. For Flash Gordon—whether it was the series syndicated in 1953, or the many episodes of the three movie serials from the 1930s—the enemies were many, the most infamous being Ming the Merciless, an outer-space version of an Oriental despot complete with Fu Manchu beard. And for Buck Rogers—whether in old theatrical serials starring Buster Crabbe, or in the short-lived ABC series—it was protecting Earth in the twenty-fifth century, as Buck did in June 1950, from such threats as the "Slaves of the Master Mind."

For eight years Captain Video rescued innocent people from all galaxies and saved moons and planets from evil men with un-American names like Vazarion, Marcus Gayo, Mook the Moon Man, Heng Foo Seng, and Kul of Eos. Captain Video even bested diabolical women, as in May 1954, when he confronted the evil female ruler of Nemos, who sought to conquer the universe. There was no way the captain could lose, however, for he was introduced each time as the epitome of political virtue:

> Captain Video! Master of Space! Hero of Science! Captain of the Video Rangers! Operating from his secret mountain headquarters on the planet Earth, Captain Video rallies men of goodwill and leads them against the forces of evil everywhere! As he rockets from planet to planet, let us follow the champion of Justice, Truth, and Freedom throughout the universe!

Such clashes between hero and tyrant were not meaningless excursions in entertainment. They were value-laden fairy tales delivered with impact. Most dramatically, they pitted the "American" do-gooder

against the forces of destruction. These may have been formulaic confrontations, but for young viewers they offered symbolic meanings.
They were stylized Cold War fantasies in which the champions of
democracy triumphed over totalitarianism. Certainly not every show
in these series treated dictatorial plots, but the theme of victory over
despotism permeated the programs.

RELIGIOUS PROGRAMMING AS PROPAGANDA

One of the most heated issues of the Cold War was the irreligious
nature of Communism. Where Karl Marx had preached that religion
was only an opiate meant to narcotize the masses, Western religious
leaders saw Marx, Lenin, and international Communism by the 1950s
as a threat to the spirituality of mankind.

American popular culture reflected this situation in two distinct
ways. First, it integrated religious matter into the mainstream of entertainment. This resulted in feature films with Biblical themes, such as
Quo Vadis?, *The Ten Commandments*, *The Robe*, *David and Bathsheba*, *The Silver Chalice*, *Ben Hur*, and *Samson and Delilah*. Even
popular music reflected this trend as songs with spiritual messages
became major hits: "Vaya Con Dios" (which reached the number 1
position on the *Billboard* magazine charts in 1953), "I Believe" (no.
2 in 1953), "He" (no. 7 in 1955), "Somebody up There Likes Me"
(no. 26 in 1956), "A Wonderful Time up There" (no. 10 in 1958),
and "He's Got the Whole World in His Hands" (no. 2 in 1958).[21]

In addition to communicating religious messages, American mass
culture assailed the militant atheism of Communism. This was frequently accomplished in an allegorical manner. In a movie such as
Sign of the Pagan, it was seen in the ignominious death of Attila, the
heathen Asian invader of Christian Europe in the fifth century. In
many other films, it was seen in the myopic paganism of ancient
Rome as it crucified and otherwise persecuted innocent Christians.

Television also presented spiritual programming, and occasionally
it was aired in prime time. In many instances such programs struck
their own blows for the United States in the East-West conflict. The
fundamental depravity explaining all Red actions was alleged to be
the atheism basic to Communism. If there was brutality within the
Soviet Union and its satellites, it was described as the result of a
Godless ideology. If Communists were threatening world peace, it
was because atheism had no respect for God and His worshippers.

Such programs stressed that suppression of the East European
peoples was suppression of the Christian faith. They suggested, how-

ever, that Providence was on the side of the downtrodden—even the Russian people held in "captivity" by Communism—and would eventually destroy the diabolical Red empire. In its own way, television conveyed the belief that the strength of anti-Communism was its alliance with the Divine.

Such themes appeared in a range of programs. In "Navy Log," "Victory at Sea," and other millitary series, images of praying servicemen illustrated the religious aspect of the American armed forces. A dramatic production such as "Cardinal Mindszenty," which appeared on "Studio One" on May 3, 1954, related the plight of the Hungarian prelate who for many years escaped Communist prisons by gaining sanctuary in the American embassy in Budapest.

Prime time dramatic anthologies occasionally utilized Cold War religious material. In "The Boy Who Walked to America," "Cavalcade of America" in January 1956 blended religion and anti-Communism in a story about a Korean boy who hitchhiked to America. After a plane flight from his homeland to Japan, the lad became the ward of an Army chaplain who eventually secured permission for the child to immigrate to Father Flanagan's Boys Town in Omaha, Nebraska. This mixture of a sweet child seeking American freedom and a loving priest arranging for his move to the United States underscored the vile nature of an enemy who would cause a child such anguish.

Sunday morning religious programs often related anti-Communist stories. Series like "Lamp unto My Feet," "This Is the Life," "The Catholic Hour," "Religious Town Hall," and "Look Up and Live" addressed ideas of freedom, patriotism, and spiritual fulfillment within a religious nation. They also dealt with the domestic threat of Communism and with escape from behind the Iron Curtain. The most zealous program of this sort was "Zero-1960."

"Zero-1960" was produced by the Blue Army of Our Lady of Fatima. It debuted in May 1957 and was nationally syndicated until 1960. The Blue Army was a decade-old organization that sought to end Communism through moral opposition. The show was named after the year in which the full message of the miracle of Fatima, partially revealed in 1917, was anticipated. The program worried less about expected holy messages than about the specter of atheistic Communism.

This was a stark political-religious presentation. The opening telecast set the pace for the entire series as Roman Catholic Bishop Cuthbert O'Gara, a missionary in China, told how the Communists had stripped him naked before his parishioners and had dragged him through the city streets. By 1958 the program handled topics such as imminent spiritual and political revolutions in the Soviet Union, the possibility of annihilation in a Russian-initiated nuclear war, the confessions of a former Soviet military officer, and the patriotic resistance by American blacks to the lure of Communism. In its last season "Zero-1960" became a religious discussion series presenting anti-Communist celebrities like the president of the Philippines discussing Red activities in Southeast Asia, and the chairman of the House Committee on Un-American Activities speaking on enemy spies in the United States.

More consistently and more grimly than other religious shows, "Zero-1960" championed the cause of anti-Communism. But its line of argument was not incompatible with the Cold War values found in other religious, and even nonreligious, TV series. Furthermore, scheduled as it was on Sunday mornings—a time usually filled with spiritual programs and public service presentations about the armed forces—church and state seemed to complement and legitimize each other.

The appearance of spiritual broadcasts in network evening hours illustrates the strategic position religion occupied in Cold War culture. Billy Graham's "Hour of Decision," for example, was a regular Sunday evening feature on ABC from 1951 until 1954. "Crossroads," an ABC dramatic series between 1955 and 1957, enacted stories from the experiences of Protestant, Catholic, and Jewish clergymen. Although this anthology series avoided the open politics found in many Sunday morning programs, it did promote a responsible and humane image of religious institutions, as well as reflecting the relevance of faith in the personal lives of most Americans.

If "Crossroads" was politically restrained, Bishop Fulton J. Sheen's "Life Is Worth Living" was openly aggressive in its anti-Communist appeal. Sheen came to the Dumont network, and then ABC, in the early 1950s. By the fall of 1953 his half-hour show on Tuesday evenings was appearing on more than 130 stations. Sheen, who was the bishop of Rochester and director of the World Mission Society for the Propagation of the Faith, left network TV in 1957 but returned in the syndicated "The Bishop Sheen Program," which ran through most of the 1960s.

Sheen was a chronically outspoken foe of Communism. During the Depression he had written hostile essays with such titles as "Communism and Religion," "The Tactics of Communism," and "Liberty under Communism." In this latter tract, published in 1937 as a response to the promulgation of a constitution in the Soviet Union, Sheen enunciated ideas that had not changed by the time he entered television two decades later.

There is no liberty under Communism because there is no Spirit. Liberty comes from the rational soul; that is why cabbages have no liberty. . . . Liberty for them [Communists] exists only when the citizens desire what the State desires, and do what the dictators order, and think only what the Party thinks. . . . Such is the liberty of dogs under the leash of their masters, and the liberty of cuckoos in cuckoo clocks, or the liberty of prisoners in prison. . . . Such are the "rights" granted to the slaves of Red Dictatorship under the new Red Constitution.[22]

On "Life Is Worth Living" Bishop Sheen lectured the nation on matters of general moral uplift as well as Cold War politics.[23] In talks punctuated by his flowing cassock and a blackboard on which he made chalk drawings, he left no doubt where he stood concerning the East-West confrontation. Sheen questioned the motives of those Americans who refused to tell congressional investigators whether they had ever been members of the Communist party. "Any good citizen, if asked by Congress if he were a member of Murder, Inc., would immediately deny it," he told viewers. "Why is it then, that some of our citizens insist on their constitutional rights when asked if they are Communists?" Sheen attacked Communists for having "perverted the notion of brotherhood into world imperialism," and for "denying God, denying morality, denying conscience, but keeping confession and guilt."

Perhaps the most publicized Sheen program occurred on February 24, 1953, when the bishop presented an energetic reading of the burial scene from Shakespeare's *Julius Caesar*. He substituted the names of Josef Stalin, KGB leader Lavrenti Beria, Georgi Malenkov, and U.N. ambassador Andrei Vishinsky for Caesar, Cassius, Mark Antony, and Brutus. When Stalin died unexpectedly nine days later, some suggested that Sheen's words might have been responsible.

In Bishop Sheen's view, the United States was to be more than the policeman of the globe—it was to be the new savior of the world by divine appointment. "America is at the crossroads—the crossroads of the starving world. It sees the world being crucified by Communism," he announced to an audience in 1953. "The long arm of Providence is reaching out to America, saying 'Take up the cross of all the starving people of the world. Carry it.'" Sheen was also forthright in explaining the future he envisioned for the United States. He pontificated on one program:

We have already saved the world from the swastika, which would cross out the cross and make a double cross. Now we must save the world from the hammer and sickle: the hammer that crucifies and the sickle that cuts life like immature wheat that it may never be one with the Bread of Life.

COLD WAR TELEVISION DRAMAS

If the strength of dramatization is its ability to exploit in emotional terms the stories of human interaction, on television the Cold War was most poignantly realized in the array of dramas presented through the medium. Whether in feature films, made-for-TV movies, live dramas, or half-hour anthologies, the political clash between Communism and anti-Communism was incorporated into America's electronic entertainment.

The networks and local stations faced a dilemma in dealing with many movies produced during World War II. In that war the Soviet Union and the United States were allies against the Axis powers. Hollywood had frequently had paid homage to this alliance, turning out wartime films praising the Russians and their accomplishments. Further, during the probe of Hollywood by the House Committee on Un-American Activities in the late 1940s, many wartime motion pictures were condemned as the products of Communist writers, directors, actors, or producers. Among those criticized during the anti-Communist "witch hunt" were *Objective Burma, Northern Pursuit, Back to Bataan, Sahara, Pride of the Marines, Destination Tokyo,* and *Action in the North Atlantic.*[24] In the Cold War, however, any historic warmth toward the Russians was considered potentially subversive. Television stations and networks had to be careful about which wartime pictures they aired.

Films like *Mission to Moscow* and *Song of Russia* had questionable content, according to the Cold War mentality. Some stations even worried about *Ninotchka*, the classic Greta Garbo feature from 1939 that actually satirized Communist dogma. The extent to which anti-Communist fears could carry television was seen in the TV version of *The North Star*, an RKO production in 1943 written by Lillian Hellman. The original movie was a sympathetic treatment of the bravery of a Russian peasant village in resisting Nazi invaders. Before it came to television, however, it was edited to diminish praise of the Russians and retitled *Armored Attack*. More strikingly, the film was given a new, contemporary ending—footage of Russian tanks suppressing the Hungarian revolution in 1956, while a narrator reminded viewers that despite the heroism of the Russian peasants, Communist leaders were as brutal now as the Germans had been in World War II.

Dramas produced exclusively for television approached the issue of Communism early but cautiously. This was especially true because the outbreak of the Korean War in June 1950 left TV without government guidelines—which had been available in World War II—explaining how to portray Communists and their ideology.

The first series to present an editorialized position on Communism was "Cameo Theater" in "Line of Duty," aired July 26, 1950, on NBC. The play concerned revolt in a European country after 20 years of Communist tyranny. At the time of the telecast, however, *Variety* remarked that the issue was not clear-cut. Many in the television industry were concerned that an attack on Communism might precipitate a demand from the Communist Party of the United States for equal time to rebut the charges. This was an especially sensitive matter in 1950, an election year, for according to Section 315 of the Communications Act of 1934, if one candidate for public office were granted facilities, equal opportunity had to be afforded all candidates.[25]

These concerns did not intimidate all broadcasters. When radio station WLIZ (Bridgeport, Connecticut) refused to sell time to the Communist party in 1950, Senator William Benton announced his support for the action. According to Paul Porter, former head of the Federal Communications Commission, such a ban was justified because "in this particular period . . . such a broadcast would tend to incite the community," and because Communists were not legitimate candidates—they were most likely exploiting the law "for the purpose of confusion."[26]

The precedent set by "Cameo Theater" made anti-Communism a popular subject for dramatic production, live and on film, during the "golden age" of TV drama. If one considers the spring and summer of 1953 as typical, the following list of programs establishes clearly that Cold War messages were prevalent:

- —"Someday They'll Give Us Guns," "The Unexpected" (April 21); in an aggressive dictatorship, a youth is trained for a regime of blood and tyranny.
- —"F.O.B. Vienna," "Suspense" (April 28); foreign agents disguised as businessmen try to smuggle vital machinery behind the Iron Curtain.
- —"Somewhere in Korea," "The Web" (May 3); U.N. soldiers escape from North Korean POW camp.
- —"The Man Who Cried Wolf," "Suspense" (June 9); clerk in Russian embassy in Mexico City steals valuable documents, then tries to exchange them for his freedom when he learns he is to be sent back to Russia to be executed.
- —"Counterplot," "Your Play Time" (June 14); American journalist tortured by Reds to get phony confession.

—"Malaya Incident," "Ford Theater" (June 18); love blooms as land-owner fights Red guerrillas in Malaya.

—"Jetfighter," "Plymouth Playhouse" (June 28); Yank pilot in trouble over Russian zone of Germany.

—"Bilshan and the Thief," "General Electric Theater" (July 5); refugee learns American patriotism from a thief.

—"The Mascot," "Suspense" (July 7); American Army deserter plans to become dictator of Mediterranean island.

—"The Traitor," "Fireside Theater" (September 1); Yank POW spies for Koreans against fellow American prisoners.

—"Two Prisoners," "Armstrong Circle Theater" (September 8); liberated POW has readjustment problems.

As the decade progressed, anti-Communism became more lavish and more expensive. "The Plot to Kill Stalin," on "Playhouse 90" in September 1958, was well received. "Darkness at Noon," on "Producers' Showcase" in May 1955 and "1984" on "Studio One" in September 1953, were famous anti-Communist novels dramatized for American audiences. "The Vanished," on "Armstrong Circle Theater" in April 1958, was based on the less renowned book *I Was a Slave in Russia*.

The plight of U.S. soldiers in Korean prisoner-of-war camps was treated in two "United States Steel Hour" productions: "P.O.W." in October 1953 and "The Rack" in April 1955. Rod Serling, who had written "The Rack," again lent his writing talent to the crusade with "Forbidden Area." A "Playhouse 90" program in October 1956, it concerned an Air Force saboteur and a sneak atomic attack on the United States set for Christmas Eve. This was not, however, one of Serling's triumphs; one critic blasted him for carelessly creating an "overall feeling [that] was one of inciting to hysteria by thinking in terms of H-Bombs, B-99s and submarines."[27]

Serling faced criticism for another military drama, "Time Element," which aired on "Desilu Playhouse" on December 8, 1958. Here, however, complaints came from the sponsor and advertising agency handling the program. The play concerned a man on December 7, 1941, who envisioned in a dream what was about to happen at Pearl Harbor. When he tried to warn the Army, he was brushed off as being a crackpot. Westinghouse and its ad agency, McCann-Erickson, protested the plot, demanding the play be rewritten so as not to portray the Army in a negative light. *Variety* reported, moreover, that Westinghouse asked for these changes "because it has a lot of contacts with the Defense Dept."[28]

In the many filmed showcases and dramatic series, there seemed always to be room for one or more episodes featuring anti-Communist themes. Such themes appeared regularly on "TV Reader's Digest," an anthology of 65 half-hour dramas in the mid-1950s. "Soldiers of Fortune" was a typical adventure series focusing on two Americans who roamed from London to the Far East, solving other people's problems and reaffirming Yankee effectiveness against international mischief. Even "Treasury Men in Action," a program treating the exploits of the U.S. Department of the Treasury, dealt with the Cold War in an episode entitled "Iron Curtain." It focused on the illegal export of American-made weapons to Communist countries.

During the 1956-57 TV season, "Wire Service" was a popular show on ABC relating tales of newspaper foreign correspondents. It was a propitious series for occasional stories about Red treachery. In "Rehearsal for Sabotage," Japanese Communists almost obtained secret Air Force documents that, the program asserted, would have precipitated a third world war and the destruction of civilization. In "Escape to Freedom," an American newsman helped a Hungarian counterpart escape certain death in Budapest during the Hungarian revolution. And in "Atom at Spithead," Communists plotted to detonate an atomic bomb during a prestigious British naval review.

One of the most graphic exploitations of Cold War fear occurred on the medical drama series "Medic." Hosted by Richard Boone, who often appeared in episodes as Dr. Konrad Styner, "Medic" had already established its reputation as a realistic program willing to dramatize medical issues usually avoided on TV. Among the more controversial topics "Medic" explored were medical malpractice, childhood leukemia, mastectomy, and postpartum psychosis. But "Medic" was never starker than in the episode entitled "Flash of Darkness," which aired February 14, 1955.

Here the topic was civil defense, and thermonuclear war actually came to the United States in this half-hour show. When Russian hydrogen bombs destroyed the downtown area, Styner and a few recruits were compelled to set up a clinic to treat the wounded in a school building. Flash fires, panic, and radioactive fallout were woven throughout the story. One child who had watched the explosion had his eyes burned out. Not all people seeking medical assistance survived. "Flash of Darkness" gave the nation a horrifying premonition of what the Communist enemy had in store for an unprepared America. But rather than express repulsion at such provocative sensationalism, critics like Jack Gould of the *New York Times* lauded this program as "genuinely educational."[29]

While dramas specifically treating Cold War issues were effective communicators of an anti-Communist ideology, this message was not always delivered so directly. Often the "truth" of *our* rectitude and *their* treachery was propagated through analogies and structural forms inherent in American entertainment genres. Whenever Joe Friday jailed a criminal on "Dragnet," TV proclaimed that the legal system was a success and that evildoers would always be apprehended. Whenever average folks won big money on quiz shows like "The $64,000 Question," the capitalist promise of material success was popularly reaffirmed. From situation comedies showing loving middle-class families working out problems using mirth and respect for one another, to daytime soap operas where the good people eventually triumphed over adversity, American popular culture preached the superiority of a social and economic system conceived in opportunity, supported by laws, and operated by a bourgeois citizenry. The genre in which this message was most fully communicated was the Western. And in the Cold War it thrived as in no time before or since.

THE TV WESTERN AS POLITICAL PROPAGANDA

The Western flourished on Cold War television. Whether in its original juvenile orientation, or in the adult formulation that emerged in the mid-1950s, the Western was relevant drama embodying the psychology of the East-West struggle. In this time of international tension and generalized social anxiety, the Western offered answers. In it powerless, perhaps frustrated, viewers found stylized tales of how their forefathers had triumphed over antisocial forces.

There were morals in the Western. The warm and friendly heroes of such programs believed in process, rules, and order. Sometimes they were law enforcement officers paid to uphold the regulations of civilized life. Sometimes they were do-gooders volunteering to rid the settlement of its disruptive elements. However they appeared, these heroes always preferred rational methods in upholding the law. But, when compelled by enemies, the Western stalwarts could be tough. These decent people were always prepared to use physical strength and firearms to achieve their just goal.

In a Cold War society where there were threats to existence and where similar toughness seemed necessary, Western heroes offered role models in resolve and courage. Their weekly exploits demonstrated a protective mentality suited to the popular perception of Cold War realities: basically law-abiding, but capable of great force in defense of civilization. As one editor pointed out at the time, "Though we are a peaceful people at heart, we let no one push us around, and find a warm kinship in reading of the Westerners who wouldn't be pushed either, or who so colorfully retaliated with six-guns, fists, or lariat."[30]

The Western was an integral part of the earliest TV programming. Directed primarily at children, relic B Western films and serials from the 1930s were inexpensive to broadcast, easy to edit for commercials, and filled with the action desired on early television. Faded cowboys stars like Tim McCoy, Hoot Gibson, and Ken Maynard had their careers rejuvenated. For William Boyd, the star of dozens of Hopalong Cassidy movies in the Depression, revitalization became a national commercial fad. By 1950 vintage Hoppy features, a new series of half-hour TV films, and a multitude of consumer products (from roller skates to bath towels) endorsed by Hopalong catapulted Boyd and his character into cultural prominence.

The success of Hopalong Cassidy opened the way for other personalities from juvenile Westerns. From movies and radio came Roy Rogers, Gene Autry, the Lone Ranger, and the Cisco Kid. And there were new heroes riding weekly in the name of justice and American civilization: Wild Bill Hickok, Annie Oakley, Buffalo Bill, Jr., the Range Rider, Kit Carson, Zorro, and even a dog, Rin Tin Tin, labored in the cause of law and order.

When they flourished in the early 1950s, the juvenile Westerns gave children emulable models of responsible American adults. The heroes of these shows were ideal relatives—the perfect father, uncle, big brother, or even mother, aunt, or big sister—the type of personality after which to shape oneself. Here, too, were paradigms of dedication to purpose and concern for positive social values. Moreover, as stylized American history, here was love of country, respect for just government, and communion with the creators of the nation.

The educative dimension of the video Western was summarized by Gene Autry in his Cowboy Code. Promulgated in the early 1950s, the code was a cowboy Ten Commandments enunciating the personal and nationalistic force inherent in the genre:

1. A cowboy never takes unfair advantage, even of an enemy.
2. A cowboy never betrays a trust.
3. A cowboy always tells the truth.
4. A cowboy is kind to small children, to old folks, and to animals.
5. A cowboy is free from racial and religious prejudice.
6. A cowboy is always helpful, and when anyone's in trouble, he lends a hand.

7. A cowboy is a good worker.
8. A cowboy is clean about his person, and in thought, word, and deed.
9. A cowboy respects womanhood, his parents, and the laws of his country.
10. A cowboy is a patriot.[31]

More finely developed as a patriotic series was "The Lone Ranger." It exhibited nationalistic qualities by being the story of a former Texas Ranger who worked altruistically to bring justice to the West of the 1870s. More specifically, patriotism was one of the basic tenets upon which producers on radio and TV constructed the show. According to the statement of standards written by its production company:

> The Lone Ranger is motivated by love of country—a desire to help those who are building the West. . . . Patriotism means service to a community; voting . . . the development of schools and churches. Patriotism includes also an obligation to maintain a home in which good citizens may be reared. Patriotism means respect for law and order, and the selection of officials who merit such respect. Patriotism consists of the preservation of the things for which our ancestors fought and died. The preservation of the rights of freedom of speech and religion.[32]

Others understood the political qualities of the Lone Ranger. Senator Homer Ferguson in 1953 lauded the character as possessing traits that were endearing to youngsters while teaching them "the principles of good citizenship, patriotism, fair play, tolerance, and a sympathetic understanding of people and their rights and privileges."[33] For George W. Trendle, creator of the program, loyalty to country was part of the general goal of making the Lone Ranger a patriotic, God-fearing, tolerant, habitless character who always used good grammer, never shot to kill, and could "fight great odds, yet take time to treat a bird with a broken wing."[34] Fran Striker, who wrote hundreds of "Lone Ranger" radio and TV scripts, also articulated the nationalistic qualities of the character. "He feels that the future of the country is in the West, so he's on the side of anyone who wants to build the West," Striker told an interviewer. "He's very patriotic," he continued, "and he believes in the right of every man to work at what he wants to do and to profit in proportion to his work."[35]

While the patriotic quality of "The Lone Ranger" was a generic appreciation of country and national past, the patriotism in "The Adventures of Rin Tin Tin" seemed more directly associated with Cold War thinking. This was an attractive program offering the alluring combination of a likable young boy, sympathetic supporting characters, and a talented German shepherd dog. More than any other juvenile Western, however, "Rin Tin Tin" glorified the military solution to problems of incivility. The series was set in a cavalry post, Fort Apache, in the Arizona Territory of the 1880s. Throughout its 164 half-hour episodes, all cast regulars except "Rinty" wore U.S. Army uniforms. This was the ultimate garrison state: few civilians except for those causing problems, soldiers everywhere, savages and other enemies outside the protective walls of the fort, and a military presence willing and able to defend American prerogatives. The series taught trust in, and dependence upon, the military. Moreover, because the young hero and his dog enjoyed the happy masculine life within Fort Apache, the program suggested that living could be fun even in a completely militarized society.

As a political statement, however, the most concentrated lesson in Cold War Americanism came from Walt Disney. In his three-part "Davy Crockett" series—broadcast in 1954-55 as part of "Disneyland" on ABC—the creator of Donald Duck and Mickey Mouse introduced the nation to a patriotic ancestor. Disney's Crockett fought and killed warring Creek Indians, but he spoke resolutely for the rights of peaceful Cherokees. With his innocent belief in direct action in the cause of truth, Crockett was elected to Congress and quickly became the voice of the honest commoner. When his friend President Andrew Jackson tried to force an unjust Indian Bill through Congress, the high-principled Crockett lashed out in unpretentiously democratic terms:

> You can fold up your grins and put 'em away, for you'll hear no jokes from Davy Crockett today. . . . Expansion is a might' fine thing. Sure, we gotta grow, but not at the expense of the thing this country was founded to protect. The government's promises set down in the Indian treaties is as sacred as your own word. Expansion ain't no excuse for persecutin' a whole part of our people because their skins is red and they're uneducated to our ways. You wouldn't be doin' the settlers no good by votin' for this Bill. You'd only be makin' rich men outta the land-grabbers and speculators that've been tryin' to get it passed.

Honest, self-sacrificing, and in love with America, Davy Crockett made the patriot's ultimate sacrifice, giving his life in the defense of the Alamo. Journeying to Texas because "Americans are in trouble" and because that was where "freedom was fightin' another foe," Crockett was killed in the cause of American imperialist expansion. Slaying Mexican soldiers with cannon, rifle, and knife, in Disney's rendition the tall frontiersman was a martyr for freedom, a model for contemporary America. This was a hero for the Cold War, part Washington, part Jefferson, and part Lincoln. Yet he was of common stock, an Everyman who loved peace and family and everyday things. Willing to heed "his country's call" to defend its political goals, Crockett was a citizen soldier convinced of democracy, repulsed by injustice, and prepared to die for his beliefs.

The Davy Crockett trilogy represented a transition in the history of the video Western. It was designed for youngsters, but it had adult appeal. Davy might outgrin a wild bear or make simple jokes with his sidekick, but there was much violence and bloodshed in the production. There was also sophistication in Davy's political philosophy, and the death of his young wife added an emotional depth to his character. Months before the "adult Western" premiered in the fall of 1955, "Davy Crockett" had shown the taste for more mature representation in this TV genre. Within a few years juvenile Westerns would be out of production and scheduled as reruns on weekend afternoons. Prime time, instead, would be packed with cowboys dramas intended for grown-ups. Still, the nationalistic relevance of the Western to Cold War thinking would endure.

With the advent of the adult Western, American television experienced a dramatic break with its past. In contrast with the flawlessly moral and one-dimensional types who were the heroes of the youth-oriented shows, the central characters in the adult programs were portrayed in more realistic terms. In an adult Western it was not uncommon to encounter the series hero drinking in a saloon, chatting amiably with a dance-hall girl, or playing poker with local gamblers. Now the star was allowed romantic interests. Others sold their talents as gunfighters or collected rewards for capturing wanted criminals. Viewers saw leading characters who sweated in the summer and complained of winter cold. Occasionally these frontiersmen exploded in anger. They also made mistakes and were compelled to suffer the consequences of their errors.

It is difficult to underestimate the acceptance of the adult Western by American society. During the next decade it would dominate popular tastes. At its height, as many as 60 million viewers per night watched Westerns. What had begun as 4 programs became 29 by the fall of 1959. In October 1957 the average Nielsen rating for 15 Westerns was 25.4, while the average prime time show rated only 20.7—a clear 23 percent higher rating for the former.[36] In 1959 almost one-fourth of prime time television consisted of Westerns. The Nielsen ratings for January 1959 also demonstrated their strength; eight of the top ten programs for the month were of that genre:[37]

1. Gunsmoke
2. Have Gun, Will Travel
3. The Rifleman
4. Wagon Train
5. The Danny Thomas Show (comedy)
6. The Real McCoys (comedy)
7. Tales of Wells Fargo
8. Maverick
9. The Life and Legend of Wyatt Earp
10. Zane Grey Theater

Despite the high number of adult Westerns, Americans were not fickle in their tastes. As Table 7 illustrates, some series lasted through hundreds of episodes and remained popular for many years.

Reasons explaining the popularity of the adult Western are plentiful. Certainly, they were engagingly written, usually well-acted, and often photographed in color, a distinct advantage at a time when color TV was being introduced to American consumers. But, most important, the explosion of the genre on television was related to historical circumstances. The Western succeeded in part because it was a political morality play for the frightened, confused, and dispirited. It contained secular parables for a nation whose citizens built

Table 7 Longevity of Leading Network Adult Westerns[38]

Program	Length of Run	No. of Episodes
Gunsmoke	Sept. 1955-Sept. 1975	649 (233 half-hour 416 hour)
Bonanza	Sept. 1959-Jan. 1973	430
Wagon Train	Sept. 1957-Sept. 1965	284
The Virginian (Men from Shiloh)	Sept. 1962-Sept. 1971	249
The Life and Legend of Wyatt Earp	Sept. 1955-Sept. 1961	226
Have Gun, Will Travel	Sept. 1957-Sept. 1963	225
Tales of Wells Fargo	Mar. 1957-Sept. 1962	201
The Rifleman	Sept. 1958-July 1963	168
Lawman	Oct. 1958-Oct. 1962	156
Zane Grey Theater	Oct. 1956-Sept. 1962	145
Rawhide	Jan. 1959-Jan. 1966	144
Maverick	Sept. 1957-July 1962	124
Laramie	Sept. 1959-Sept. 1963	124

bomb shelters in their backyards, whose government leaders threatened massive nuclear retaliation against evil "bad guys," whose external enemies seemed perpetually poised for attack, and whose internal politics generated fear of subversion and disloyalty.

In three distinct ways video Westerns suited the emotionality of their times. First, they reaffirmed the desirability and superiority of innocent American-style civilization. Second, they offered a system of justice that was efficient and effective. Third, they justified nationalism in terms of a moral code that may have sounded secular, but had at its base a Judeo-Christian religious heritage.

Westerns paralleled the popular understanding of the East-West struggle. They were social allegories in which honest, hard-working American folk were threatened, without good reason, by evil forces. Innocent ranchers, settlers, and town dwellers inevitably found their world under attack from criminals. The honest folk never asked for this trouble, never did anything to precipitate it. But it was now upon them, and it called for heroic intervention by a brave soul.

This is the stuff of which myths are made. Indeed, the TV Western projected a mythical interpretation of reality. This was legend, not documentary. It was the past shaped for the present, the fabulous justifying the contemporary. Always the Westerns suggested that the society defended by these video champions was well worth defending. By implication they argued for similar defensive actions by contemporary heirs of that which was forged in the Old West.

How often did audiences encounter the value of responsible social freedom? How often did such programs applaud democratic themes—tolerance, equality, dignity—among those settling the wilderness? How frequently did the frontier heroes operate among those symbols of the superiority of American social arrangement—the church, the schoolhouse and the schoolmarm, the fence, the ranch house, the graveyard, the wife, and the child? And how often did video Westerns underscore the desirability of such capitalistic tenets as individuality, hard work, and self-reliance?

While all such programming stressed obedience to law and the arrest, execution, or redemption of the lawbreaker, the television Western suggested a facile image of the American legal system. Legal complexities so frustrating in reality were absent in these series. Lawyers were usually nonexistent, and where they did appear, they were frequently shown to be shysters. Court technicalities were also unimportant, since the genre on TV seldom treated restraining orders, changes of venue, grants of immunity, plea bargaining, appeals, and trial delays. Instead, decisions were swift and justice was well served. Here was a universe where good men thwarted villainy, and viewers generally concurred in the courses of action taken by their heroes to restore law and order. In its streamlined and obvious way, then, television invited its audience to become interpreters of the law, experts in legal sophistry. It was also an alluring model through which to understand the Cold War.

For many seeking to comprehend the complexity of world and national politics in the 1950s and 1960s, television Westerns offered a straightforward answer: strong action unencumbered by legal sophistry—the political equivalent of the quick draw or the night in jail. This attitude was espoused by William F. Rickenbacker, writing in 1962 in *The National Review*. He argued that the video Western embodied the aspirations of the nation. When a stalwart told an interloper to leave town, Rickenbacker suggested, the stranger had better depart. "That's the kind of thing a hundred million Americans would like to see someone say to Nikita Khrushchev," he contended.

Further, in the stereotype of a pioneer rancher refusing to be intimidated by the threats of rustlers, the author saw a situation analogous to popular resistance to the encroachment by central government. "Several thousand city officials throughout the country," he alleged, "would all do us a service if they took this attitude toward the schemes the Federal Government has for making over the face of the country in the image of Washington (D.C., alas; not George)."[39]

If in the Western Rickenbacker recognized patterns of action for the politically abused, David Shea Teeple argued in *American Mercury* magazine in 1958 that the direction of foreign policy could be enhanced were American diplomats required to view TV Westerns. He argued that television stressed models of the successful "rough and ready character," rather than the impotent "dressed-up dude rancher." According to Teeple, the popularity of these series proved that the "American public . . . wants to abandon the grey philosophies of fuzzy minds and return to the days when things were either black or white—right or wrong." In a colorful argument, Teeple called upon an array of video champions to substantiate his points.

> Would a Wyatt Earp stop at the 38th Parallel, Korea, when the rustlers were escaping with his herd? Ridiculous! Would a Marshal Dillon refuse to allow his deputies to use shotguns for their own defense because of the terrible nature of the weapon itself? Ha! Would the Lone Ranger, *under any circumstance*, allow himself to be bullied and threatened by those who sought to destroy the principles by which he lives? Would

"Restless Gun" or Jim Hardy of "Wells Fargo" attempt to *buy* friends who would fight for the right? Can you imagine Paladin of "Have Gun Will Travel" standing aside, while women and children were being massacred? Can you imagine Cheyenne living in a perpetual state of jitters because he feared the next move of some gun slinger? Would Judge Roy Bean release a murderer on some technicality devised by a slick lawyer? Would Wild Bill Hickok sell guns to the badman?[40]

If the TV Western proffered an interpretation of law and its enforcement, it also dealt with the morality fundamental to American civilization. In fact, legality and morality were often synonymous. This was succinctly stated in "Scorpion," an episode of "The Virginian," when one character remarked, "We have laws here, Mr. Pierce, to hold all of us in. . . . Law and morality have to be the same thing." In this way Western heroes were moral as well as legal agents. In their actions were ethical, even religious, judgments as well as juridical assessments. It is important that two of the more compelling contemporary explanations of the Western on TV suggested that the genre held great religious significance.

For Peter Homans in 1962, the Western was essentially "a Puritan morality tale in which the savior-hero redeems the community from the temptations of the devil." Undoubtedly, most viewers did not consciously register such a relationship each time Bill Longley on "The Texan" or Johnny Yuma on "The Rebel" stopped a criminal and saved a town. But as a pattern of social action, the formula closely resembled the fundamental motif of Christian faith: the single savior giving his life for the salvation of the multitude. In Homans' view, the Western hero was a religious operative, moving within a secular environment to reaffirm the Judeo-Christian morality originally planted in American civilization by the Puritan forefathers. "Tall in the saddle," Homans noted, the Western hero "rides straight from Plymouth Rock to a dusty frontier town" where "his Colt .45 is on the side of the angels."[41]

Even more theological in its direction was the argument put forward in 1957 by Alexander Miller in *The Christian Century*. Miller stressed the appearance within the genre of many of the great dialectical issues of Christian theology. Pilgrimage and rest, justice and mercy, war and peace—basic contradictions between which religious man fluctuated—were integral to the TV Western as well as faith. Miller contended that the cowboy hero was a fatalistic, yet moralistic, individual. "A man does what he has to do," noted Miller, "and justifies it in one way or another." Like modern religious man, the central

character in the television Western possessed "the incorrigible yearn-
ing after virtue, the inevitable implication in sin, the irrepressible inclination to self-justification." Miller concluded that in the genre
"every theological theme is here, except the final theme, the deep
and healing dimension of guilt and grace."[42]

In the mix of moral, legal, and social self-justification that was
the Western, throughout the Cold War millions each night saw the
taming of the savage and the Americanization of the wild. Truly, to
employ the phrase of Chuck Connors, star of "The Rifleman" and
"Branded," the Western is "the American fairy tale."[43] As such its
political message—appropriate at all times, but singularly suited to
the spirit of anti-Communism—was welcomed. It was reassuring to
see the shooting of the vicious gunslinger or the jailing of an anarchis-
tic malcontent. It made the world a safer place in which to live. In
their allegiance to law and order, TV Westerns defended the American
system against divisiveness and subterfuge. The heroes of these series
were mythic outriders of freedom, defeating enemies of democratic
civilization and ensuring for law-abiding people the right to pursue
happiness. William F. Rickenbacker again touched upon the nationalistic flavor of the TV Western when, at the time of the Cuban missile crisis, he wrote that such programs

> ... speak a language very close to the heart of the American Dream:
> the dream of righteousness, the flowering of personal virtue and the
> power that flows therefrom, the selfless battle against Evil, a simple
> moral code, a sense of community, the respect for the poor, for the
> downtrodden, for the tempest tossed.[44]

The recurrent message of Cold War television came across loudly
and clearly: America was threatened by a sinister, dictatorial power;
in order to survive, the United States—with leadership primarily from
government through its political officials, espionage agencies, and
armed forces, plus a large dose of citizen cooperation—would have to
root out subversives at home, outmaneuver enemy agents overseas,
and win over the uncommitted and enslaved populations of the world
through generosity, efficiency, bravery, and strength. It was a tall
order. But it was accomplished each time culture heroes like Herb
Philbrick, Biff Baker, China Smith, Steve Canyon, or any of the many
cowboy good guys won another battle against treachery.

Indeed, there were countless occasions on which such propagan-
dizing champions had the chance to win. Typically, during the week
of February 1-7, 1958, the seven stations servicing Minneapolis-St. Paul

Table 8   Cold War Programming, Week of February 1-7, 1958[45]

Saturday

8 Western movies	The Silent Service	"For God and Country,"
12 Western series	China Smith	speech by American Legion
Flash Gordon	Rocky Jones	commander
Combat Sergeant	Navy Reporter	The Big Picture

Sunday

Religious Town Hall,	Look Up and Live,
"Struggle for Freedom"	discussion of the film *Time Limit*
Victory at Sea	The Big Picture
4 Western movies	Spy film, *The House on 92nd Street*
8 Western series	The Man Called X
Orient Express	The 20th Century,
Foreign Intrigue	"D-Day Buildup," Part I

Monday	*Tuesday*
2 Western movies	1 Western movie
6 Western series	7 Western series
I Led 3 Lives	Phil Silvers Show
Superman	China Smith
O.S.S.	The West Point Story
Uncommon Valor (U.S. Marines)	I Led 3 Lives
Crusader	Cold War film, *He Stayed for Breakfast*

Wednesday	*Thursday*
1 Western movie	5 Western series
4 Western series	The Silent Service
I Led 3 Lives	Men of Annapolis
China Smith	2 Navy Log episodes
	This Is Your Navy
	TV Reader's Digest
Friday	Matinee Theater, *The Man Without a Country*
8 Western Series	Wartime film, *They Lived Dangerously*
I Led 3 Lives	I Led 3 Lives

---

and the two outlets in Fargo, North Dakota, offered the programming shown in Table 8.

When a society entertains itself with the slogans and symbols of its political, nationalistic rhetoric, it runs the risk of misinforming its citizenry, distorting the exchange of information and ideas, and developing an insularity that is unhealthy for social, intellectual, cultural, and political growth. It is one thing for a partisan legislator to use TV to persuade the electorate of his or her political values. It is quite another when unsuspecting people sit down to watch an evening of television, only to discover those political values are an integral part of their entertainment. In most cases, viewers do not recognize politics in their amusements. They do not discover the propaganda amid the diversion. With little information with which to evaluate what they see, innocent viewers are tempted to believe that the imagery on television is both accurate and universally accepted.

To a great degree, American society in the 1950s was marked by this mentality. It was noticeable, however, to a wide range of foreign viewers. The London *Times Literary Supplement* in October 1954 painted an ominous picture of American television and the society it served. An article in this conservative journal described the "climate of fear" in American TV, which "strips the medium of so much reality and truth." While the anonymous author deplored "the rigid, constrictive commercial framework" of broadcasting in the United States, he was especially hostile to the impact of Cold War politics on the maturation of television. "The greater tragedy may be," he remarked, "that the first crucial years of development will have been experienced during the deepest political reaction America has ever known."[46]

The newspaper of the Soviet government, *Izvestia*, complained in early 1961 about the "spy mania" on American TV. The journal blasted American video in general, terming it "a horrible mixture of criminality and advertising, low-quality shows, and radically cut films." Yet, itself a communications medium heavily infused with government propaganda, *Izvestia* was most angry about politicized entertainment on American television:

> An American is sitting in front of his television set, and if a murderer is not aiming at him, a spy is creeping up on him. What kind of spy? A "Communist" spy, of course, a "Soviet" spy, and always with a knife between his teeth and an atomic bomb in his hand.[47]

What had been missing in video in the 1950s was a persistent, rational presentation of the issues and motives in the East-West confrontation. TV exploited nationalistic loyalty instead of creating a thoughtful, informed public. An intelligent dialogue through which honest information might have challenged propaganda was absent from postwar American TV. The result after more than a decade of such imbalance was a nation of patriotic, trusting citizens left underinformed and fearful. It was a citizenry that in the 1960s was hardly in a position to criticize its political and military leaders when they began to slide inexorably into that tragic anti-Communist war in Southeast Asia.

4

FROM COLD WAR TO HOT WAR: THE VIDEO ROAD TO VIETNAM

As had no appliance before it, television experienced massive acceptance in its first years. Whereas there were few privately owned receivers in the mid-1940s, by 1960 there were TV sets in 89.4 percent of American homes. More people had television sets than had electric toasters, vacuum cleaners, or washing machines. And still there was a demand for sets. Between 1959 and 1961, manufacturers produced 6 million receivers annually.

Americans also used their television sets. The average household in 1961 watched TV for 5 hours and 22 minutes each day. At any minute between 7 A.M. and 1 A.M., almost 14 million homes—representing 29.6 percent of all sets in the nation—had a television set turned on. In the evening hours, between 6 P.M. and 1 A.M., that figure was even higher. At that time sets were operating in more than 21 million homes, accounting for 44.9 percent of all receivers.

Needless to say, as mass acceptance of television increased, so did corporate revenues. Whereas in 1948 the total revenue earned by networks and stations was $8.7 million, in 1958 the industry grossed more than $1 billion. In 1960 total revenue was $1,268,600,000.[1]

More important than the quantitative acceptance of video, the American people quickly assimilated TV into the quality of their lives. Receivers were placed in bedrooms, living rooms, dens, and other areas where families relaxed in the informality and security of home.

Parents often used TV sets as diversion for their children. TV watching became a national practice in the prime time evening hours. Increasingly, as daytime and late-night programming improved, Americans spent more time watching during those hours.

Yet, more than an entertainment appliance, television was a one-way medium of communication bringing an interpretation of the world directly into the American household. In news-related and entertainment programming, audiences received value-laden images and spoken messages. In the privacy of the home—where viewers were not necessarily defensive or skeptical of what they were told—the popular attitudes of a generation were shaped in the first decade of the medium.

Significantly, viewers quickly came to trust video. A Roper poll in late 1959 indicated that this early in its history, television rivaled schools, local government, and traditional communications media in terms of popular believability. Asked to rate the quality of the job being done by social institutions, the respondents gave the following ratings:

Institution	Excellent to Good	Fair to Poor	No Opinion
Schools	64%	26%	10%
Newspapers	64	30	6
TV stations	57	32	9
Local government	44	43	13

When asked if only one could be kept, which communications medium they would most want to save, television won a plurality.[2]

Television	42%
Newspapers	32
Radio	19
Magazines	4
No opinion	3

The industry may not have expected or wanted it, but in little more than ten years television had created for itself a great responsibility. Americans received their frivolity and their seriousness from the medium. Americans learned of life from video. TV news informed increasing millions. TV comedy and drama offered viewers an outlook on life as well as a few hours of escape each night. The medium was now fundamental to the personal and national lives of all Americans. Whatever video "said" affected millions every minute of every day. It is little wonder that by 1960 television was the primary national instrument used by Americans to select the leader of their republic, the president of the United States.

JOHN F. KENNEDY AND TELEVISION

Never in history did an American chief executive owe so much to the broadcasting industry—and specifically to television—as did John Fitzgerald Kennedy. Since the time of Calvin Coolidge radio had been important to the electing of presidents. In 1928 and 1932 Herbert Hoover spent heavily for air time to speak to the nation. Franklin D. Roosevelt took advantage of radio, delivering many speeches and fireside chats. Harry S. Truman and Dwight D. Eisenhower slowly made the transition from radio to radio *and* television coverage of their speeches, news conferences, and reports to the nation. For Kennedy, TV was the principal medium of communication and persuasion.

Throughout his congressional career, Congressman and then Senator Kennedy was aware of the importance of video in making his face and name familiar to the national audience. Many times during the 1950s he shared his ideas and TV personality with viewers. Whether it was on a panel discussion program where he spoke of domestic and foreign problems, or on shows such as "Person to Person" when—with his lovely bride, Jacqueline Bouvier Kennedy at his side—on October 30, 1953, he chatted amiably from his Manhattan apartment with Edward R. Murrow, all such appearances contributed to making a burgeoning political force out of this young, handsome, articulate, and telegenic politician from Massachusetts.

For JFK, television could turn defeat into victory. At the Democratic National Convention in 1956 he was unsuccessful in a bid for the vice-presidential nomination. Ironically, Kennedy lost to another TV senator, Estes Kefauver of Tennessee, whose national reputation had been created several years earlier when he chaired televised hearings into crime in America. Still, from the loss to Kefauver, Kennedy gained increased national exposure and political credibility. Further, with the defeat of Adlai Stevenson and Kefauver in the elections that fall, the young senator emerged a formidable contender for the Democratic presidential nomination in 1960.

TV was strategic to the Kennedy campaign for that nomination, and for the election in 1960. The image so carefully crafted by JFK and his staff—chiefly his campaign manager and brother, Robert F. Kennedy, and Guild, Bascom & Bonfigli, the San Francisco-based advertising agency that fashioned his TV commercials—was crucial in sweeping away liabilities that Kennedy possessed: his religion, his youthfulness, his inexperience and lack of international standing. More important, video enabled JFK to overcome his toughest obstacle, Richard Milhous Nixon, the popular vice-president of the popular retiring President Eisenhower.

Nixon had credentials. Eight years a successful vice-president, after Ike's heart attack in 1955 he literally had been that "heartbeat away" from the presidency until Eisenhower fully recovered 143 days later. Nixon knew well the importance of TV as a political tool. Late in the 1952 campaign he had used the medium to explain away charges of financial irregularities. In the famous "Checkers" speech on a half-hour of national TV time purchased by the Republican National Committee, Nixon had delivered an exemplary performance, convincing the nation that he had no political slush fund, that he should remain as Eisenhower's running mate, and that no matter what his fate, he would not return the spaniel puppy, Checkers, that one supporter had given his children.

The election in 1960 was a TV contest. The "great debates" staged in the fall gave millions of viewers a chance to see their candidates in a conflict of ideas and issues. But television also allowed viewers to assess the "looks" of the candidates, to determine which one looked more honest, appeared more confident, and came across as more presidential. Nixon relied heavily upon the debates and only late began a campaign of TV commercials. The Kennedy campaign, however, supplemented the debates with appearances on talk shows and the evening news, and with a multimillion-dollar campaign of television commercials that began weeks before Nixon's TV spots.

Importantly, Kennedy had not been a spectacular legislator. In neither the House of Representatives nor the Senate had he sponsored significant legislation. He was not a major party leader. He had conducted no spectacular investigations. In fact, as a young lawyer, his brother Robert had worked on the staff of Senator Joseph R. McCarthy during the height of its anti-Communist activities. But John F. Kennedy *looked* good on TV. He knew how to exploit the new medium to deliver the image of leadership. For a nation increasingly dependent on television for the creation of cultural heroes and role models—from Disney's Davy Crockett to the suave "cool" of private eye Peter Gunn—the dashing senator appeared to know what he was doing.

TV is an image medium. It thrives on pictures, attractive personalities, action, and lightness. It was no coincidence that early television popularized the flamboyance of wrestlers like Gorgeous George and the compelling movement of roller derby. In its first years, TV also revived vaudeville—a world of slapstick, pratfalls, pies and pillows in the face, garish costumes, and facile jokes most effectively realized in the "vaudeo" style of Milton Berle.

Except for the visual hyperbole of this early fare, politics on television operated similarly. The best video politician was the person who attracted viewers, appeared self-assured, and was pleasant to watch—all within the boundaries of what was politically possible. Senator Kennedy realized this. Writing in *TV Guide* in 1959, he expressed approval of glamorized politics. He spoke of "a new breed of candidates" that was successful because of a "particular reliance on TV appeal." Most of this new breed were young men, for youth, according to Kennedy, "is definitely an asset in creating a television image people like and (most difficult of all) remember." While he admitted that video could be "abused by demagogues, by appeals to emotion and prejudice and ignorance," JFK endorsed the new type of TV politician:

> Honesty, vigor, compassion, intelligence—the presence or lack of these and other qualities make up what is called the candidate's "image." While some intellectuals and politicians may scoff at these "images"— and while they may in fact be based only on a candidate's TV impression, ignoring his record, views and other appearances—my own conviction is that these images or impressions are likely to be uncannily correct.[3]

For its part, TV responded to the Kennedy image. Unconsciously swept up in his alluring video persona, distinguished television newsmen abandoned substance in favor of glamour. This was amply demonstrated on "Person to Person" on September 20, 1960. Seven weeks before the elections, host Charles Collingwood avoided tough questions of policy, preferring to pursue the flattering family side of Kennedy. As the following excerpt from his conversation with Mrs. Kennedy suggests, the homey perfection communicated by this program could not hurt the Democratic nominee locked in a close contest with Richard Nixon.

Mrs. Kennedy: . . . Would you like to see her?

Collingwood: Oh, I'd like to very much. Are you sure it is all right for us to intrude on the young lady?

Mrs. Kennedy: Well, we will see, Charles, keep your fingers crossed.

Collingwood: Hello, Caroline.

Mrs. Kennedy: Can you say hello?

Caroline: Hello.

Mrs. Kennedy: Here, do you want to sit up in bed with me?

Collingwood: Isn't she a darling?

Mrs. Kennedy: Now, look at the three bears.

Collingwood: What is the dolly's name?

Mrs. Kennedy: All right, what is the dolly's name?

Caroline: I didn't name her yet.

Mrs. Kennedy: You didn't name her yet?

Caroline: No.

Mrs. Kennedy: When are you going to name her?

Collingwood: Is that her favorite?

Mrs. Kennedy: It is her favorite as of this minute.

Collingwood: Oh, just like all little girls.

Mrs. Kennedy: What do you think you will name her tomorrow? What color are her shoes?

Caroline: White. Like mine.

Mrs. Kennedy: Like yours. What color is your dress?

Caroline: Pink.

Mrs. Kennedy: And why has she got a hat on?

Caroline: [Indistinct]

Collingwood: I didn't quite get that.

Mrs. Kennedy: She has to have a hat on because the wind blows her hair.

Collingwood: Oh, Caroline, you are a very, very pretty little girl and I should think, Mrs. Kennedy, that the proud father would get mighty lonesome for her when he is out on the campaign trail.

Mrs. Kennedy: Well, I think he does. We will go down and join him now.

Collingwood: Oh, that will be a treat for him.

Mrs. Kennedy: Shall we go see daddy?

Caroline: Yes.

Mrs. Kennedy: Can you take us to the parlor?

Caroline: Yes.

Mrs. Kennedy: And we will go see daddy?

Caroline: Yes.

Mrs. Kennedy: All right, let's go see daddy.[4]

From the beginning of his presidency, Kennedy demonstrated great TV skills. The inauguration on January 20, 1961, was a masterpiece. First, there was Marian Anderson to sing "The Star Spangled Banner." The great black operatic singer, who had once been denied the right to perform in Washington, D.C., because of her race, was now welding the future of Afro-Americans to the new administration. No matter that poet Robert Frost stammered and appeared confused while reciting his original poem for the ceremony. Television recorded that the new president had brought another cultural giant into his inauguration, the nation's greatest living poet testifying to refinement within the New Frontier.

Kennedy also presented a handsome image. Dressed in top hat and waist-coat, and accompanied by his radiant young wife, the new leader cut an impressive figure for the 59.5 percent of American homes viewing the ceremony. Camelot was taking shape in the national capital, and TV was showing the metamorphosis.

Even more dynamic, however, was the president's inaugural address. It was perfect for the time and for television. It exhorted the public to patriotic sacrifice. It challenged the Russians. It spoke of an idealistic future. And there were those memorable phrases so crucial to making any speech live beyond its delivery. When JFK declared, "The torch is passed to a new generation," he touched young Americans who saw in his youthfulness a reflection of their own importance and vitality. When he proclaimed, "Ask not what your country can do for you, ask what you can do for your country," Kennedy appealed to an altruism basic to the American character but submerged in the self-centeredness of American culture during the 1950s.

Since the late 1940s American liberalism had been on the defensive. The forces of Senator McCarthy and others had castigated liberals for being unpatriotic, not harsh enough in their anti-Communism, too supportive of the "socialistic" legacy of Roosevelt and the New Deal legislation. In this one speech, JFK became not only the spiritual heir of FDR but also the man who restored patriotism as a outspoken value for liberals. Kennedy's address was a nationalistic, anti-Communist manifesto delivered from the American moderate left. Now liberals could wave the flag and not feel as though they had joined the ultrapatriotic John Birch Society. As a starting point there were many Cold War slogans that Kennedy employed in his inaugural speech. He spoke of "defending freedom in its hour of maximum danger," and he warned that the United States would "support any friend, oppose any foe to assure the survival and success of liberty." In addition, Kennedy pledged that "One form of colonial control shall not have passed away merely to be replaced by a far more iron tyranny," and he declared an unwillingness "to witness or permit the slow undoing of those human rights to which this country has always been committed."

While avoiding specific policy recommendations, the new president indicated future directions. Like FDR, JFK favored government action to alleviate poverty and injustice at home. Similarly, he favored an interventionist foreign policy to protect American interests and to influence the direction of the decolonizing movement. To "old allies" Kennedy pledged "the loyalty of a faithful friend." To "those nations who would make themselves our adversary," he called for increased American military strength tempered by negotiations on arms control, technological cooperation, and general international understanding so that "a beach-head of cooperation may push back the jungle of suspicion."

Significantly, Kennedy spoke also to the newly emerging nations of the world. He promised "those people in huts and villages of half the globe" that the United States would be active in helping them help themselves "for whatever period is required." He suggested, moreover, a moral dimension, alleging that his motivation was to help the underdeveloped world not "because the Communists may be doing it, but because it is right."

John Kennedy's political thoughts were not unknown to television audiences before his inaugural address. Throughout the 1950s he had presented his views on camera. What had emerged from those thoughts was a philosophy in harmony with the anti-Communism of the times. On "Meet the Press" on December 2, 1951, he sided with Republican critics of President Truman, urging the president "to clean house" and to end "corruption" in his administration. Kennedy also urged strong military commitments in Europe. Having only 28 divisions in Europe to counter 175 Russian divisions, he said, "We're going to be in the most critical time in Western Europe that we're ever going to be, about next March."

Even more significant on that "Meet the Press" program were Kennedy's views on East Asia. Recently returned from a trip to the region, he appeared now as an Asian expert. On the Korean War, he agreed that in some strategies General MacArthur was correct. Kennedy urged greater reliance upon air power to win the war, but he did not favor the bombing of Manchurian sanctuaries, since that "would take the chance . . . of bringing us into a war with the Soviet Union." Kennedy was also critical of Truman's policies in Southeast Asia. He called for greater assistance, better propaganda, and a bypassing of the French, going directly to the indigenous people, since "You can never defeat the Communist movement in Indochina until you get the support of the natives, and you won't get the support of the natives as long as they feel the French are fighting Communists in order to hold their own power there." For Kennedy there had to be an alternative to Communism other than continued French imperialism. That alternative was native nationalism, to "give this country the right of self-determination and the right to govern themselves." Otherwise, Kennedy noted, "This guerrilla war is just going to spread and grow and we're going to finally get driven out of Southeast Asia."

Kennedy was committed early to the rivalry with Communism in Asia. On October 7, 1952, on Dumont's program "Keep Posted," he explained the necessity of keeping American troops in Korea. "Unless we want to withdraw completely from Korea," he remarked, "it seems to me that we have no alternative but to stay. . . . because the South Koreans cannot hold the line against a nation of over 400 million [Communist China] unless they are given assistance."

Increasingly, the senator's anti-Communist attentions were focused on Southeast Asia. Shortly after the Geneva Accords, which in 1954 terminated French colonial control of the area and prescribed unifying elections for Vietnam within two years, Kennedy was on NBC radio to bemoan the agreement. On "The University of Chicago Roundtable" on July 25, 1954, he spoke the classic language of the domino theory, envisioning that "the future of Southeast Asia is indeed dark" as a powerful Communist China was surrounded by weak, neutralist nations—from Laos and Cambodia to India, Ceylon, Burma, and Indonesia. These countries, in Kennedy's view, were vulnerable because, as neutrals, they were outside any "system of mutual guarantees" the United States might erect against the Peking government.

Kennedy urged a military buildup to meet the Asian challenge. "We must recognize that we are the leaders of the Free World," he told his audience, and "We offer because of our strength, not because of our desires, the only real counter to the Communist forces." Further, he said, "We must be willing to bear the burdens of leadership regardless of how difficult they may be if we are not to see the balance of power in the world tilt in favor of the Communists."

Most specifically, Kennedy revealed his thinking on Vietnam in a speech before the influential lobby organization the American Friends of Vietnam. Speaking on June 1, 1956, he lauded "the amazing success" of the organization's hero, Ngo Dinh Diem, whom the United States had installed as premier of South Vietnam two years earlier.[5] JFK saw Vietnam as strategic to American policy, calling it "the proving ground of democracy in Asia" and "a test of American responsibility and determination in Asia." In addition he reiterated his belief in the domino theory. Kennedy claimed that Vietnam represented ". . . the cornerstone of the Free World in Southeast Asia, the keystone to the arch, the finger in the dike. Burma, Thailand, Indonesia, Japan, the Philippines, and obviously Laos and Cambodia are among those whose security would be threatened if the red tide of Communism overflowed into Vietnam."[6]

With such public declarations in his background, it was no wonder that on the CBS yearly review program "Years of Crisis: 1960," David Schoenbrun foresaw the foreign policy objectives of the president-elect. From his perspective in Europe, Schoenbrun claimed JFK was "African-minded, Asian-minded," convinced that "the real problem now is to save freedom and democracy in Africa and Asia."

While JFK found television crucial to his election, as president he continued to manipulate TV for political purposes. Within weeks of the inauguration, ABC political commentator Bill Shadel anticipated as much, telling a fan magazine, "I believe Kennedy has discovered he's a new TV idol. I have no doubts that he'll go on TV whenever he really wants something, such as a piece of legislation passed." Significantly, Shadel added, "He'll use television as FDR used radio, to get the people to go along with his policies."[7]

During his almost three years in the presidency, Kennedy delivered 19 speeches on live TV, 9 of these being reports to the nation on matters as diverse as the Cuban missile crisis and the racial integration of the University of Mississippi. JFK was also regularly on the evening news as network journalists centered attention on the dynamic and likeable young leader. He sat for lengthy TV interviews with Walter Cronkite of CBS, Bill Lawrence of ABC, and Eleanor Roosevelt representing educational television.

Even Jacqueline Kennedy promoted the handsome, youthful presidential image. Most successfully, on February 14, 1962, she accompanied Charles Collingwood and 24.5 million viewers of CBS and NBC on a videotaped tour of the White House. This hour-long excursion was seen in 73.9 percent of all American homes having TV sets. The program was repeated two days later on most ABC stations. In promoting the telecast, *TV Guide* printed Collingwood's flattering description of the First Lady.

> Mrs. Kennedy isn't at all like I imagined. She has a shy manner, even a sort of shy way of moving. She is very girlish and youthful, yet with all her youth and shy manner she gives you an impression of being quietly assured, though not arrogantly so. . . . She speaks very precisely, enunciating carefully. She has a beautiful smile. She was perfectly groomed—with a simple, two-piece, plum-colored wool dress with a boat neck and a three-strand pearl necklace. And low-heeled shoes.[8]

One month later, when the First Lady toured India and Pakistan, she received extensive TV coverage. ABC supplemented its regular news reportage with daily five-minute summations of her activities. These afternoon "news specials" were sponsored by Maybelline cosmetics. When Mrs. Kennedy returned, NBC summarized her tour in a one-hour TV special.

Such exploitation of network TV by the Kennedys, and such fawning appreciation by distinguished journalists prompted George Rosen to write in *Variety* in March 1962: "There's a growing awareness in the television industry of how President Kennedy and the First Lady are collectively and individually wrapping TV around their little finger."[9]

The folksy image of JFK perhaps reached its peak on December 17, 1962, when he engaged in a wide-ranging conversation at the White House with newsmen Sander Vanocur of NBC, George Herman of CBS, and Bill Lawrence. In a one-hour filmed program aired by NBC, JFK answered questions about his first two years in office. But what made this telecast especially effective was that throughout the discussion the president was seated comfortably in a rocking chair. Solid, traditional, practical, and reliable—the traits of the rocking chair seemed to imbue the chief executive with authority and an aura of Americana. Coming at Christmastime—less than two months after the Cuban missile crisis took the planet to the brink of nuclear annihilation—the "rocking chair conversation" allowed viewers at home and around the globe (it was distributed to markets accounting for 82 percent of the non-Communist world) to find confidence in the relaxed, mature figure presented by Kennedy.

Of all his TV formats, however, Kennedy was most adept at the live news conference. Upon the strong recommendation of his press secretary, Pierre Salinger, the new chief executive became the first to open his press gatherings to live video coverage. During his tenure, JFK held 64 news conferences, and 14 of them were on live television. With no editing and no time for retakes, this was TV realizing its destiny of informing the citizenry, bringing the news source into the experience of the home viewer.

What emerged in these confrontations with the news media was the image of a bright, personable, and articulate national leader, a man whose instincts were right and whose purposefulness appeared undaunted. Those in the video audience responded. Viewers complained that their president was not being treated with enough respect when "rude" newsmen and newswomen rustled papers, yelled and waved their hands to get Kennedy's attention, and mumbled or coughed when questions were being asked. Historian Arthur M. Schlesinger, Jr., described these conferences as "a superb show, always gay, often exciting, relished by the reporters and by the television audience."[10]

Kennedy's televised news gatherings had as their principal goal not the informing of the press but a direct communication between the president and the voters. During the campaign JFK had received little support from newspapers, the vast majority of them editorializing in favor of Richard Nixon. Now, via television, he could bypass the print medium and approach the citizenry directly. As adviser Theodore Sorensen explained it, the purpose was "to inform and impress the public more than the press" and to provide "a direct communication with the voters which no newspaper could alter by interpretation or omission."[11]

Audiences reacted favorably to the president's confrontations with the press. His first conference, conducted January 25, 1961, was seen by 65 million people in 21.5 American homes. While viewer interest waned as the novelty of these news forums faded, Kennedy's televised press gatherings averaged 18 million viewers. A survey in 1961 showed that 90 percent of those polled had watched at least one of the first three conferences—and 85 percent of that total had watched on purpose.[12] Further, another poll that same year showed overwhelming support for live televised press conferences: 79.6 percent felt they were a good idea, and only 7.8 percent called them a bad idea.[13]

In action before the 200 to 400 jounalists at his conferences, the president was masterful. Bill Lawrence conceded that "Reporters, those friendly and not-so-friendly, never cease to be amazed at the facts and figures at the President's command."[14] Merriman Smith of United Press International, the senior wire service correspondent who opened and closed Kennedy's press conferences, felt that JFK's intelligence and preparation intimidated journalists. The president, according to Smith, "is exceptionally well-briefed on current events and a reporter who tackles him poorly prepared is liable to be shown up before a nationwide audience."[15] Writing several years after Kennedy's death, William Small, news director and bureau manager of CBS News in Washington, argued that "Handsome John Kennedy was a perfect President for television exposure." In Small's words, Kennedy "loved intellectual combat with the press. He had wit and grace and was always well-prepared. He was an instant public success. The President was continually curious about his ratings. . . ."[16]

A glamorous president in a medium that thrived on the attractive, JFK developed a powerful influence over the national press. His ability to turn aside tough questions with grace and to employ charm and wit in avoiding embarrassing answers masked the great deal of preparation Kennedy put into each news conference. Before such confrontations he conferred with advisers, anticipated questions, and prepared his responses. At the conferences he could masterfully employ facts and figures or charming rhetoric to handle his questioners. He seldom faced tough follow-up questions. At his press conferences and in his general relationship with the press, Kennedy soon precipitated charges of news management because of such practices as planting questions with reporters, the use of controlled news leaks, highly visible political tours for himself and other administration members, and even pressuring privately for the suppression of news. In this light, the attack upon TV as a "vast wasteland" delivered in May 1961 by Newton P. Minow, chairman of the FCC, takes on a political dimension.

While Minow was criticizing video for airing violent and banal programs, he also was urging broadcasters "to service the nation's needs." While threatening to make the license-renewal procedure a means to force the upgrading of programming, Minow warned, "We cannot permit television in its present form to be our voice overseas." While saying "I am deeply concerned with concentration of power in the hands of the networks," he chastized the mediocrity he perceived in TV:

> And I would add that in today's world, with chaos in Laos and the Congo aflame, with Communist tyranny on our Caribbean doorstep and relentless pressure on our Atlantic alliance, with social and economic problems at home of the gravest nature, yes, and with technological knowledge that makes it possible—as our President has said—not only to destroy our world but to destroy poverty around the world—in a time of peril and opportunity, the old complacent, unbalanced fare of action-adventure and situation comedies is simply not good enough.[17]

This was an unnerving speech. At a time of quiz-show and payola scandals, network power was being assaulted more directly than at any time in the history of broadcasting. When asked his views at a press conference, Kennedy preferred to let Minow's words speak for him. Yet, privately Kennedy told Minow to "keep it up," and Attorney General Robert Kennedy joined the criticism. In July 1961 he met with CBS president Frank Stanton and board chairman William S. Paley to indicate his interest in seeing changes in video programming.[18]

Still, early in his tenure television was swept up in a Kennedy craze. On February 28 and April 11, 1961, NBC presented two "JFK Report" programs, tracing his life story, introducing his family, spending a "typical" day in the Oval Office. On its "Close Up" documentary series, ABC offered "Adventures on the New Frontier." Aired March 28, the program took JFK through his primary victories, to Inauguration Day, and finally to relaxation at the end of a day's work. While he approved of flattering programs such as these, JFK's press secretary, Pierre Salinger moved quickly to quash the trivialization of the presidency that seemed to be developing. "The press conference is not a network show," Salinger reminded public service TV executives on April 11, "it is a news event." In a time of domestic and international tension, Salinger was upset by those in TV who asked "what people [in the White House] eat for lunch, what color paper the First Lady writes on, what soap is used by the President." Salinger wanted programs that demonstrated "what we are doing in Washington," and not the trivial stories that "clog up the communications channels and are a waste of the administration's talent and time."[19]

Nonetheless, for an administration wanting in-depth coverage, in Kennedy's first great crisis in foreign policy the administration was less than candid with network TV. The Bay of Pigs incident occurred in mid-April 1961, when a brigade of about 1,500 Cuban refugees attempted an invasion of their homeland and the overthrow of Fidel Castro. The invaders had been trained, equipped, and financed by the Central Intelligence Agency. In fact, they had been groomed by the CIA since 1960 at secret bases in Guatemala. After Kennedy took office, he decided to permit the brigade to launch its invasion of Communist Cuba. Kennedy made his decision on April 4.

At his press conference on April 12, Kennedy was duplicitous when asked if a decision had been made on how far the United States would go in helping an anti-Castro uprising or invasion in Cuba. Kennedy promised that "There will not be under any conditions an intervention in Cuba by the United States armed forces. And this government will do everything it possibly can—and I think it can meet its responsibilities—to make sure there are no *Americans* involved in any actions inside Cuba."

If JFK was publicly deceptive, in private he moved adroitly to control the American press. He persuaded high-level editors at the *New York Times* and *The New Republic* not to print articles on the American role in the imminent invasion. Further, anticipating reactions by American journalists once the hostilities commenced, just before the attack Kennedy penned a note asking, "Is there a plan to brief and brainwash key press within 12 hours or so?"[20]

American spy planes photographed Cuba for the invaders. American frogmen led landing parties, and American trainers eventually flew combat missions over the island. A U.S. Navy task force maneuvered off the Cuban shore. A radio transmitter owned by the CIA beamed propaganda broadcasts toward Cuba throughout the operation. And four American citizens died in the ill-fated invasion. The anti-Castro forces, however, were wrong when, while boarding ships in Nicaragua on April 13, they assured President Kennedy that Fidel Castro could be overthrown without direct American military intervention.

Denials of U.S. complicity were most eloquently presented by Adlai Stevenson, now the chief American representative at the United Nations. He denied Cuban accusations as "charges without any foundation." He explained that two anti-Castro airplanes in Florida were actually Cuban Air Force jets flown to the United States by defectors from Communism. To prove his point, he showed photographs of the planes. Apparently, Stevenson was not aware of CIA and Kennedy involvement in the invasion. The photographs he displayed had nose guns where Cuban aircraft had no such armament.

The Bay of Pigs invasion was a short-lived operation. It began on April 15 with an air strike by CIA-owned airplanes against Castro's paltry Air Force, knocking out all but three training jets. Troop landings began the following day. Unfortunately for the invading brigade, those unscathed Cuban jets were able to destroy air and sea support for the operation. Also, there was no spontaneous anti-Castro uprising on the island as had been expected. Cuban militia with Russian tanks and superior firepower badly crippled the rebels, forcing them to surrender on April 19.

For the Kennedy administration, the incident was a fiasco. Kennedy alienated anti-Communists in the United States who felt this to be the opportunity to aid the insurgents and introduce American military might to crush Castro. Kennedy, however, refused to commit direct U.S. military power to the invasion. To many liberals the affair was an unnecessary loss of life, secretly plotted by the CIA and the president, with no input from Congress or the citizenry.

In international affairs, the new administration was seriously compromised. Its spokesmen and supporters, from Stevenson, Salinger, and Secretary of State Dean Rusk to Senator Wayne Morse and the president himself, were all caught in public lies. In addition, foreign leaders openly criticized the American action. Castro, and especially the Cuban delegate to the United Nations, Raul Roa, assailed the "Vandalistic aggression" and "imperialistic piracy" of the Kennedy government. They likened the CIA to the Gestapo. Khrushchev pledged "all necessary assistance" to the resistance, and the Russian delegate urged the United Nations to assist Cuba against the assault. Prime Minister Nehru of India accused the United States of having encouraged the adventure. By April 21, even bitter anti-Castro rebels were assailing the CIA for its "monumental mismanagement" of the invasion.[21]

At home Fidel Castro was hailed as a hero. If ever his power over the Cuban revolution had been questioned, he emerged from the Bay of Pigs incident as the uncontested head of state. Moreover, if ever Communism had not been totally accepted as the Cuban destiny, the failure of the invasion permanently discredited democratic or anti-Communist influences on the island.

American television was curiously quiet following the collapse of the counterrevolution. One of the few introspective TV programs was "WCBS-TV Views the Press," seen only in the New York City area on April 23. Aired at 3:45 P.M. on Sunday, this program raised several questions about the silence of American journalism in the face of colossal government military initiative. Charles Collingwood pointed out that the secret invasion had not been too clandestine, since it was mentioned in the *Hispanic American Review* in October 1960, and on the front page of the *New York Times* in January 1961. Collingwood was critical of those journalists who pleaded ignorance of the CIA intervention. He accused the press of dropping news leaks and not carrying through on leads. George Rosen described this program as presenting "a stinging rebuke of U.S. journalistic standards and practices."[22]

But 15 minutes of criticism on a Sunday afternoon in New York City did not shake American journalism. On April 20 the president spoke to the American Association of Newspaper Publishers and referred to the invasion as "a struggle of Cuban patriots against a Cuban dictator." The anti-Castro insurgents became "a small band of freedom fighters [that] has engaged the armor of totalitarianism." Admitting no wrongdoing, Kennedy offered a staunchly anti-Communist speech in which he said the United States would never concede Cuba to Communism, and although no new invasions were contemplated, Yankee patience with the island was "not inexhaustible." The speech was broadcast live on network television.

The following day, at his nontelevised press conference, Kennedy refused to elaborate on the U.S. role in the invasion. He dodged several inquiries on the subject and referred reporters to his defensive speech of the previous day. The closest the president came to a public admission of error was "There's an old saying that victory has a hundred fathers and defeat is an orphan." The important matter, he declared, was that "I am the responsible officer of the government."

By the time of his press conference on May 5, Kennedy had to answer only two questions about Cuba. To one, he spoke of a possible trade embargo against the island; to the other, he responded that he had no plans to train an invasion force of Cuban exiles in the United States or elsewhere "at this time."

By early May the crisis had passed. The New Frontier and its journalistic chroniclers were back in high gear. While he evaded further questions about the Bay of Pigs, Kennedy sparked national excitement when he spoke of speeding up the American space program, of beating the Russians in the race to land a man on the moon. A week before the invasion, the National Aeronautics and Space Administration (NASA) had announced that the administration was accelerating its timetable, and instead of the "beyond 1970" target date envisioned in Eisenhower's space program, Kennedy's NASA was predicting a lunar landing by 1969-70—or perhaps as early as 1967. This annoucement was made all the more credible when, on May 5, Navy Commander Alan B. Shepard, Jr., aboard his "Freedom 7" capsule, was launched 115 miles into space and returned to earth 15 minutes later. America had its first spaceman.

Generating still more favorable publicity, the New Frontiersmen were off to visit the world with TV crews reporting their expeditions to the American people. In mid-May, Vice-President Lyndon B. Johnson visited Asia and, most important, South Vietnam. The following month Adlai Stevenson journeyed to Latin America. The president himself was an active and visible traveler. On May 16-18, JFK and his wife visited Ottawa in what *Variety* termed "basically a television show," filled with speeches, inspection of honor guards, and close-ups of Mrs. Kennedy accepting compliments in French and English.[23]

At the end of May the president was off on his most glorious international visit. He and Mrs. Kennedy visited Paris, London, and Vienna, where he met with Nikita Khrushchev. As abusive as Khrushchev was at that conference, the presidential tour was wondrous television. The image of the American leader operating easily with other heads of state was reassuring. That wit and style for which the president had become known were never better evidenced than in Paris on June 2, when he opened a question-and-answer session with the self-effacing comment, "I do not think it altogether inappropriate to introduce myself to this audience. I am the man who accompanied Jacqueline Kennedy to Paris, and I have enjoyed it." Kennedy topped his whirlwind visits with a televised report to the nation on June 6 and a news conference on TV two days later.

With so much engaging dynamism, few in American TV paid much attention to the direction Kennedy's anti-Communist politics were taking. In the speech delivered to publishing executives on April 20, as well as rationalizing the Bay of Pigs adventure, the president on several occasions reaffirmed his constant interest in Southeast Asia. Arguing that wars between large armies with nuclear weapons were inappropriate for solving contemporary problems, JFK hinted that this was now the time of the guerrilla—"subversion, infiltration, and a host of other tactics steadily picking off vulnerable areas, one by one, in situations which do not permit our own armed intervention." In facing "the insidious nature of this new and deeper struggle," the president said, "we dare not fail to grasp the new concept, the new tools, the new sense of urgency we will need to combat it, whether in Cuba or South Vietnam."

In that speech JFK argued that "the message of Cuba" was being communicated elsewhere by Communist voices: "The complacent, the self-indulgent, the soft societies are about to be swept away with the debris of history. Only the strong, only the industrious, only the determined, only the courageous, only the visionary who determine the real nature of our struggle can possibly survive." Clearly, the American chief executive—like the population that applauded his charming intelligence—had lived down the Bay of Pigs affair and was ready to accept other international challenges. Just as clearly, the next target of his attention would be Southeast Asia.

By the end of 1961, Kennedy had demonstrated his intention to alter American commitments in the Far East. Following the vice-president's visit to Vietnam, JFK dispatched Stanford University economist Eugene Staley to assess the South Vietnamese economic condition. In October he sent his military representative, General Maxwell D. Taylor, to Saigon to report on military realities. When Allen B. Dulles resigned in the wake of the abortive Cuban invasion, Kennedy named John D. McCone as the new CIA director. As described by *The New Republic*, McCone was "the kind of man who hates Communism, not because it betrayed the revolution, but because he assumes it *is* the revolution."[24] And as Henry Fairlie has shown convincingly in his book *The Kennedy Promise*, the president spent much of late 1961 surrounding himself with long-time Cold Warriors—many of them Republicans—in preparation to wage "Total Cold War."[25]

It is important, too, that during the last half of 1961 Kennedy perfected his thinking on the need to fight Communist guerrillas with American guerrillas. Young, tough, aggressive, and agile, John Kennedy—the hero of those touch-football games on the lawns of Hyannisport—was now convinced that similar virtues of self-discipline would be required for this new breed of American fighting man: the U.S. Army Special Forces, popularly and erroneously called Rangers in the early 1960s (this because American guerrillas in World War II and the Korean War were the U.S. Army Rangers), but later known as the Green Berets.

The stealth and purposefulness of the Communist guerrilla was passing to organized American troops. If large armies and nuclear weapons were incompatible with subversive infiltration, the new anti-Communist response would have to be in kind. For a nation raised on Cold War television—with its facile images of good guys and bad guys, protectors and defilers, honorable American ingenuity and Communist perfidy—the Green Berets were a characteristic response.

The Green Berets seemed well-suited to the culture of the United States in the early 1960s. In their recognizable green standard Army uniforms highlighted by a unique shoulder patch and the engaging beret worn tilted to the right, these specially trained, specially dedicated troops were akin to the heroes of the many TV Westerns of the day. Where Paladin had a chessman on his holster, the Lone Ranger had silver bullets, Wyatt Earp used twin Buntline Special pistols, and several heroes owned specially modified rifles, the essence of the Special Forces was embodied in the beret—signifying skill, spirit, and education. These jungle fighters were more than guerrillas. As Senator Richard B. Russell of the Armed Services Committee remarked so appropriately in early 1961, "I rather associate guerrillas and bushwackers to be on the side of the bad folks on television, and the Rangers and the Boy Scouts on the side of purity and justice."[26]

Kennedy did not create the Green Berets—the initial Army Special Forces unit was activated in July 1952, and the familiar berets were first worn publicly in June 1955. But the vigor, intellect and commitment of the Green Berets paralleled the personal values of the young president. Kennedy in 1961 increased the number of Special Forces from 800 to 5,000. Although the Army high command in 1956 forbade the wearing of the beret—fearful of creating an elite military force within the regular Army—Kennedy in late 1961 requested that Special Forces personnel resume wearing the headpiece. The relationship between the president and these counterinsurgency soldiers was such that after the assassination of JFK in 1963, the 1st Special Forces Group was permitted to add a black border to the all-yellow shield worn on its berets.[27] The Green Berets—described by NBC News as "those highly-trained men, designed particularly to handle the so-called limited wars"—were a prominent part of the funeral ceremonies for the slain President Kennedy.

By the end of 1961 the president had decided to react more aggressively against Communism in Vietnam. The Army and militia of the Republic of South Vietnam increased greatly. The level of U.S. aid was raised. American troop commitments were boosted. Where there had been 875 advisers in South Vietnam when Kennedy came to office, in one year he raised the figure to 3,164. Many of these advisers were Green Berets who now accompanied South Vietnamese troops into battle areas. President Kennedy was moving the United States into the Vietnam War, and American television was practically silent on the matter.

In the years after his presidency, defenders of the Kennedy administration have contended that South Vietnam never commanded much of JFK's attention, and that had he lived, he would have extricated the United States from Southeast Asia following the elections of 1964.[28] Implicit in such argumentation is the conviction that Kennedy did not start the Vietnam War, that the true culprit was Lyndon B. Johnson, who took a few thousand military advisers and turned a defensive military assistance program into a full-scale war.

Privately, the president was cautious about his increasing commitment in Southeast Asia. Each magnification of the American role in Vietnam was taken after consultations with advisers—some more interventionist and anti-Communist than he—and considerations of American domestic politics. It was an equivocal JFK who slid inexorably into that Asian conflict.

But Kennedy did not share his doubts with the American people. On television he never left the impression that Vietnamese affairs were of peripheral interest, or that he was uncertain about the American course of action in that area. Southeast Asia was a frequent topic in his public utterances during his first months in office. From mid-1961 until the day he died, the president openly reaffirmed his determination to fight world Communism by stopping its spread into South Vietnam. In his special message to Congress on urgent national needs,

Kennedy on May 25, 1961, decried those "adversaries of freedom" who

... send arms, agitators, aid, technicians, and propaganda to every troubled area. But where fighting is required it is usually done by others— by guerrillas striking at night, by assassins striking alone—assassins who have taken the lives of four thousand civil officers in the last twelve months in Vietnam alone. ...

When he spoke before the United Nations on September 25, 1961, Kennedy reiterated the domino theory, noting that "the smoldering coals of war in Southeast Asia" were threatening all of Asia, for "if they are successful in Laos and South Vietnam the gates will be opened wide." He touched on Vietnam in his State of the Union addresses in 1962 and 1963. He skillfully answered questions about Vietnam in many press conferences. On "Washington Review" on September 23, 1962, he told David Schoenbrun that "If we stop helping them, they will become ripe for internal subversion and a Communist takeover. ... if we can keep these countries free, then we can help the peace and keep our freedom." In his "rocking chair" TV conversation in 1962, Kennedy saw American military commitments in a historically unique perspective, telling Sander Vanocur, "We have a lot of Americans in South Vietnam" (11,326 military personnel by December 1962) but that "No other country in the world has ever done that since the beginning of the world—Greece, Rome, Napoleon, and all the rest always had conquest. We have a million men outside and they are trying to defend these countries."

When Kennedy spoke to the nation about his civil rights program on June 11, 1963, he mentioned the Vietnamese commitment. When CBS and NBC expanded their evening news to a half-hour format, JFK appeared on their premiere broadcasts and touched upon Southeast Asia. On September 2, 1963, he told Walter Cronkite that "unless a greater effort is made by the [South Vietnamese] government to win popular support," the war could not be won. "We are prepared to continue to assist them," he added, "but I don't think that the war can be won unless the people support the effort. . . . ." On September 9, JFK spoke with Chet Huntley and David Brinkley, returning to the domino theory, defending the CIA against charges it was operating in Vietnam without White House guidance, and concluding:

What I am concerned about is that Americans will get impatient and say because they don't like events in Southeast Asia or they don't like the government in Saigon, that we should withdraw. That only makes it easy for the Communists. I think we should stay. We should use our influence in as effective a way as we can, but we should not withdraw.

On November 1, 1963, the Diem government was overthrown in a coup d'état agreed to by President Kennedy. In the coup the autocratic South Vietnamese leader was murdered. Kennedy's response was to resume economic aid to South Vietnam, to recognize the new provisional government, and—as he told a press conference on November 14, 1963—to convene administration leaders in Honolulu to assess "how we can intensify the struggle, how we can bring Americans out of there."

The Vietnam War was a major part of John Kennedy's foreign policy. He consistently treated it in his television appearances. The last speech the president delivered before his assassination was concerned with the war. Speaking to the Fort Worth Chamber of Commerce, Kennedy seemed more wedded than ever to his military commitment. He boasted that his administration "increased our special counterinsurgency forces which are engaged now in South Vietnam by 600 percent." He argued that "without the United States, South Vietnam would collapse overnight." The president continued, "We are still the keystone in the arch of freedom, and I think we will continue to do as we have done in the past, our duty, and the people of Texas will be in the lead." Ironically, a few hours later Kennedy was dead and a Texan was sworn in as his successor and the new leader of the Free World.

TV AND THE COMING OF THE VIETNAM WAR

It is ironic that while it was silent, even ignorant, about the coming Vietnam War, television had prepared the nation for just such a battle. It was not a conscious brainwashing, but a subtle persuasion acted out over a dozen or more years of programming. TV told Americans the world was black and white, good and bad. TV showed that American virtues always trimphed, that American answers were best for mankind, and that Americans were selfless, wanting only to help others. Simplistic in its anti-Communism, increasingly venerative of national political leaders, and traditionally superficial and biased, TV indicated there was no need for profound analysis or for skepticism. Whether fiction or actuality, child-oriented or intended for adults, video ill served the public. It offered too many distorted images of the non-American world. It provided far too little information with which to assess world affairs. At a time when Americans depended upon the medium for honest diversion and accurate reportage, television offered too much propaganda and shallowness.

At no time in the nation's history did the United States go to war as in Vietnam. There were no cries of "Remember Pearl Harbor!" or "Remember the Maine!" Vietnam was not an openly declared "police action" taken in conjunction with a vote of the United Nations. Kennedy did not go before Congress, as had Woodrow Wilson and other wartime chief executives, to obtain a constitutional declaration of war. The Vietnam War was eased into. Without open debate and without popular comprehension of the issues, motives, or consequences, Americans one day simply found themselves in an Asian land war. The anti-Communist action that under Truman and Eisenhower had been only a holding action in Southeast Asia now became an active American war undertaken on the basis of secret decisions by Kennedy and his advisers.

The first television exposure of the Vietnam War was made by James Robinson, the NBC correspondent stationed in Hong Kong. On "Projection '62," televised January 5, 1962, Robinson seemed to flabbergast his colleagues when he bluntly declared to anchorman Frank McGee, "Well, Frank, like it or not—admit it or not—we are involved in a shooting war in Southeast Asia." No American broadcast journalist or network had ever described the actions of U.S. advisers in Southeast Asia as did Robinson.

In his analysis Robinson left no doubt that American forces were not just training South Vietnamese troops to resist Communist insurgents:

> American troops in battle uniforms, fully armed, are being killed [by] and killing Communist-led rebels in South Vietnam. American officers are in full command authority of important military operations there. And our active military participation in this war is on the increase. Our involvement stems from the fact that the South Vietnamese are unable, and in some instances, unwilling to make the necessary sacrifices to save their land from Communist take-over. United States officials there have told me we must win this war, even if we have to militarily attack North Vietnam, the present source of Red infiltration and aggression.

Perhaps the most objective correspondent at NBC, Robinson refused to see the struggle in Vietnam in terms of anti-Communist clichés. Instead, he explained the conflict more realistically:

> The Asian Communist strategy to conquer South Vietnam is not based on ideology. Rather, it's self-survival. The Red regimes in Peking and

Hanoi are proved economic failures. They simply can't feed their subjects. They must have the surplus food of South Vietnam in the very near future, and eventually in all Southeast Asia, or they'll collapse.

Robinson recognized that the new Vietnam War was the result of political and military decisions made in Washington. But he warned against overestimating American prowess and underestimating the strength of the enemy. "The presence of American soldiers in this battlefield doesn't necessarily guarantee victory," noted Robinson, "for U.S. involvement will trigger increased efforts for the Asian Communist camp." He added ominously, "Is President Kennedy willing and able to cope with this avalanching military challenge in the Far East? Many there doubt it."

To this date network TV had communicated the battle between Communists and non-Communists in Vietnam as classic Red guerrilla subversion valiantly resisted by freedom-loving, religious South Vietnamese. When Vice-President Johnson visited the South Vietnamese premier in mid-1961, he called Diem "the Winston Churchill of Asia"—this to go along with Diem's other sobriquet, "the Abraham Lincoln of Southeast Asia." As for the American role in Diem's struggle, it had been protrayed as advisory, helping the South Vietnamese to help themselves—and economic, providing financial aid to bolster the South Vietnamese economy. This was the essence, for example, of the two-part CBS documentary "Guerrilla," which aired on "The 20th Century" on November 12 and 19, 1961.

That James Robinson startled his peers on "Projection '62" is apparent from the following discussion of his assessment.

> McGee: Now, Jim, let me get this clear. I think it's important. You're saying that we are not simply training South Vietnamese troops over there to fight, but that American soldiers in uniform are carrying guns and shooting at the enemy?
>
> Robinson: That's absolutely right. Also, our Navy is patrolling in South Vietnamese waters to seal off infiltration from the North. We have our Air Force in combat operations there. Rangers and Special Forces are out in hand-to-hand combat in the jungles and in the delta regions of South Vietnam.
>
> Cecil Brown: Jim, a few dozen helicopters and a few thousand troops do not represent a very extensive commitment. . . .

Sander Vanocur: . . . Jim, I think that your evaluation is much too strong. We are not in a war there, we don't consider—a local operation . . . .

Robinson: Well, Sandy, in a sense this is a pretty shocking political morality from Washington. Because we have already promised officially to South Vietnam that we will go to any efforts to save that country from the Communists. And what are we doing? Carrying out an experiment now in American lives there without knowing really what we're going to do?

Bernard Frizell: Well, I think the question, Jim, really is: Is this going to develop into another Korea?

Robinson: It certainly is! It already *has* developed into another Korea! We have many countries anxious to get in there. Many countries already participate in the war there. You have Malaya sending considerable amounts of equipment. England has sent advisers. You have the Philippines and Thailand ready to send troops in there.

The only comment more unnerving than Robinson's revelations of active participation this early in the Vietnam War, was his prophetic final statement on what Americans might expect in Vietnam in 1962: "Tragic news will shock, sadden many American families in 1962—news of deaths of Americans killed in Southeast Asian conflicts."

The Kennedy administration offered television journalists a wide variety of crises and program innovations to fill the evening news and documentary specials. From civil rights at home to the Peace Corps abroad, from Cuba and Berlin to the Alliance for Progress in Latin America and new initiatives in central Africa—there was under JFK a news dynamism absent from politics under Eisenhower. Moreover, with television technologically more mature by the 1960s, visual communication of domestic and international challenges to Kennedy's activism could be more thoroughly presented.

American TV, however, seemed more fascinated with the Kennedy personality than the Kennedy policy. The surprised and defensive reactions of those NBC correspondents to James Robinson's report—essentially a "radio" report with no pictures nor film to enhance his points—reveal the shallowness of TV news when it gravitates to personality instead of thorough, objective analysis. On January 12, 1962, NBC aired its eleventh hour-long "JFK Report" without having fully probed developments in South Vietnam. On February 25, 1962, that network broadcast a "White Paper" entitled "Red China," again without looking at American policy in Southeast Asia. The administration continued to exploit the president's aplomb in short-answer news conferences and succinct statements taped for the nightly news. By late March, Senator William Proxmire, a Wisconsin liberal Democrat, publicly urged Kennedy to use television more responsibly by speaking to the nation in detail about administration policies.[29]

On the matter of South Vietnam, the president at his news conferences was seldom pressed for details when he mentioned American commitments. Without a probative retort, on January 31, 1961, he announced, "The situation in Vietnam is one that's of great concern to us. . . . The United States has increased its help to the government." On February 7 he spoke of U.S. economic aid to Vietnam, and the existence of "training groups out there which have been expanded in recent weeks as the attacks on the government and the people of South Vietnam have increased," but there were no follow-up questions asking for specifics. Nor was there a press reaction to JFK's appeal for caution in reporting on South Vietnam. He told the journalists on February 7:

> Now, this is a danger area where there is a good deal of danger, and it's a matter of information. We don't want to have information which is of assistance to the enemy—and it's a matter which I think will have to be worked out with the government of Vietnam, which bears the primary responsibility.

When asked to explain developments in Vietnam because "We don't have any overall coverage. . . . [and] because the Pentagon won't put out anything," Kennedy on March 7 brushed off his questioner: "I don't think you could make a judgment of the situation," he remarked, adding, "It's very much up and down, as you know, from day to day and week to week, so it's impossible to draw any long-range conclusions." A month later, in his conference of April 11, the president lamented the death of American soldiers in South Vietnam, but quickly added, "We cannot desist in Vietnam." Again, however, there were no follow-up questions.

As presidential evasion continued, television, by the spring of 1962, finally began to analyze the situation in South Vietnam. On May 8, NBC aired "Viet Nam—Last Chance," an hour-long analysis narrated by Edwin Newman and James Robinson. *Variety* described the program as "at a superficial level . . . a good war story in motion pictures, and at its most profound . . . a balanced, purposeful study of U.S. policies, native politics, and armament in Southeast Asia."[30] More revelatory was the May 23 ABC telecast of "Howard K. Smith with News and Comment." Since leaving CBS in the fall of 1961 and moving to prestige-hungry ABC News, Smith had been given a prime-time commentary program in which to treat issues he felt most pressing. In this installment Smith's topic was "What is Kennedy going to do about the Cold War that past administrations didn't do?" Specifically, he focused on South Vietnam and "one of his conspicuous new approaches, Mr. Kennedy's interest in guerrilla warfare."

Smith opened areas never fully explored on network TV. He told how in one year Kennedy had raised the number of American Special Forces from slightly more than 1,000 to a projected 10,000. While all were volunteers, Kennedy "passed down word that promotion will be faster for regular Army men who . . . volunteer for guerrilla service." Further, Smith reported American "troops pouring into Thailand."

There were administration spokesmen to pronounce the necessity of increased U.S. intervention. Walt Whitman Rostow, chief State Department policy planner, described Communist guerrilla warfare as "a type of war they [Communists] feel they can impose on a transitional society at a certain moment in vulnerability in the course of its movement towards modernization." Roger Hilsman, the director of intelligence for the State Department, likened the Communist guerrillas to the gangsters in Chicago in the 1920s—lacking true popular support, but operating freely because local government was not effective in controlling their terror and retaliation.

Secretary of Defense Robert S. McNamara was both manipulative and forthright when he discussed the Vietnam situation with Howard K. Smith. After Smith had presented strong criticism of Diem's autocratic regime in Saigon, McNamara spoke glowingly of the premier's accomplishment "to move his country toward a democratic structure." When quizzed more specifically by Smith, the secretary of defense admitted that in Vietnam "autocratic methods within a democratic framework were required."

More frankly, McNamara held out little hope for a quick victory over Communism in South Vietnam. When asked to estimate "how long it's going to take to settle this issue in South Vietnam," his answer was not encouraging. "I can't, but I'm certain it isn't a matter of months," McNamara responded, "rather a matter of years. I would guess three to five at a minimum."

It is important to note that throughout this program—in fact, throughout the several years that Howard K. Smith broadcast commentaries for ABC—he was not opposed to the anti-Communist commitment in Southeast Asia. This program was filled with encouragement for the administration to upgrade its performance, militarily and psychologically. Smith also subscribed to the domino theory, which envisioned the collapse of countries like Burma and Thailand should Communism be victorious in Indochina.

Journalistically, Smith was a product of World War II. One of Edward R. Murrow's young protégés covering the war in Europe, Smith gave one of the war's most powerful broadcasts when, in May 1945, he described conditions in bombed-out Berlin—once the fourth largest city in the world, now in ruin because of Allied bombing and occupation. Like so many from that era, words like "appeasement" and "isolation" were to Smith synonymous with the advance of Fascism; and Hitler's policy of conquering one independent country after the other was a political pattern never to be allowed again.

Smith was an anti-Communist, but within a liberal framework. He called for the overthrow of Castro because the Cuban leader was like Hitler. On his program of September 30, 1962, he declared:

> My completely personal view is that Castro's Cuba has become a threat to U.S. security—a more important threat than the Communist invasion of South Korea was. . . . I think Castro's satellite government has to be removed. Cuban patriots, aided by us, should do it. But if Russian guns have made that too difficult, direct American action should be contemplated. . . . For us, this is a little like watching Hitler's march into the Rhineland. He could have been stopped easily then.

Smith also viewed Communist China with values from the Hitler experience. "In China the need for living space is not out of date," he told his audience on March 7, 1962. "In China, *Lebensraum* may become the sharpest of all issues. . . . the huge Chinese population is way out of control. It's going to have to move somewhere sometime unless Chinese technology improves immensely." Still, he could be pragmatic. He was willing to recognize, for example, that China and the Soviet Union had national interests that differed, and this meant a world of Communisms to be dealt with diplomatically. Thus, on December 12, 1962, he could suggest:

> . . . it is all a rich opportunity for us. . . . If Communism is no longer monolithic, our attitude in dealing with it should cease to be a solid monolithic opposition. The use of Western trade to reward moderate Communist countries and to punish radical, aggressive Communists—this while standing firm on basic commitments—might change the course of history by peaceful action.[31]

In the early years of the American slippage into the Vietnam War, television journalists failed to offer informed rebuttal or even healthy doubt when the government explained the imperatives for a military commitment in Southeast Asia. Smith was the only network newsman regularly editorializing; there were no opposing voices urging a full exposure of the issues in Vietnam, a weighing of all sides, a full national debate of the advisability of the American actions, or an adherence to constitutional processes in the expanding military role of the United States in Southeast Asia.

In many cases, moreover, American TV journalists held political views that matched administration perceptions. Like Kennedy, many newsmen saw Communist China as an aggressive anti-American power threatening to establish hegemony over all of Southeast Asia—and perhaps all Asia. The two CBS correspondents stationed in Asia, Bernard Kalb and Peter Kalisher, saw Chinese Communism behind Asian upheavals. On "Years of Crisis: 1962," Kalb contended the Chinese never made a secret that Communism for all Asia was their goal. "Their objective," said Kalb, "is to brainwash all of Asia, rattle Asia, weaken Asia, and then make Asia ripe for the taking over by the Communists." For Kalisher, "Red China sees world domination for Communism, with Red China at the head of the band."

The principal Chinese weapon, according to Kalisher, was manpower. Because "You can't tell a Chinese from the Vietnamese or from any of the other races—most of them—in Asia," he contended, the Chinese were able to pour "men and enthusiasm into all these trouble spots in Asia." This tactic, he said, allowed the Chinese to feel they "can bring us [the United States] down where the Russians can't with atomic might." Therefore, Kalisher said, the Chinese "think that this nonsense about paying lip service to American atomic might is ridiculous because they've got ways of getting around it."

One of the few newsmen to see weakness and conservatism in Communist China was Marvin Kalb of CBS. On "Years of Crisis: 1963" he argued with Kalisher, contending, "I question very much any marked success either in Chinese internal or external policy." According to the younger Kalb brother, "The only mild success that Communist China has had in several years has been in conveying the impression to the Soviet Union and to many other Communists that they stand for something very revolutionary. But the fact is that Chinese foreign policy has been marked by *great* caution throughout Asia."

While Kalisher, the Far Eastern correspondent, continued to claim Communist China was the disruptive, aggressive force in Asia, Marvin

Kalb was the CBS correspondent at the State Department. And Kalb's view seemed less an independent conclusion than a reflection of a "new look at Communist China" he described as taking place at the State Department. Here in the first weeks of the presidency of Lyndon B. Johnson, Kalb suggested that "We are now taking a more pragmatic, less emotional, . . . dispassionate and calm look at China," especially at "the second echelon of authority and power in the Chinese Communist party . . . the younger generation coming up. . . ."

If the opinions of many correspondents might have been affected by Cold War slogans and official government policy, even more questionable were those journalists who worked for the government. Two of the most prominent TV newsmen, Chet Huntley and Walter Cronkite, on more than one occasion lent their talents and prestige to the making of government propaganda films. Specifically, they narrated and appeared in Defense Department motion pictures extolling the anti-Communist goals of the U.S. armed forces.

Early in 1960, while coanchor of the top-rated "Huntley-Brinkley Report," Chet Huntley narrated "The Ramparts We Watch," a propaganda movie lauding the cooperative efforts of the four major branches of the American military. The half-hour motion picture opened with a statement from Secretary of Defense Thomas Gates, Jr. It included footage and voice recordings of President Eisenhower and the joint chiefs of staff. The film suggested to its viewers—most likely would-be recruits and trainees—that despite modern technology, the soul of the armed forces remained man. Huntley's narration was accompanied by pictures of American GIs operating machinery, and carrying out human assistance programs in Hong Kong with "refugees from Red China" and with children in a Taiwanese kindergarten. While the modern military carried out missions in outer space, Huntley reminded his viewers, "We still face the need for defending the Free World's ramparts on Earth." What was needed, he suggested, was traditional and human: "The nuclear soldier may look different from today's soldier, but [he] must have the same patriotic fighting spirit and more specialized training."

Even more professionally compromising was Huntley's narration of "The United States Navy in Vietnam." Produced in 1966, this propaganda piece was a 30-minute commendation of the Navy's role in the Vietnam War. Huntley stood dockside and lauded "vertical envelopment," amphibious landings, and other new techniques the Navy was using "to help the people of Vietnam protect themselves." Viewers saw "civic action" as sailors gave boots to an old villager and clothing to a Vietnamese infant. Here was the latest naval equipment: destroyer-frigate, jets, and helicopters strafing enemy positions, big guns pummeling the Viet Cong enemy from offshore, and the massive aircraft carrier, the U.S.S. *Enterprise*. At a time when millions of Americans watched Chet Huntley weeknights on NBC for a better understanding of the war in Southeast Asia, he was contracting with the Pentagon to appear on camera and narrate its patently propagandistic motion pictures. At a time when his profession needed the utmost in objectivity to report accurately to the American citizenry, with uplifting music in the background Huntley lavished praise on the "Navy man":

> Vietnam has already written a new chapter in the annals of naval history. Never before has the potential of the Navy-Marine team been so fully realized. And yet, one important thing remains unchanged: the success of the overall effort will rely, as it always has, upon the acts of the individual man. Whatever credit is due will rest with many thousands of individual men who stand behind the aircraft, the ships, the boats, and the rifles, from the delta to the South China Sea. And whether he serves ashore or in the rivers and coastal waters, at sea or in the skies above, he will shoulder the responsibility for final success or failure. And he will be the one to make the needed sacrifice. And it is important to remember, that no matter what his job or whatever his duty, he is the Navy's greatest single asset: the individual man. This is the American Navy in Vietnam, moving quickly where and when needed, displaying the flexibility of modern sea power, controlling the seas, extending its influence on land, and holding superiority in the air—a three-way force for peace geared to meet aggression at any spot on the globe.

More aggressively anti-Communist were the government films narrated by Walter Cronkite. Although he began working in 1950 for CBS News, in 1953 Cronkite narrated a Defense Department film, "The Price of Liberty." The motion picture dealt with the role of women in the American armed forces. But clearly, from Cronkite's opening words, this 15-minute movie had other purposes: "Liberty is the most expensive commodity in the world today," proclaimed Cronkite while seated at a typewriter. "We have it only because we are willing and able to pay the price for preserving it against Communist aggression." This was a time of "the fight for world freedom," said Cronkite, and "Today armed vigilance must back every truce in the war between freedom and slavery." And, he suggested, "Military strength is still the only practical answer to the menace of Communism."

Throughout his career Cronkite's programs on CBS were marked by their reliance upon the Pentagon for film footage, statistical information, and interviews with prominent military men. This was the case with "The 20th Century," "Air Power," and "The 21st Century." Still, only a few months before he replaced Douglas Edwards as anchorman of the CBS evening news in April 1962, Cronkite narrated "The Eagle's Talon" for the Department of Defense. Ostensibly a report from Secretary McNamara on his first year in office, the film was a paean to the Kennedy administration for strengthening American military power. Cronkite declared the Soviet Union was "the opponent" of America, and all those Polaris, Minuteman, Nike-Hercules, Nike-Zeus, and other rockets were intended to protect the United States from a first strike by the Russians. While he noted that thermonuclear war started by the Soviets "would mean disaster for themselves," Cronkite reminded viewers "that does not mean Communism has curbed its ambition for world conquest." According to him, "Communist China even now has plans to dominate Asia by mass murder as in Tibet, destroying ancient civilizations." On Cuba, he remarked, "Right next door is a nation we freed in 1898, Cuba, as Communist tyranny holds sway and whiskers do not hide the naked face of dictatorship."

This was powerful propaganda. Oversimplified, well-scored, graphically illustrated, and stridently narrated, the Defense Department film described a world in which the U.S. Army "is face to face with Communism around the world." To meet the threat, the film alleged, the Kennedy administration was enhancing the nuclear and nonnuclear potentials of the armed services.

In classic propaganda style, after having frightened viewers with images of thermonuclear war and threats of savage Red aggression, Cronkite reassured them that with Kennedy everything would be fine. "No matter what the future holds, there is no need to fear for America," Cronkite guaranteed, for "The President, as Commander-in-Chief, keeps the decade of decision alert to Washington's advice, still timely today: 'To be prepared for war is one of the most effectual means of preserving peace.'"

There were several significant instances of network news personnel having close ties to government. Edward R. Murrow left CBS to head the United States Information Agency (USIA). He died, however, before returning to broadcast journalism. John Chancellor of NBC left the network in 1965 to become director of the government's chief propaganda outlet, the Voice of America. After several years in that capacity, he returned to NBC. In a reversal of the movement from broadcasting to government service, James C. Hagerty became the head of ABC News in 1961 after having been President Eisenhower's press secretary through most of Ike's two terms.

Corporate executives in the television industry also were closely associated with the partisan political interests of government. While it was common during World War II for broadcasting leaders to work for the Roosevelt administration, the practice was not widespread in the 1960s. Yet, at least two major TV executives were active in the Johnson administration: Frank M. Stanton and Robert E. Kintner. Stanton was president of CBS while also a trustee and chairman of the RAND Corporation, a government-supported think tank that one journalist described as "an annex of the Pentagon."[32] He was also appointed by President Johnson to head the Committee on Information Policy, an advisory group offering advice on government propaganda policy. Stanton, furthermore, was a close friend of the president. He and his wife once considered building a house on LBJ's Texas ranch.[33] Kintner, the president of NBC in the mid-1960s, was also a personal friend of Lyndon Johnson, that relationship extending back to Washington during the New Deal. As he did with Stanton, the president occasionally telephoned Kintner to complain about TV coverage or to seek advice. When Kintner left NBC in 1966, he accepted a Johnson appointment as special assistant to the president.

Government found TV networks and producers eager to assist in U.S. propaganda efforts around the world. By late 1961, according to *Broadcasting*, the USIA was receiving the greatest possible cooperation from commercial TV interests. Whether the agency wanted an hour-long NBC documentary on Ernest Hemingway, a CBS drama about the Berlin wall, or a David M. Wolper documentary production concerning the great black athlete Rafer Johnson, American television was cooperative. To ensure this harmonious relationship, however, President Kennedy and Edward R. Murrow were careful to meet in the fall of 1961 with the network chiefs, impressing upon industry executives that the government wanted easier access to network archives. While there had always been a cooperative relationship between TV and the propaganda agencies of the U.S. government, beginning with the Kennedy administration, access was simplified, streamlined, and generally enhanced. As one USIA official reported in late 1961, "Our arrangements with them are working well. . . . We're in touch almost daily. . . . We're getting material all the time."[34]

While conflicts of interest and bias among broadcast journalists were discernible in most cases, a less obvious influence on TV news came from personal and corporate self-interest within network management. While he defended the integrity of news operations "at the news department level," Louis G. Cowan, former president of CBS, rebuked unnamed executives "at the network level." Speaking in 1967, Cowan chided those executives who were more concerned with profits than with network responsibility to cover the news, even "the news that does not get an audience. Certainly they have not done as much as they might have about news."[35]

Robert MacNeil, a former NBC-TV newsman and presently co-host of "The MacNeil-Lehrer Report" on the Public Broadcasting System, echoed Cowan's criticism of network news. According to Mac-Neil, "The news executive may, under unusual provocation, stand by a principle and threaten to resign. . . . Yet control remains beyond his grasp." This inherent weakness in network news, MacNeil pointed out in 1968, was socially dangerous. Because TV was for many Americans "the primary source of information"—and because it was "increasingly invaded by politicians and under great pressure from powerful officeholders, especially in the White House, to present issues in a manner favorable to them"—TV news more than ever needed to be a thorough and honest presentation. Instead, he argued, "the system of many compromises" that is television journalism "is simply not good enough, for the product is compromised."[36]

In the United States, news is a commercial product. It has sponsors, Nielsen ratings, and other measurements of its popularity with the audience. As early as 1955 there was talk of a possible Senate probe of TV news to ascertain the influence of sponsors and other economic interests in suppressing and slanting the news.[37] Although the investigation never materialized, the phenomenon of Camel cigarettes (CBS), Gulf Oil (NBC), and other corporations bringing the news to mass America was not without its critics. On December 22, 1968, Senator John O. Pastore told an audience on the National Educational Television Program "PBL" ("Public Broadcasting Laboratory") that the networks allowed competitive considerations and pressures from advertisers to affect news coverage. The root of this situation, according to the chairman of the Senate Communications Subcommittee, was "Money. Money. Advertising. The Hooper [Nielsen?] ratings. Money. Money is the source of all evil. . . . And there's lots of money in broadcasting."[38]

While it is difficult to pinpoint instances where corporate sponsorship interfered with story selection or actual reportage, the fact that something so crucial to American society—the latest information on domestic and world events—was associated with a specific commercial product raised the potential for undermining the quality and respectability of TV news. There were numerous instances in entertainment television where sponsors and advertising agencies exerted censorship over programs they purchased. Thus, by inference there was a possibility for news to be affected similarly.

Even more potentially influential, however, were the economic interests of TV corporations themselves. While the networks were reporting the news of the Vietnam War, for example, in many cases their parent corporations were making millions of dollars supplying the military with war materials. The Radio Corporation of America, the parent company of NBC, was ranked twenty-fourth among Defense Department contractors in 1965. That year RCA obtained almost $214 million in military contracts. As the war escalated in 1966, that figure rose to $242.4 million. And the RCA-NBC situation was not unique. General Electric, with extensive interests in TV and radio, had government contracts totaling $824.3 million in 1964 and $1.187 billion the following year. The contracts of General Tire and Rubber, which owned the RKO-General broadcasting enterprises, rose from $302 million to $327.3 during the same time span. Kaiser Industries owned TV stations and earned $218.8 on government contracts in 1964 and $441.4 the following year. Westinghouse owned the Group W radio and TV outlets and had Defense Department contracts totaling $260.9 million in 1965 and $348.7 million in 1966.[39]

While ABC and CBS were not corporate subsidiaries, in the mid-1960s there were moves toward merging these networks with larger corporations. The legal moves to merge ABC with International Telephone and Telegraph were thwarted principally by a scandal at ITT in 1968. ITT was a major defense contractor with $206.7 million in 1965 and $219.8 million the next year. There were also tentative maneuvers toward merging CBS with either Litton Industries or International Business Machines. Both of these corporations were major war contractors.

Add to these financial influences the fact that many network advertisers were also profiting from the Vietnam War. Table 9, listing the top 30 Defense Department contractors, suggests that many companies—selling everything from telephone service and automobiles to refrigerators and typewriters—made billions of dollars from the war.

There were, however, a few voices in the wilderness asking for an analysis of the relationship between what Americans saw of the

Table 9 Leading Defense Department Contractors, 1965[40]

Company	Contracts (in millions)
1. Lockheed Aircraft	$1,715.0
2. General Dynamics	1,178.6
3. McDonnell Aircraft	855.8
4. General Electric	824.3
5. North American Aviation	745.8
6. United Aircraft	632.1
7. American Tel and Tel	587.6
8. Boeing	583.3
9. Grumman Aircraft Engineering	353.4
10. Sperry Rand	318.4
11. Martin-Marietta	315.6
12. Ford	312.0
13. General Tire and Rubber	302.0
14. Raytheon	293.4
15. Hughes Aircraft	278.3
16. Ling-Temco-Vaught	264.7
17. Westinghouse	260.9
18. Northrop	255.9
19. General Motors	254.4
20. Bendix	234.9
21. Avco	234.2
22. General Telephone and Electronics	222.5
23. Kaiser Industries	218.8
24. Radio Corporation of America	213.9
25. International Telephone and Telegraph	206.7
26. Todd Shipyards	196.6
27. Textron	195.7
28. Litton Industries	189.9
29. International Business Machines	186.2
30. Newport News Shipbuilding and Drydock	184.8

Vietnam War and the influence upon TV by profiteers. In 1966 Bill Greeley wrote in *Variety*:

> No accusation will be here stated of any government propensity in news coverage by the subsidiary of defense contractors, but such charges are made privately and semi-privately by critics. No specific evidence can be charged, but it will be recalled that it wasn't too many years ago that $100 payola put radio deejays off the air.[41]

The following year *Variety* returned to the issue, wondering "Can a major news medium like television do a thoroughly honest job when it is owned and controlled by a parent corporation that has a financial involvement with the government?"[42]

Nicholas Johnson, an outspoken member of the Federal Communications Commission in the late 1960s, several times rebuked the networks for failure to discuss economic interests in the Vietnam War. Appearing on "PBL" on December 22, 1968, to discuss TV journalism, Johnson spoke of "a form of self-imposed censorship" that was the failure of television to cover, or cover well, "those things which affect its economic interests and the economic interests of its suppliers and the economic interests of others who share the basic philosophy and background and participation in the industrial establishment that broadcasting shares."[43] Several months later in *TV Guide*, Commissioner Johnson returned to this theme, pointing out that "We have been shown miles of film from Vietnam, it's true. But how much has television told you about the multibillion-dollar corporate profits from war?"[44]

Americans wanted and needed accurate, in-depth information from their television receivers. A study in 1960 by Gary A. Steiner, published as *The People Look at Television*, revealed a great demand for more news and informational programming. Although Steiner's statistics showed that only 16 to 20 percent of those surveyed actually watched news-related TV, part of the reason was that with the exception of nightly newscasts, most such programs were relegated to commercially poor viewing hours: Sunday mornings and afternoons.[45]

In the spring of 1960, at the same time Steiner was drawing his conclusions about TV news, Frank M. Stanton, the president of CBS, explained to a group of television executives that electronic journalism was now "as important as printed journalism and as much a part of the lives of Americans." Stanton was there to defend video journalism and to speak against Section 315 of the Communications Act of 1934. Section 315 had two important dimensions as far as broadcasters were concerned. First, it stipulated that candidates for election must be given free equal time should an opponent be allowed to use radio or television without charge; should a candidate buy air time, opponents must be allowed to purchase a similar amount of air time at the same fee. This "equal time" aspect was augmented in 1949 with the so-called "fairness doctrine." By this broadening of Section 315, the FCC ruled that all sides in controversial issues must be treated fairly by broadcasters in news and commentary. Stanton spoke for most network executives when he called Section 315 a "straitjacket," a regulation that "strips broadcast journalism of both the right and the responsibility of news judgment."

Unfortunately for viewers of news-related television, this function of TV needed no enforcement of Section 315 to be journalistically compromised. Inherent in the corporate structures and personal politics of important newsmen were conflicts of interest that eroded the objectivity and thoroughness of broadcast journalism.

Stanton knew the inadequacies of his industry. Yet, he insisted that TV news was crucial to the viability of American society. "It is, in sober fact," he told his audience, "a battle to meet the increasingly urgent need for information if this society is to survive." Still, he blamed Section 315, alleging that because of it the "use of television as education for democratic living and, indeed, for democratic survival is plagued and choked."[46] The CBS president was correct to conclude that by this date the survival of democratic society in the United States was dependent upon the educative information received through television. But the provision for equal time and fairness was not the culprit. It was television journalism itself that betrayed the American people by the consistent dissemination of propaganda instead of complete truth, clichés instead of wide-ranging analysis. And by the late 1960s, as the nation faced its greatest domestic unrest since the Civil War, the situation was caused in greatest part by the misinformation, and even deceit, regarding the Vietnam War, transmitted by TV.

POLITICIZED TV IN WARTIME AMERICA

If in the earliest years of the Vietnam War television failed the public in its news functions, as a vehicle of mass diversion it compounded that shortcoming with programming conducive to militaristic adventurism. Now, video lionized democratic champions of war; it lauded the "just" hero, even one willing to overlook legal processes and employ direct action to solve the problems of others.

In the early 1960s the composite adventurer in prime-time entertainment was a handsome white male—almost always an American—who responded with strength and bravery in his weekly selfless undertakings. His foe might be a Nazi, a Communist, or some other dictatorial type. Invariably, however, his enemy was never the autocrat of a nation supported by American foreign policy. The video hero of the early 1960s was loyal, unquestioning, stalwart—but under it all he was basically a commoner. While he remained dedicated to the cause for which he struggled, he was frequently shown helping a child in distress or pursuing a romantic conquest.

This composite character might be an historic figure whose self-sacrifice was recalled in a documentary series or moralistic drama. He could be a fictional soldier, cowboy, or secret agent. His purpose was revealed in war dramas, situation comedies, spy stories, and Westerns. Wherever encountered, this champion proffered a role model for a nation at war: an unswerving representative of the best of things American—the product of democracy—the protector and/or savior of the downtrodden—not so committed as to be a zealot, but sufficiently sketched in human terms as to be recognizable and emulable.

More than entertaining, this composite hero was propagandistic. By his actions and attitudes, he communicated the honorableness of his activities. While he amused a nation of TV watchers, he politicized that audience, offering without rebuttal a rationalization for the Cold War becoming increasingly hot. Archibald MacLeish, poet, playwright, and Librarian of Congress understood this. He once suggested to a group of broadcasters that images disseminated in entertainment shows were more influential than information delivered in "serious" programs. Speaking in 1959, MacLeish concisely delineated the political importance inherent in televised popular culture.

> What you [broadcasters] do matters more over the long run (if our civilization has a long run ahead of it) than what anybody else does. Because you are more persistently shaping the minds of more people than all the rest of us put together. . . . The programs lumped together as entertainment have as great an influence on the minds of the human beings who watch them as programs which claim a more serious purpose. Indeed, they have a greater influence. . . . Every program you put on is "doing" and will have a consequence, whatever you may call it.[47]

There was in the 1960s, however, a continuity with Cold War programming of the previous decade. Westerns continued to mix glamorized Americana with the crusade to establish democratic order in a hostile wilderness. There also continued to be entertaining documentaries reminding viewers of great military triumphs of the past. The first such series of the Kennedy and Johnson years was "Winston Churchill—The Valiant Years," which ABC twice telecast in prime time: in 1960-61 and as a rerun in 1962-63. The 26 episodes of this Emmy-winning program showed the British leader as a determined national hero waging war on totalitarian dictatorship. In the context of the Cold War, historic Churchill became a contemporary model of tenacity in the search for justice. Playing down his strong imperialistic views and his detestation of anticolonial leaders such as Mohandas Gandhi of India, the series stressed Churchill's patriotism, his love of Anglo-Saxon democracy, and his inspirational words for a nation at war. For instance, on the episode entitled "The Crisis Deepens," Churchill assumed the prime ministership with stirring words still appropriate for the United States locked in the Cold War:

> Come, then, let us to the task, to the battle, to the toil, each to our part, each to our station. Fill the armies. Rule the air. Pour out the munitions. Strangle the U-boats. Sweep the mines. Plow the land. Build the ships. Guard the streets. Succor the wounded. Uplift the downcast. And honor the brave. Let us go forward together in all parts of the Empire, in all parts of the island. There is not a week, nor a day, nor an hour to lose.

Success with "The Valiant Years" led to other historical documentaries. "Battle Line" was a syndicated series in the 1962-63 season that investigated World War II through the eyes of Allied and Axis survivors of significant battles. In the fall of 1964, viewers relived World War I. In the CBS series "World War I," and in a syndicated British production, "The Great War," Americans encountered two 26-part dissections of the causes, events, and consequences of that great conflict to make the world safe for democracy. At the same time, "Decision: The Conflicts of Harry S. Truman" premiered as a syndicated series—complete with opening statements by the former president and historic film footage—that flatteringly showed Truman facing and solving problems during his presidency. Also premiering in 1964 was the 32-part syndicated series "Men in Crisis," in which historic struggles between moral forces—Chamberlain versus Hitler, Castro versus Batista, Mussolini versus Haile Selassie, Darrow versus Bryan— were recalled in documentary film. In January 1965, moreover, ABC returned with "F.D.R.," a 27-part program from the producers of "The Valiant Years."

Perhaps the most widely viewed documentaries in this style were the 91 half-hour histories in the "Biography" series. Narrated by Mike Wallace, this syndicated program first appeared in 1962. "Biography" presented the lives of people as diverse as Pius XII, Grace Kelly, David Ben-Gurion, and Babe Ruth. It featured many American war heroes— among them generals Eisenhower and MacArthur, and Admiral Chester Nimitz. Stalin, Mao Tse-tung, Fidel Castro, and Ho Chi Minh were less approvingly chronicled.

Even more dedicated to Cold War tensions was "The 20th Century." This CBS series, which began in 1956 and ran until 1966, consistently spent much effort reviving great military achievements of the past, reporting on technical and operational conditions in the modern American armed forces, and spotlighting the East-West struggle. In 1963, for example, the series treated World War I in "Verdun: End of a Nightmare" (December 8), and World War II in several installments, among them "Beachhead an Anzio" (February 10), "Attack on Singapore" (February 24), "Typhoon at Okinawa" (June 2), and "Get the Graf Spee" (October 6). At the same time it continued to praise the American military in such productions as "From Jet to Dyna-Soar" (January 13), "Frogmen of the Future" (April 28), and a two-part program, "SAC: Aloft and Below" (December 15 and 22).

The Cold War, another familiar theme of "The 20th Century," frequently was broached directly. "Zero Hour in Greece" (January 6) traced the history of the Greek struggle against Nazi invaders in World War II and Communist revolutionaries in the postwar era. "Finland: Tug of War" (February 3) concerned the politics of modern Finland, trapped between a Soviet neighbor and Western inclinations. Fear of Soviet espionage against the United States was explored on "Red Ships off Our Shores" (March 24). "End of an Empire" (September 1) stressed the role of Communist China in assisting the Vietnamese nationalist movement to oust the French from Southeast Asia. And "The Road to Berlin" (November 10) traced the history of that divided city during the Cold War.

Less frightening were those pastoral reflections on American life and culture treated on the "Project XX" series during the 1960s. Under the control of producer Donald B. Hyatt, NBC here presented documentaries in praise of America and its uniqueness. "Laughter, U.S.A." concerned native humor, and "The Story of Will Rogers" treated an eminent American humorist. "The Red, White and Blue" was a Flag Day program filled with marching bands, county courthouses, veterans' organizations on parade, and old-time flag-waving. Interestingly, this patriotic documentary wondered wistfully what had happened to diminish popular participation in such demonstrations of Americanism. From George Washington to the Plains Indians, from immigrants arriving at Ellis Island to Christian religious themes in great art, "Project XX" lovingly offered America and its proud dreamers, testifying to the overriding goodness of the nation.

Only once in the 1960s did "Project XX" return outspokenly to the Cold War themes that marked its productions in the 1950s. "That War in Korea" was a 90-minute retrospective on the Korean War. It relied on wartime film shot by NBC cameramen and added contemporary footage of American soldiers patrolling near the thirty-eighth parallel, for ten years the demilitarized border between North and South Korea. The program was a lesson in preparedness, a story of national sacrifice that leaders might have to ask of Americans again. Aired less than two days before President Kennedy was assassinated, whatever national discussion the program may have generated was lost in the dislocation precipitated by events in Dallas.

Whether as nostalgia for a perceived simplicity in the past, or as historic sketches of wars, celebrated democrats, or infamous Communists, entertainment TV supplemented the evening news and its images of moral conflicts in the world. Further, as the values of anti-Communism found increasing acceptance by those on the right wing of American politics, TV became a favorite medium for the dissemination of intolerant interpretations of world Communism. By January 1962, *Broadcasting* could alert its readers to "look for [a] rash of anti-Communist TV documentary series to break out during 1962 on both network and syndication levels."[48]

The first program reflecting this new stridency was a live special, "Hollywood's Answer to Communism." This three-hour extravaganza —consisting of a seminar held by the California School of Anti-Communism, plus a live rally of 12,000 people at the Hollywood Bowl— was televised on October 16, 1961, on 35 stations in 6 Western states. It was produced by the Christian Anti-Communist Crusade, and was financed by the politically conservative Schick Safety Razor Company and Technicolor, Inc. Among the prominent people appearing on the program were C. D. Jackson, the publisher of *Life* magazine, and Dr. Fred C. Schwarz, the fiery crusader whose controversial book *You Can Trust the Communists (to Be Communists)* vilified the Soviet Union and placed him at the forefront of the growing right wing. Clearly the treat of the program, however, was the many Hollywood celebrities who appeared to assert their patriotism and to assail the Red threat. Mixing conservative politics with the allure of Jane Russell, Roy Rogers, Pat O'Brien, Robert Stack, James Stewart, and Jack Warner—plus host (and eventually U.S. Senator) George Murphy —the right wing was learning in a video age how best to communicate its message. Films of "Hollywood's Answer to Communism" were televised two weeks later in New York City and other major markets.

The success of this TV special opened the way for other such anti-Communist programs in the early years of the Kennedy administration. In many local productions, syndicated series, and network products, hostility toward Communism gained popular expression. In October 1961, on the King Broadcasting stations (KING-TV in Seattle, KREM-TV in Spokane, and KGW-TV in Portland, Oregon), "The Threat" was a 90-minute program filled with anti-Communist speakers and a question-and-answer session with a studio audience. WTVJ in Miami offered a drama special, "The Day Miami Died," a fictionalized version of how Reds took over the city. Although primarily exploiting radio for their fundamentalist Protestant anti-Communism, media evangelists like Billy James Hargis and Carl J. McIntyre gained increasing TV exposure for their warnings about the Reds.

And there were important syndicated productions. "Communism: R.M.E." ("a *R*iddle wrapped in a *M*ystery, inside an *E*nigma") was a 13-part series narrated in 1962 by Art Linkletter and promising "authentic revelations of life behind the Iron Curtain" as well as clarification of "the fundamental differences between Communism and the Free World." Less ambitious was "The Rise and Fall of American Communism." Released in 1964 by David L. Wolper Productions, this was an hour-long documentary telling the story of Moscow-directed Red radicalism in the United States.

Network TV was not immune to the national fervor being generated by the energetic political right. While the "CBS Reports" documentary "Thunder on the Right" (televised February 22, 1962) presented a neutral examination of the phenomenon—from the paramilitary Minutemen preparing a guerrilla force to protect America from invasion in the next war, to the middle-class members of the John Birch Society and the "conscience" of American conservatism, Senator Barry Goldwater—in the early 1960s the networks generally exploited the mounting paranoia over the Communist challenge. "Communism has suddenly emerged as the hottest new program subject idea in television," proclaimed *Broadcasting* in January 1962. "No fewer than 100 programs, including five series for syndication to stations, are currently in the planning and production stage," the trade magazine continued, "not counting a mounting volume scheduled or planned by individual stations."[49] Both in the reiteration of democratic myths and in the reproach of Communism, network television offered political lessons. There were docudramas and stylized historical accounts of great patriots. "The Great Adventure" on CBS in 1963-64 presented stories of nationalistic heroes such as Nathan Hale, Harriet Tubman, Sam Houston, and Wild Bill Hickok. During the following season NBC presented "Profiles in Courage," dramatizations of the lives of those heroic men and women treated in John F.

Kennedy's Pulitzer Prize-winning book of the same title. In "Saga of Western Man," ABC documentarian John H. Secondari, Jr., between 1963 and 1966 created 13 lavish productions that traced the development of American society by emphasizing pivotal years—"1492," "1776," "1898," and "1963"—as well as crucial events and influences: "The Puritan Experience" and "Custer: To the Little Big Horn."

Also significant was the NBC News presentation "Profile on Communism." Aired in the first months of 1963, this series of four, hour-long films probed Communism from various perspectives. "The Death of Stalin" (January 27) and "The Rise of Khrushchev" (February 3) offered still another historical treatment of modern Russian history. With Chet Huntley as narrator of both films, the former treated Stalin in terms of police-state terrorism and the Russian despot's belief that "war with the imperialists is inevitable." The latter program traced the five-year rise of "a country bumpkin" from Communist bureaucrat to leader of the Communist world in the post-Stalin era.

On "Who Goes There?" (March 1), the third program in this NBC limited series, correspondent Robert Abernathy took viewers on a historical tour of Marxism-Leninism, focusing upon Soviet ideology, revolution, totalitarianism, and imperialism as "the four faces of Communism." In closing, Abernathy described the meaning of Communism in familiar Cold War rhetoric: "Can our power and our will check their imperialism? Can our self-discipline match their totalitarianism? Can we wipe out the conditions that invite revolution? Above all, can our freedom and our faith deny their ideology? We think we can."

The final installment of "Profile on Communism" was a survey of the Communist world, "An Encylopedia of the Divided World of Communism" (April 10). Narrated by Chet Huntley, this installment dealt at length with the split between China and the Soviet Union. But it suggested, in the words of President Kennedy, that "Hope must be tempered with caution, for the Soviet-Chinese disagreement is over means, not ends. A dispute over how to bury the West is no ground for Western rejoicing."

As sophisticated as NBC made this series, it still suffered from a strong anti-Communist bias. In his preface to a bound edition of the scripts of these four programs—distributed to the public free of charge —William R. McAndrew, then executive vice-president of NBC News, gave clear evidence that while the series expanded its perspectives on Communism, it did so with familiar prejudices. "Most people know it as a menace to their way of life, to their institutions, to themselves," wrote McAndrew of Communism. "They know that it tramples freedom, tries to level ambition, preaches atheism. And oversimplify, as is our custom, to 'it's the bad boy' and 'we are the good boy.' " Clearly, too, NBC felt the United States could defeat Communism. As McAndrew phrased it, the purpose of "Profile on Communism" was to help Americans triumph over Communism, for "you must know your enemy before you can defeat him."[50]

In the two years and three months between the outbreak of World War II in Europe and American entry into that conflict following Pearl Harbor, network broadcasters carefully avoided programs that appeared militaristic or biased toward U.S. involvement in the war. Twenty years later, as the United States drifted into undeclared war in Vietnam, TV was anything but neutral toward the issue of war. Soldiers were plentiful on television in the 1960s. In many cases they were fictional combatants, the entertaining central characters in war adventure series.

Never in the history of American broadcasting had there been so many war programs. Even during World War II, radio discouraged excessive amounts of fictional drama re-creating battles and other forms of military violence. In the 1950s there were military series on television, but only one, "Combat Sergeant," was set permanently in a war zone. During the Vietnam War, however, TV presented a procession of soldier heroes fighting for freedom in weekly dramatic series.

The time frame of most such shows was World War II. While one program was set in the Civil War ("The Americans") another in peacetime ("The Lieutenant") and still another was in a militaristic future ("Voyage to the Bottom of the Sea"), none, ironically, took place in Southeast Asia. The pacesetter in this trend was ABC, which in 1962 premiered "Combat" and "The Gallant Men." In fact, of the series listed in Table 10, only "Convoy" (NBC), "The Lieutenant" (NBC), "The Americans" (NBC), and "Jericho" (CBS) were not ABC programs.

The most significant programs of this genre were "Combat," "Twelve o'Clock High," and "The Rat Patrol." They lasted longer, enjoyed higher ratings ("Combat" was the tenth most popular program in the 1964-65 season, and "The Rat Patrol" was ranked twenty-fourth in its first season), and generally provided more action than the other series. If TV news never consistently went into battle with the troops, and if GIs in Vietnam were nameless or appeared once and then were reabsorbed by the conflict, fictional war dramas gave "flesh and blood" to the American fighting man. Characters became

Table 10 War Drama Series on Network TV[51]

Program	Years of First-Run	No. of Episodes
The Americans	1961	17
The Gallant Men	1962-63	26
Combat	1962-67	152
The Lieutenant	1963-64	29
Twelve o'Clock High	1964-66	78
Voyage to the Bottom of the Sea	1964-68	110
Convoy	1965	13
Jericho	1966-67	16
Court Martial	1966-67	26
The Rat Patrol	1966-68	58
Garrison's Gorillas	1967-68	26

familiar, and viewers "got to know" the serviceman. He was wise and understanding, like Lieutenant Gil Hanley (Rick Jason) and Sergeant Chip Saunders (Vic Morrow) on "Combat." He was also brave like Brigadier General Frank Savage (Robert Lansing), who lost his fictional life after one season on "Twelve o'Clock High." That same series also illustrated the character development possible with wartime responsibility as Joe Gallagher (Paul Burke) took two seasons to evolve from a cocky young captain to a wise and courageous colonel.

Here were role models for a nation unquestioningly sliding into a war in Asia. Here also were "insights" into the way men acted in war. At least that was the argument in mid-1962 of Selig Seligman, producer of "Combat." According to him, the program was "a searching in our history for the ideals and heroism that can sustain the American people in a troubled time."[52]

While "Twelve o'Clock High" and "Combat" were Hollywood creations, they frequently used actual war film. The former employed authentic aerial combat footage, since the series concerned a bombardment group fighting in the European theater of operations. At the end of each "Combat" episode, special thanks were given to the Department of the Army for its production assistance. But for glamour and adventure, the most compelling war series was "The Rat Patrol." For outside help, this show was indebted only to Warner Brothers and United Artists for sharing props and other war material left after completion of the feature films *The Battle of the Bulge* and *The Great Escape*.

"The Rat Patrol" was set in the barren North African desert. Although filmed in Spain and on the MGM studio lot in southern California, the series focused on the war against General Erwin Rommel and the German Afrika Korps. Four young soldiers—one Briton and three Yanks—skimmed across the desert on jeeps with mounted machine guns blazing. They fought Nazi evil, Arab treachery, and the cruelty of the desert—and they did so with conviction that their cause was just. Furthermore, none of the Rat Patrollers ever died. No matter that on the evening news American deaths were rising in the reality of Vietnam; in TV fiction the brave young warriors seemed immortal.

Interestingly, only one military drama series was openly anti-Communist. Although inspired by the nineteenth-century French writer Jules Verne, "Voyage to the Bottom of the Sea" was conceived as a Cold War program. In an advertisement for the premiere of the series, ABC showed footage from coming episodes—including one scene where the heroic Admiral Harriman Nelson interrogated four enemies, one looking like Lenin, another like Ho Chi Minh, and the others having generally malevolent Asiatic features—while the announcer heralded the coming of a new series.

> Now! To the television screen! The most incredible adventure series ever filmed! "Voyage to the Bottom of the Sea!" This is the sea. Uncontrolled, a devastating force, as mighty as any on earth. But below that destruction lies another power. The *Seaview*! You'll live in the year 1973 with the most extraordinary submarine in all the world. Its public image, an instrument of marine research. In actuality, the mightiest weapon afloat, secretly assigned to fight an evil power dedicated to the destruction of freedom. Richard Basehart as Admiral Nelson, David Hedison as Captain Crane, lead their men to incredible, exciting adventure. From the terror that lies on the ocean floor, to the super-modern weapons of their enemy in a war at the top of the world. In "Voyage to the Bottom of the Sea." Every week on ABC.

During the first season, Admiral Nelson and his crew fought Communist saboteurs and secret agents seeking to thwart the mission of the *Seaview*. The heroes foiled Red revolutionaries in Latin America. They safely delivered a young monarch to his Far Eastern kingdom following the assassination of his father by Communist revolutionaries. In "Hail to the Chief," aired December 29, 1964, Nelson and his men successfully fought off enemy agents seeking to murder the president of the United States after an accident in South America forced the touring chief executive to seek emergency treatment aboard the *Seaview*.

In later seasons, "Voyage to the Bottom of the Sea" abandoned the Cold War in favor of the Hollywood gimmick war. Evil now came in the form of strange alien monsters with amazing powers and dastardly purposes. Still, as in "Deadly Cloud," broadcast on March 12, 1967, the admiral employed recognizable Cold War weaponry—in this case a nuclear bomb—to destroy evil invaders intent upon destroying the earth.

War as entertainment allowed TV viewers to empathize with the agony of conflict, and rejoice in victory with clean-cut video heroes. Television also gave the public much to laugh about. The military situation comedy flowered in TV during the Vietnam War. Where in the late 1950s Phil Silvers' rascalish Sergeant Ernest E. Bilko had been the first successful comedic soldier in broadcasting history, in the next decade TV abounded with comedies set in most branches of the armed services. As Table 11 suggests, even more than war drama series, Americans approved of military comedies.

These situation comedies suggested that there was something basically light and recognizably human about the military.[53] On "F Troop" audiences laughed at zany soldiers and daffy Indians on a cavalry post in the days of the Wild West. Incredibly, "Hogan's Heroes" brought high jinks to a Nazi prisoner-of-war camp where Hitler's henchmen were bumblers and the internees produced more guffaws than resistance to Fascism.

Table 11 Military Situation Comedies on Wartime Network Television[54]

Title	Years of First-Run	No. of Episodes
Hennesey	1959-62	96
McKeever & The Colonel	1962-63	26
Don't Call Me Charlie	1962-63	13
Ensign O'Toole	1962-64	26
McHale's Navy	1962-66	138
No Time for Sergeants	1964-65	34
Broadside	1964-65	32
Gomer Pyle, U.S.M.C.	1964-69	150
Mr. Roberts	1965-66	30
The Wackiest Ship in the Army	1965-66	29
Mona McClusky	1965-66	26
F Troop	1965-67	65
I Dream of Jeannie	1965-70	139
Hogan's Heroes	1965-71	168
It's About Time	1966-67	26

TV found much laughter in the South Pacific during World War II. The clowns of "McHale's Navy" began amusing audiences in 1962. On "Broadside" predictable jokes emerged from a situation where a group of U.S. Navy WAVES was stationed on an island filled with male sailors. The hero of "Mr. Roberts" wanted to see real battle action, but had to content himself with generating humor on a cargo ship far from the fighting. The most convoluted premise, however, occurred with "The Wackiest Ship in the Army." In this series the U.S.S. *Kiwi* was a schooner commanded by a Navy lieutenant when at sea, and an Army major when in port. Ironically, this premise was derived from an actual wartime development.

There were also military situation comedies set in peacetime. "No Time for Sergeants" concerned a Southern "hick" in the Air Force. "Gomer Pyle, U.S.M.C." featured another Southern stereotype, a simple but likable Marine from the mountains of North Carolina. The heroine of "Mona McClusky" was an actress, but her husband and comedic foil was an Air Force sergeant. "McKeever and the Colonel" was about life at a military school. "Hennesey" dealt with the humorous adventures of a Navy medical officer stationed in San Diego. The short-lived "Don't Call Me Charlie" concerned an Army veterinarian stationed in Paris. The focus of "I Dream of Jeannie" was an attractive female genie owned by—and later married to—an Air Force astronaut living on an air base. And misdirected astronauts were the central characters in the farcical "It's About Time," a comedy set in the Stone Age and later updated to contemporary Los Angeles.

In one sense military comedies and dramas on TV were simple adventures in escapism and business. Their engaging tales and formulaic humor were meant to amuse an audience of enough millions to garner good Nielsen ratings. This enabled the networks to increase profits by selling commercial time at higher rates. In turn, the networks ordered new militaristic series and more episodes of already successful productions.

There was in this escapism, however, a sociological dimension. These war stories and comedic encounters prolonged the inability of the American citizenry to confront the reality of war. TV showed stylized armed conflict in which virile Yank soldiers triumphed in the end and comedic farce stripped war of its brutal, violent, murderous nature. No one on "McHale's Navy" was killed in its make-believe world war. Colonel Bob Hogan's heroic charges constantly joked with their Nazi guards. Gomer Pyle innocently made rube humor during a Marine Corps bayonet drill. Sergeant Saunders spent five years on "Combat" walking around the eucalyptus trees and potted plants of a Hollywood film lot, acting out a popular fantasy that war was somehow part moral crusade, part athletic event. There were grenades, machine guns, mortars, and the like, but there was no real blood, no authentic death in entertainment warfare. Furthermore, set as so many were in World War II, there was certainty among viewers that the Americans would win—because in actuality they did win that war. Somehow, the uncritical early television coverage from Southeast Asia made the Vietnam conflict seem an extension of American popular culture.

This cultural propensity to commercialize and be entertained by streamlined re-creations of reality was most glamorously achieved in the many spy series that flourished in TV in the mid-1960s. As Table 12 indicates, the counterespionage operative was a popular part of American viewing during the Vietnam War.

The video spy as suave, handsome man-on-the-go was realized first in John Drake (Patrick McGoohan), the dashing investigator for NATO governments in "Danger Man," and exclusively for the British government in "Secret Agent." Like his more lavish counterpart in the James Bond feature films, Drake ate well, fought well, and loved well as he roamed the globe on dangerous assignments. The most attractive

Table 12 Spy Series on Television in the 1960s[55]

Program	Years of First-Run	No. of Episodes
Danger Man	1961	39
Espionage	1963-64	24
The Man from U.N.C.L.E.	1964-68	99
The Prisoner	1965	17
Secret Agent	1965-66	45
Amos Burke, Secret Agent	1965-66	17
Secret Squirrel	1965-66	26
The Double Life of Henry Phyfe	1965-66	17
I Spy	1965-68	82
Get Smart	1965-70	138
The Baron	1966	16
Blue Light	1966	17
The Man Who Never Was	1966-67	18
The Girl from U.N.C.L.E.	1966-67	29
The Avengers	1966-69	83
Mission: Impossible	1966-71	171
It Takes a Thief	1967-70	65

American entry in this style was Napoleon Solo (Robert Vaughn), the man from U.N.C.L.E. Working for the United Network Command for Law and Enforcement, Solo and his partner, Illya Kuryakin (David McCallum), fought the international crimes of their archenemy, THRUSH, a sinister organization plotting to control the world. While "The Man From U.N.C.L.E." had elements of satire and even ridicule, it contained the essential ingredients of the spy genre and struck a responsive chord among viewers in the mid-1960s.

There were funny spies in "Get Smart" and "The Double Life of Henry Phyfe," and romantic spies in "It Takes a Thief" and "Amos Burke, Secret Agent." The first Afro-American spy appeared in "I Spy," the first female agent, in "The Girl from U.N.C.L.E." In "The Avengers" the formula to save the world consisted of technical gadgets and stereotypic British certainty. In "Mission: Impossible" masterful disguises and technology helped American agents penetrate the Iron Curtain, thwart Latin American revolutionaries, and exert American will around the globe.

The anthology series "Espionage" was inspired by historic spies. "The Man Who Never Was," "The Baron," and "Blue Light" relied more on foreign locations than compelling scripts. In "The Prisoner" Patrick McGoohan played a British agent—called only Number 6—who was mysteriously imprisoned and spent every program resisting the brainwashing schemes of his anonymous but evil captors. Even children had an espionage hero in Secret Squirrel, a Saturday morning cartoon secret agent who with his pals in intelligence activities, Morocco Mole, Winnie the Witch, and Squiddly Diddly, pursued the archvillain Yellow Pinky, an obvious twist on James Bond's foe Goldfinger.

TV spy programs were at once elaborate detective stories preaching that crime does not pay, patriotic war dramas in which intelligence agents risked their lives as much as any soldier, and romantic escapades highlighting beautiful people in exotic locations. Whether serious or satirical, video secret agents worked for modern, efficient-sounding agencies that were often identified by acronyms. Alexander Mundy, the reformed jewel thief turned American agent, defeated enemies and kissed beautiful women for the SIA. Zany Maxwell Smart of "Get Smart" worked for C.O.N.T.R.O.L., and against K.A.O.S. Scholarly Henry Phyfe was an agent for the CIS—the Counter Intelligence Service. And the masters of espionage on "Mission: Impossible" labored for the Impossible Mission Force, the IMF.

The permeation of American society with fictional TV soldiers and spies did not end with the hundreds of episodes listed in Tables 10 to 12. While these programs might have popularized such characterization, servicemen and secret agents were found in other types of shows. Dramatic anthologies like "Bob Hope Presents the Chrysler Theater" used war stories. Military themes appeared occasionally on programs such as "Run for Your Life," "Star Trek," "The Name of the Game," and "The Invaders." Even tongue-in-cheek "Batman" dealt with would-be conquerors defeated by selfless heroes. Professional sports, especially football, which in the 1960s supplanted baseball as the national pastime, also reflected militaristic values. Half-time pageantry often saluted American troops in Southeast Asia. The most celebrated football leader of the decade was coach Vince Lombardi of the Green Bay Packers, a successful molder of players with his emphasis upon Spartan dedication and the supremacy of will. Even the terminology of football—the bomb, the blitz, and the shotgun formation—assumed the quality of warfare.[56]

There were spies galore in nonspy programs in the 1960s. Erik Barnouw has described how "The FBI" became increasingly concerned with Communist agents in the United States. Espionage came also to "77 Sunset Strip." Barnouw even detected this theme infiltrating situation comedies such as "Mr. Ed" and "The Lucy Show," as well as "Tarzan," "Mr. Terrific," and "Super 6."[57]

Glamorized, flashy, and stressing heroes with panache, the spy genre supplemented military images on prime time television. Again, however, international rivalry was trivialized, reduced to a morality play between positive and negative stereotypes. In many cases such shows were burlesques, gaudy exaggerations of the real world of international intelligence operations. At a time when Americans needed solid, unbiased information with which to understand and influence national policies, television—the only truly national medium of communication—once more offered diversion from the real and frivolity in place of substance.

Militarized American society was reflected even in television commercials. An ad in the mid-1960s for a new flavor of Jello featured a trenchcoated spy calling from a phone booth. A commercial for Aerowax showed bullets bouncing off the top of a jet plane cockpit. There were public service announcements that exploited the Vietnam War specifically. One ad for the USO showed a group of weary soldiers relaxing in the jungle while a female voice sang wistfully that "The cruel war is raging, Johnny has to fight. I want to be with him from morning to night." As the woman continued, an announcer declared, "Where-ever he goes, your thanks go with USO. USO is there only if you care." Actual footage of an American helicopter crew in Vietnam was used in an advertisement for U.S. Savings Bonds. With film of the helicopter emphasizing its polished machine gun, the announcer said:

> This is Vietnam. And these are Americans on the job. The hours aren't nine to five, but they don't complain. They work for freedom, and sup-port it with their dollars, too. Seven out of ten of our men overseas buy United States Savings Bonds through the Payroll Allotment Plan. Buy Bonds where you work. They do.

Even more plentiful were militaristic commercials pitched at American children. In his study of juvenile programming, *Saturday Morning TV*, Gary H. Grossman contended that television for young-sters in the 1960s essentially avoided politicized Cold War topics.[58] However, he failed to describe the heavily politicized advertisements on Saturday morning video. These ads were especially bombastic when describing the guns, tanks, and assorted war toys available to kids. One commercial invited children to share the wartime experience with a plastic gun:

> Your patrol is in position. You're in a tough spot. But you have the amazing new Multi-Pistol 09. Fire grenade that bursts. Aim through telescopic sight. Fire bomb that blasts. And if you're trapped, surprise! Out comes your secret derringer. You have done it with Multi-Pistol 09. The only pistol that gives you all this: exploding grenades, cap-loaded bomb, fires short-range bullets, fires long-range bullets, fires message missile, anti-armor rocket, and the secret derringer cap pistol. There's never been anything like it before for action, excitement, firepower. Get it all in this rugged carrying case. Get Multi-Pistol 09! Multi-Pistol 09! Multi-Pistol 09! by Topper.

War toys were plentifully displayed throughout the decade. TV told children they could play with G.I. Joe war dolls, or breech-load, command, and fire Tiger Joe—a "gigantic" battery-powered plastic tank complete "with walkie-talkie operator, machine gunner, Tiger Joe. Rugged. Powerful. Ready for battle." Battlewagon was a large plastic ship filled with rockets, torpedoes, and the other paraphernalia of naval warfare. The ad for this toy featured a young boy screaming orders: "Fire missiles!" "Battle stations!" "All stations fire!" As a background chorus sang "Battlewagon! Battlewagon!" A sonorous male announcer interjected: "It's the mightiest warship you'll ever see," "A blinker light signals 'Enemy Approaching,' " and "Now, you can be Captain of [chorus sings] 'Battlewagon!' "

Such hard-sell commercials were not limited to war weaponry. TV also kept children abreast of the latest spy toys. Secret Sam was a multipurpose attaché case equipped with a gun that could be converted to a long-barrel rifle. It also had a periscope and a hidden camera so youngsters could "find the master spy." Even more prepossessing was Zero-M Sonic Blaster, a plastic air gun that, as announcer William Conrad explained it, was a must:

> You must not fail, Zero-M. This mission's critical. This is the most unusual weapon. It is specially designed for counterespionage. For agent Zero-M. It's called a Zero-M Sonic Blaster. This is why! It fires a massive blast of compressed air. And this tremendous roar is the actual sound. For training purposes, this special action-delayed target comes with it. Get Mattel's powerful Zero-M Sonic Blaster wherever toys are sold. Remember the password: Zero-M.

Television in the 1960s was highly politicized theater. Seldom tolerant of programs criticizing national government activities or American foreign policy, network TV turned escapism into politicization, diversion into indoctrination. From news actualities and heroic war dramas to militaristic situation comedies, romanticized tales of secret agents, and even commercials, Americans saw the world divided into two incompatible camps. There were few gray areas in this dichotomy. On the other hand, areas of compromise were not required, for those video shows told audiences continually that Americans were always right, Americans never lost, and that as selfless rescuers of the world, Americans wanted little except a pat on the back, a kiss from a pretty girl, or a child's smile.

Fed such propagandistic fare for more than a decade, viewers seldom protested—or recognized—the partisan political quality of this programming. In fact, protest was reserved almost exclusively for productions containing views not in accord with TV's traditional political outlook. Television had a history of censorship and political intolerance dating from the earliest years of the Cold War. Now, in the early years of the Vietnam War, there was no reason to expect a change of attitude by the networks or the public.

On one level the blacklists were gone by the 1960s. TV shows on occasion even dealt with the adverse effects of blacklisting upon individuals and the society that tolerated the practice. Typical was "A Claim to Immortality," an episode of the ABC series "Channing," aired February 26, 1964. "Channing" presented dramas about college life, and this episode starred Telly Savalas as a brilliant professor who rejected a major academic appointment. The professor feared that a routine background check for the new job would reveal that his wife was involved with campus Communists while a college student in the 1930s.

Even more impressive was writer Ernest Kinoy's "Blacklist," an episode of the civil libertarian series "The Defenders." Telecast January 18, 1964, this drama starred Jack Klugman as a blacklisted actor who, after ten years, received a dramatic part, only to be protested by a group of local anti-Communists. This poignant drama won Emmy awards for both Kinoy and Klugman.

And there were other signs, such as the appearance of a script by Millard Lampell, "No Hiding Place," a drama about racial bigotry and the shallowness of much white liberalism. It was televised December 2, 1963, on "East Side/West Side," a CBS dramatic series about social workers in New York City. Two years later Lampell wrote an Emmy-winning drama, "Eagle in a Cage," for "Hallmark Hall of Fame." It was televised October 20, 1965, and concerned the exile of Napoleon to St. Helena. The significance of these achievements was that Lampell himself had been blacklisted for a decade. He had been a creative writer and musical performer in the 1940s—a member of the leftist Almanac Singers folk group and author of provocative radio dramas. But because of his progressive politics he, like Napoleon, was socially ostracized. As he accepted his Emmy, Lampell received an ovation when he whimsically informed the audience of his peers, "I think I ought to mention that I was blacklisted for ten years."[59]

Nevertheless, such achievements did not signal the end of political censorship in network television. In January 1962, The Weavers were banned from a scheduled appearance on "The Jack Paar Show." NBC explained that members of the folk group would not sign a loyalty oath before appearing. Two days later ABC informed sponsor Sara Lee that it had no prime time openings for "Folksong Festival," a musical special being assembled and spotlighting The Weavers.[60] Another ABC program, "Hootenanny," banned The Weavers even before it premiered in April 1963. This prompted folk singers such as Joan Baez to refuse to perform on that show.[61] In the fall of 1963 ABC agreed to invite Pete Seeger, lead singer of The Weavers, to appear on "Hootenanny," provided he signed a sworn affidavit regarding past or present affiliations with the Communist Party or its front organizations. Seeger never appeared on "Hootenanny."[62]

There also continued to be trouble with TV drama. In January 1968, writer Rod Serling quit television. According to the originator of "The Twilight Zone" and many distinguished dramatic productions,

TV restricted too much what a writer could say. Serling was particularly discouraged by the refusal of CBS to accept for its "CBS Playhouse" what he called "a slightly pacifist" drama set in World War I.[63]

Network documentaries were also not without difficulties. To its credit, ABC aired "Cuba and Castro Today" on April 19, 1964. It was a relatively objective look at the Cuban revolution, highlighted by lengthy talks with Fidel Castro and interviews with Cuban citizens for and against the revolution. Together with a Canadian filmmaker and a Hungarian-refugee photographer, network newswoman Lisa Howard, in the words of Murray Horowitz of *Variety*, "returned TV news coverage of Cuba to where it belonged: her base was Cuba itself, not Miami."[64]

Erik Barnouw has praised "Cuba and Castro Today" for its frank questions and answers, its unique look at the Cuban leadership, and its overriding theme—as stated toward the end of the program by Senator J. William Fulbright, chairman of the Senate Foreign Relations Committee—that it might be time for a reevaluation of American policy toward Cuba, even though that might "lead to distasteful conclusions." Barnouw also pointed out that no advertiser would underwrite the program, that it was aired inconspicuously on a Sunday afternoon, and that it was preceded by an appeal by the International Rescue Committee for money to assist refugees from "Castro's tyranny."[65]

LYNDON B. JOHNSON AS TV COLD WARRIOR

The succession of Lyndon Baines Johnson to the presidency brought to power a man with mixed feelings toward television. Johnson was more cautious about the way in which he appeared on TV, yet he exploited the medium, appearing more often than any of his predecessors. Where Kennedy relished the atmosphere of spotlights, cameras, reporters competing for attention, and millions of viewers assessing his style perhaps more than his substance, LBJ lived less dangerously on TV. Since his wife had owned a station in Austin, the new president was well aware that a misstatement or a poor visual image on live TV would be disastrous to a political career. Thus, he preferred to deliver prepared comments or a special message to the nation. In his first week as president this pattern was apparent. On November 26 he was on live TV reading remarks about Kennedy's Latin American economic program, the Alliance for Progress, to representatives of the Latin American nations. The following day, before a national video audience, he delivered an address to Congress. And on November 28, he offered a Thanksgiving message to the American people.

Johnson was more cautious in approaching the open news conference, mindful of his need to remain a dignified leader in this time of national crisis, and aware that in a spontaneous press gathering he might embarrass himself and his office. Nevertheless, LBJ did not hide from the press. During his six years as chief executive, he held 126 news conferences; and during his first 22 months in office, 17 conferences were on live TV (three more appearances than by Kennedy in his 34 months in office). Still, not until February 1, 1964, his fifth meeting with the nation's journalists, did he allow the networks to televise the conference.

The president clearly preferred the structure and controllability of the staged event. It might be a formal speech to a university or business group, then excerpted for the evening news. On live TV, it could be a regular event, such as his State of the Union address to Congress, or a talk made directly to the American people. Johnson also made bill-signing ceremonies into nationally televised events. In all cases, however, LBJ and his aides were concerned about his video image. He had his face made up. He abandoned glasses for contact lenses. He used a TelePrompter—its scroll rolling before the camera lens, but invisible to viewers at home—from which he read his written speech. His media advisers worked, moreover, to lessen his Texas drawl and to curb his "cornpone, benign paternalism."[66]

Once comfortable with television as he wanted it, President Johnson was an incorrigible exploiter of the medium. In his first 22 months in office, he made 59 live appearances—more than Eisenhower in two full terms, and more than double Kennedy's complete record. Add to this figure the countless times he was photographed for the nightly news, and his many appearances during his successful campaign for election in 1964. Furthermore, compared with his two immediate predecessors, a considerably higher percentage of Johnson's video exposure was in prime time.[67]

Kennedy was a tough act to follow. Relative to the urbane JFK, the new president was slow, rural, less intelligent, and—in a TV era of anti-Southern civil rights images and "dumb, but quaint Southerner" programs like "The Beverly Hillbillies," "Petticoat Junction," "The Andy Griffith Show," and later "Gomer Pyle, U.S.M.C.," "Mayberry R.F.D.," "Green Acres," "O.K. Crackerby," and "No Time for Sergeants"—Johnson had a strong Texas accent that to many Americans marked him as a "hick."

Johnson also was not a handsome man. Compared with Kennedy's boyish good looks, LBJ was homely and grandfatherly. Even his short-tenured "court historian," Eric F. Goldman (replacing Kennedy's long-time insider-historian, Arthur M. Schlesinger, Jr.), conceded that "Television, strange instrument, has its favorites, whom it somehow shows at their best, but it also has its stepchildren, and television had certainly done nothing for this man."[68] The long face, big ears, deeply furrowed face, and thinning hair all contributed to an unattractive TV image for Johnson.

But before the camera Johnson did possess a trait not as evident in his predecessor. With Kennedy, glamour and wit sometimes undermined his attempts to appear sincere. Johnson, however, had the ability to speak from the heart, to appear and sound genuine and candid in addressing his constituency. There seemed to be true sadness in his words when, in his first televised national message, he said, "A great leader is dead; a great nation must move on. . . . let us also thank God for the years that He gave us inspiration through His servant, John F. Kennedy." And he sounded more sincere than naive when later he pledged a billion dollars for rehabilitation of the Mekong delta, if only the Viet Cong and North Vietnamese would agree to peace terms.

Under Johnson, television remained a strategic medium for the manipulation of public opinion. In news conferences he took much time at the beginning to make announcements and describe policies. This maximized his control of the meetings by cutting into the time allotted for reporters' questions. Johnson also had questions planted in his news conferences. Sympathetic reporters were told what to ask, and the president then called on them. Where Kennedy has done this with one or two questions per meeting, according to Robert MacNeil, "Johnson often tried to plant a great many. The practice rankled some members of his staff because they felt it was being overdone."[69]

Although he ran the risk of TV overexposure or upsetting the public by preempting, postponing, or interrupting popular programs, Johnson found video a means of maintaining broad support for his Vietnam policies. Discontent with the course of the war might translate into diminished approval as reported in public opinion polls. Yet a speech or news conference carried on national television usually remedied the situation and increased the size of the majority favoring the American commitment in Southeast Asia. After one address, support for the Johnson policy in Vietnam rose by 30 percent. According to the influential pollster Lou Harris, there existed a noticeable "correlation between televised presidential speeches and increased public acceptance of the President's positions."[70]

Johnson had little sensitivity toward the television industry. He often gave reporters and the networks short notice that he was ready to go on the air. While this might be slightly disconcerting for journalists, it created havoc with the networks. Johnson insisted upon beginning one address on Vietnam at 9:55 P.M., during the climactic minutes of prime-time programming. On several occasions his speeches were not carried by all networks simultaneously. In these cases network executives decided a certain address would not be significant, so it was carried by only a single network, the others offering it on a tape-delayed basis later in the evening. If he was angered by the way the networks responded to his demands for air time, according to Newton Minow, "President Johnson was quick to let broadcasters know in no uncertain terms when they displeased him."[71]

Johnson's reliance upon television to spread his influence was enhanced by the growing importance of the medium as a source of information for the American people. A Roper poll conducted in November 1963 dramatized how by this date TV had become the principal medium of news for the nation. By a rate of 36 percent to 24 percent, people found television a more believable medium of information than newspapers. Those same people found TV the least unbelievable —30 percent naming newspapers as least believable, while only 7 percent cited TV. Further, asked to choose which medium they would select if only one could be maintained, 44 percent preferred television, 28 percent named newspapers, 19 percent cited radio, and 5 percent preferred magazines.[72]

From the beginning of his presidency, LBJ spoke openly of the course he would take in Vietnam. In his first policy address, a speech to Congress delivered November 27, 1963, Johnson declared, "This nation will keep its commitments from South Vietnam to West Berlin." That meant that with 18,000 Americans presently operating in South Vietnam, the new chief executive would pursue Kennedy's goal of defeating Communism in Asia. As LBJ told a State Department audience eight days later, his intention was "to win the struggle there and bring victory to our group."

Like so many in government in the early 1960s, Lyndon Johnson had been young and powerless during those gathering years of World War II. As Nazi Germany, Fascist Italy, and imperial Japan conquered their weaker neighbors, non-Fascist countries seemed impotent to stop them. From Manchuria to Ethiopia to Austria, the dictators forcefully absorbed new territory while others offered no resistance. The climax of this policy was reached in the fall of 1938 at Munich. Here, to placate German threats of invading hapless Czechoslovakia, the four major European powers—Great Britain, France, Germany, and Italy —convened. The Czechs were not invited. Thanks primarily to Prime Minister Neville Chamberlain of Great Britain, the Nazis were ceded strategic portions of Czech territory without firing a shot.

From that experience of impotence in the face of aggression came the disdainful connotation of the political word "appeasement." From that experience, too, came a lesson for those who later fought World War II to reverse the legacy of appeasement: that never again should a militaristic nation be allowed to conquer its neighbors while on its way to world domination.

For many Americans who experienced the rise and fall of the dictatorships, the Russians after 1945 became the new would-be world conquerors, and Communism became new Nazism. Rather than recognize Communism as a legitimate response to social, economic, and political shortcomings within a nation, American leaders saw it as a monolithic extension of the Soviet Union. They argued that Communism was being exported by the Red Army and by subterfuge by foreign agents. Whatever their nationality, Communists were painted as traitorous pawns of the Russian government instead of concerned citizens struggling against the abuses of individual governments.

President Johnson—like Kennedy, Eisenhower, and Truman before him—argued that the success of revolutionary Communism was analogous to the spread of Fascism, and that failure to halt this contagion would necessitate even greater military sacrifice later. Certainly, LBJ eventually recognized different types of Communism. By October 1964 he argued that because of the power rivalry between Moscow and Peking, and because of varied Communist styles around the world, "There is no longer one Cold War. There are many. They differ in temperature, intensity, and danger." Still, the president believed that accommodation with Communist expansion was appeasement.

As early as February 29, 1964, Johnson compared his military policy in Vietnam to the Normandy invasion of 1944. Among his advisers on foreign affairs were other antiappeasers such as Secretary of State Dean Rusk and National Security Council adviser McGeorge Bundy. As LBJ wrote to his biographer Doris Kearns in 1970, "Everything I knew about history told me that if I got out of Vietnam and let Ho Chi Minh run through the streets of Saigon, then I'd be doing exactly what Chamberlain did in World War II. I'd be giving a big fat reward to aggression."[73] It mattered little that Johnson had a poor sense of history, that his comprehension of contemporary problems was inadequate if based upon the experience with Hitler. As Eric Goldman wrote, Johnson "like so many other people who do not read history, was peculiarly a creature of it, and perhaps a prisoner of one particular interpretation of it. . . . President Johnson was determined, as he once snapped, 'No more Munichs.' "[74]

LBJ shared with Kennedy many of the anti-Communist stereotypes of the day. First, he never abandoned his belief in the domino theory. In "A Conversation with the President," a one-hour special aired on the three national networks on March 15, 1964, Johnson told his interviewers—Bill Lawrence, Eric Sevareid, and David Brinkley—that if Vietnam were lost:

"I think the whole of Southeast Asia would be involved and that would involve hundreds of millions of people, and I think . . . . it cannot be ignored, we must do everything we can, we must be responsible, we must stay there and help them, and that is what we are going to do."

Second, like his predecessor, Johnson explained American military action in Vietnam as a function of largess, one country simply helping another to defend itself. "We have a very difficult situation in Vietnam," Johnson remarked at his news conference on February 29, 1964. "We are furnishing advice and counsel and training to the South Vietnam Army," he continued, "And we must rely on them for such action as is taken to defend themselves." Despite the fact that thousands of U.S. soldiers were in Southeast Asia, that his policy in that area cost $1.125 billion that year, and that Americans were killing and dying there, Johnson asserted—and most Americans believed—that this was a selfless action meant to help a friendly government requesting help. As LBJ explained it so convincingly on "A Conversation with the President":

We are very anxious to do what we can to help those people preserve their own freedom. We cherish ours and we would like to see them preserve theirs. We have furnished them with counsel and advice, and men and material to help them in their attempts to defend themselves. If people would quit attacking them we'd have no problem, but for ten years this problem has been going on. . . . but we are a patient people, and we love freedom, and we want to help others preserve it, and we are going to try to evolve the most effective and efficient plans we can to help them.

This was a grossly simplistic way to explain American intervention in a civil war in Southeast Asia. But for a people indoctrinated with idealistic, escapist entertainment in which gallant American heroes were always successful—in 30 or 60 minutes—when they risked their lives to help innocent victims of aggression, the Vietnam commitment was a chance to play the role for which television had prepared the nation.

The Vietnam War was more than Matt Dillon, Captain Midnight, or the Rat Patrollers stopping the bad guys and saving the town, nation, or planet. The war was a complex admixture of nationalism, Communism, Confucianism, Buddhism, Christianity, and ethnic affiliations. It also involved issues beyond the borders of Vietnam, among them the American containment policy toward Communism, the struggle between the Soviet Union and Communist China, the breakup of Western colonial empires, economic rivalries between individual countries and between capitalists and Communists for raw materials and markets, the political solidification of the large area that had been French Indochina, and the contest for power and prestige within the nations of the Free World. To explain American actions in Vietnam as the honest impulse of a do-gooder was inadequate and deceptive. To have communicated unquestionably this interpretation of the U.S. role in Southeast Asia—as did TV journalists and American citizens for the most part—was even less responsible.

It is self-deluding to believe that President Johnson actually felt that the struggle in Vietnam was a contest between Good and Evil. Yet he often used such simplistic rhetoric to explain his actions. At his news conference on June 2, 1964, for example, he spoke of the "four basic themes that govern our policy in Southeast Asia." According to the chief executive, these themes were: "America keeps her word"; "the issue is the future of Southeast Asia as a whole" [domino theory]; "our purpose is peace"; and "this is not just a jungle war, but a struggle for freedom on every front of human activity."

Privately, the president and his advisers knew that the Vietnam War was more than an extended version of "Combat" or "The Gallant Men." Johnson inherited and was trapped in a land conflict in Asia. To win, he concluded, his commitment would have to be increased. Withdrawal was not possible. With a presidential election approaching in the fall of 1964, and with an anti-Communist "hawk" like Senator Barry Goldwater as his conservative Republican opponent, LBJ would have been vilified as a traitor and a coward had he brought home the

American troops. As a senator, Johnson had experienced Republican attacks upon Truman and Dean Acheson for having "lost" China when the Communists took power in 1949. If anything, the Republicans were already hammering at Johnson for being "soft on Communism," and many clamored for bombing raids against the enemy in North Vietnam.

Johnson had another option. President Charles de Gaulle of France suggested that Vietnam might be unified and made politically neutral. But this was also unacceptable in Washington. To have made de Gaulle the peacemaker in Southeast Asia would have elevated Johnson's main rival within the Western world. Further, a neutral Vietnam—as suggested by the disintegration of the Laotian neutrality negotiated in 1962—might only have postponed an inevitable Communist triumph.

South Vietnam had been artificially created following the Geneva conference of 1954. Where the division between North and South Vietnam was to be temporary, the United States moved quickly to recognize and stabilize the anti-Communist Saigon government. Where elections to unify the country were to be held by 1956, the South Vietnamese and the Americans—neither a signatory of the Geneva agreement—refused to honor the commitment. Now, ten years later, Johnson had the problem of assisting a government in South Vietnam that had neither popular support nor military power. That government controlled less than half its 43 provinces. Furthermore, since the murder of the dictatorial Diem in 1963, government instability in Saigon added to Johnson's concerns.

Johnson's third alternative was to remain in Vietnam, even if that entailed increasing the size and scope of the American commitment. This was the course he chose from the outset of his presidency. But to accomplish his goal, Johnson needed sizable support at home. For an unelected, Southern-based chief executive in a nation with roots planted deeply in isolationism, such popular backing was not a foregone conclusion. LBJ and his advisers, however, were not averse to obtaining such support through the manipulation of television and the information it disseminated. This was demonstrated in the Tonkin Gulf incident and the political reaction it precipitated.

The incident was a two-phase affair, taking place over the period August 2-4, 1964. The first phase involved a Navy destroyer, the U.S.S. *Maddox*, which was shot at by North Vietnamese PT boats while in the Gulf of Tonkin on the evening of August 2. The second phase occurred two days later when the *Maddox*, now accompanied by the destroyer U.S.S. *C. Turner Joy*, reported another attack by enemy

PT boats, this time involving torpedoes launched against the American ships.

President Johnson used the incident to "get tough" in Vietnam. He ordered air strikes against four ports and an oil storage depot in North Vietnam. It was the first time the United States officially had bombed north of the seventeenth parallel. LBJ went on national television at 11:36 P.M. (EDT) on August 4 to announce the raids, to praise the bravery of the naval commanders and their crews, and to repeat again, "We still seek no wider war." Johnson also used this crisis message to announce his desire for a congressional resolution "making it clear that our government is united in its determination to take all necessary measures in support of freedom and in defense of peace in Southeast Asia." That Tonkin Gulf resolution, passed three days later by votes of 414 to 0 in the House and 88 to 2 in the Senate, became Johnson's rhetorical equivalent of a formal declaration of war. He would use the resolution many times in the future to defend himself against critics who said he was acting illegally or presumptuously in Vietnam.

In light of information made public several years after the Tonkin Gulf incident, it seems obvious that the president and his subordinates misrepresented and manipulated the naval events of August 2 and 4, and overreacted for political reasons. Two days before the first attack on the *Maddox*, American-supplied South Vietnamese boats had shelled two important North Vietnamese islands. The *Maddox* was ordered to check North Vietnamese radar and communications on those islands. On August 1 and 2, the *Maddox* approached within four miles of the attacked islands. Followed into international waters after these provocations, the *Maddox* exchanged fire with three North Vietnamese patrol boats. Fire from the destroyer and four support aircraft quickly routed the enemy, leaving one boat dead in the water while the others returned to port. The *Maddox* incurred one bullet hole.

Authorities at the Pentagon decided that the naval skirmish had been a local error by the North Vietnamese, perhaps mistaking the *Maddox* for the South Vietnamese craft that had attacked them earlier. A Defense Department spokesman publicly termed the incident "unwelcome but not especially serious." Dean Rusk seemed content that "The other side got a sting out of this. If they do it again, they'll get another sting."[75]

There is strong evidence to suggest that the second phase of the Tonkin Gulf incident was a nonevent, that no enemy boats attacked the *Maddox* and *C. Turner Joy*, and that reports of such attacks were seriously in error. The "attack" occurred on a night described by Captain John J. Herrick of the *Maddox* as "completely dark, ink dark," while the destroyers were moving through rain squalls and high seas. Earlier that day specialists had repaired the *Maddox*'s broken sonar equipment and its IFF (Identification Friend or Foe) device, which allowed the ship to identify nearby ships as friendly or otherwise. Further, both commanders were nervous about possible enemy attack in light of what had occurred on August 2.

The radar sightings that prompted the destroyers' firing were highly questionable. Given the weather conditions, the inexperience of the *Maddox*'s radar and sonar operators, the fact that no enemy was ever seen, and that the two ships nearly fired on each other in the dark, even the captain of the *Maddox* questioned his first short-wave reports of enemy attack with torpedoes in the water. Soon after reporting the "attack," Herrick radioed that his first messages were not accurate and that "many reported contacts and torpedoes fired appear doubtful." He blamed his sonarman, the weather, and the lack of visual sighting or intercepted enemy communiqués during the battle. Herrick urged "complete evaluation before any further action." This message was received at the Pentagon at 4:46 P.M. on August 4. By that time, however, the punishing American response had been set in motion. No change of mind in the Tonkin Gulf could stop it.[76]

The nonevent in the Tonkin Gulf was well suited to the president's immediate political needs. By bombing North Vietnam, he could silence Goldwater's criticism and undermine the senator's belligerent campaign appeal. The raid also buttressed the crumbling Saigon regime of General Nguyen Khanh, who had seized power in a coup seven months earlier and was now being challenged by Army rivals. Moreover, as a one-time response the bombings satisfied Johnson's desire to show Hanoi the destructive potential of an angered United States, but to avoid a prolonged, costly escalation during an election. The air strikes also demonstrated that liberals could be stern in their anti-Communism—but without seeking a wider war. This was escalation without responsibility, and it made LBJ all the more attractive to voters fearful of Goldwater's belligerence.

The Tonkin Gulf incident was a major turning point in the Vietnam War. It demonstrated America's willingness to extend its commitment from simply helping the South Vietnamese defend themselves to taking aggressive military action in North Vietnam. It also demonstrated that the United States, the richest, most advanced technological power in the world, would employ much of its mighty arsenal against a militarily fourth-rate, agrarian country. The North Vietnamese had no air force. Understandably, the retaliatory raid on August 5 destroyed half their navy of small boats.

Further, the attack against North Vietnam extended the American interpretation of the war. Until this time the war officially involved the Viet Cong—South Vietnamese revolutionaries who were Communists and were supplied through North Vietnam—and the South Vietnamese government. Now the United States signaled its intention to hold Hanoi directly responsible in the future.

Twenty-five years earlier it would have been inconceivable that President Roosevelt, although willing to involve the United States in World War II, would have done so by using his powers as commander in chief to order troops to Germany and Japan. American public opinion would never have tolerated such a usurpation of power. Loyal but strong opposition would have risen to stop the president. Even after Pearl Harbor, FDR came to Congress as prescribed by the Constitution. He asked for a declaration of war against Japan according to time-honored legal processes. And several days later, Americans entered the European theater of World War II because Germany and Italy first declared war on the United States.

But now the United States was escalating its military commitment, and few asked for a declaration of war. Congress was especially supine before the power plays of the Johnson administration. The Republican Party, the loyal opposition, was indeed loyal—but it offered no opposition. Public opinion, with what it did know of the facts, rallied behind the president.

Television was crucial in persuading the American public to accept this radical change in policies. Of course, there were precedents and extenuating circumstances. Truman in Korea and Kennedy in Vietnam had waged war without formal declarations. The United States was now the cornerstone of the Western world, and as such it had to be willing to move decisively to protect its interests. The concentration of power in the presidency—the so-called imperial presidency—rendered the legislative branch of government secondary. And, some argued, the United States needed flexibility to answer sudden military challenges with instant retaliation, unencumbered by rigid rules written in the late eighteenth century, when the country was an isolated, agricultural backwater. But it was TV that made protracted, undeclared war acceptable.

Like it or not, the medium had become fundamental to popular comprehensions of world affairs. As reading and other forms of information gathering waned among the American people, TV gained in stature as the principal medium of national communication. While television was playing an important part in enlightening the public about civil rights inequities and social poverty within the nation, it was to be expected that the medium would also spread balanced, honest information about the Cold War, and specifically about hostilities in Vietnam.

But television was a failure in this regard. Throughout its existence it interpreted foreign affairs in simplified terms. Its journalists seldom probed with sustained curiosity the nature of the East-West rivalry, the motives of the national leaders, or the American involvement in Southeast Asia. Further, the medium presented a steady diet of stylized adult fairy tales about uncomplicated virtue in combat with evil. Such ignorance and indoctrination made the American public a predictable, manipulable entity—especially when approached through its source of information on international affairs, television.

Throughout its history, moreover, executives of the TV industry continued to praise the contributions of video to world understanding and education. Calling for "an intellectual explosion, a new age of questioning, of probing, of discovery," for example, CBS president Frank M. Stanton could proclaim in 1962 that now, with "the miracle of Telstar," the first U.S. communications satellite in orbit, video "can transmit pictures, sound, and action simultaneously across the continents and oceans."[7] In this regard, too, it seemed duplicitous when Robert Sarnoff, the NBC board chairman, told a university audience a year later, "The public must recognize and consider that television's flaws and fallibilities are to a great degree a reasonable mirror of its own."[8]

Unlike the Soviet Union, where the control of information coming into the society enables state leaders to mold public opinion relatively easily, in the democratic United States, with its freer press and tradition of open inquiry, the manipulation of public opinion is a finer art. Throughout the 1950s and 1960s it depended upon conscious and unconscious cooperation among government, corporate, educational, military, industrial, labor, and communications institutions. It meant a single-mindedness in approaching the threat of Communism. It meant understanding the world and America's role in it from a common point of view. It also involved the discouragement of intellectuality when thought offended ideological sameness. It entailed ignoring dissident opinion and ostracizing independent thinkers. It meant understanding protest as potentially subversive. It meant masking economic interests behind the prose of patriotism. And it meant the accomplishment of this program through persuasion of the American public, a manipulation most effectively realized through television.

The Tonkin Gulf incident made for exciting TV. After the first attack on August 2, key Democratic and Republican legislators were briefed by State Department and White House personnel. On "Face the Nation" that day Senator Hubert H. Humphrey praised the Navy for reacting "in an admirable, creditable manner." Journalists covering others, such as senators Everett Dirksen, Richard Russell, and Thomas Kuchel, found them also sounding righteously wronged.[79]

On the evening of August 4, in response to the unsubstantiated attack that Captain Herrick was now questioning, government and TV worked in unison. Television time was requested by the White House. During prime-time hours there were promotional announcements advising that the president would be speaking later that evening. When Johnson finally did appear, he was especially somber as he announced his decision to bomb North Vietnam and requested a resolution of congressional support. When he ended his speech, saying of U.S. "firmness in the right" that "Its mission is peace," the networks switched to the Pentagon, where Secretary of Defense McNamara used maps, a pointer, and a detailed chronology to justify the retaliatory air raids.

This was dramatic TV produced by the White House. But the networks themselves followed the incident with similarly supportive, uncritical coverage. This was demonstrated in "Brink in Vietnam?," an "ABC News Reports" program televised August 6, a day before the important resolution passed Congress. From the opening, host Ron Cochran interpreted the naval incident in nationalist terms. He began by speaking of "our swift retaliation [which] has brought far greater losses to the enemy." He later employed the domino theory, remarking that "Vietnam stands like a domino between Red China and Laos, Cambodia, Thailand, and Malaysia." Cochran closed by editorializing that President Johnson's "strong and determined stand against Communist attackers has surely shown Hanoi and Peking that the United States was no paper tiger." According to him, "We have said strong words. We have backed the words with strong deeds."

There were others on the program who expressed similar notions. Senator Goldwater seemed somewhat disarmed now that LBJ could no longer be called "soft on Communism." He expressed agreement with the president's decisions, adding a simple adage, "When the bees bite you, attack the hive." Government spokesmen, however, were more manipulative. Scenes from a press conference that day showed McNamara explaining U.S. actions and raising the possibility of Communist Chinese military intervention. None questioned the authenticity of the attack upon the *Maddox* and *C. Turner Joy* when the secretary of defense confided, "I think it probable that the Communist Chinese will introduce some aircraft into North Vietnam in support of them." When asked why he felt this probable, McNamara credited intuition, noting, "I have no indication of it, but I would think that that would be a likely response. . . . As they have no combat aircraft of their own, I would assume they would make such a request and that it would be answered." McNamara only increased concern when he assured news reporters that "We have no indication that there have [sic] been any substantial movement of Communist Chinese forces, either land or air."

Equally alarming was William Bundy, the assistant secretary of state for Far Eastern affairs and the chief architect of the Tonkin Gulf resolution. He confused the actual attack of August 2 with the non-event of August 4. This avoided the necessity of explaining why re-taliation against North Vietnam waited until a second naval clash, or what really happened during the second encounter.

Throughout the program, network journalists displayed little understanding of the Communist adversary. They accepted totally what the Johnson administration was saying. No one bothered to interview Senator Wayne Morse, although he was mentioned as opposing the Tonkin Gulf resolution. When Bundy confused the two naval engagements, John Scali never asked what American warships were doing in North Vietnamese waters, or why the bombing was ordered only after the second attack, if the naval incidents were provoked by the Americans, and whether there was solid evidence to prove that the attacks at sea actually occurred.

There was bias when Charles P. Arnot described General Khanh as "South Vietnam's fighting premier," and Ron Cochran pictured Ho Chi Minh as one who "has tried to sell himself as a smiling, popular leader. But the experts consider him a ruthless dictator, bent on the conquest of all Vietnam." When this stereotype was challenged by Professor Bernard Fall, a distinguished expert on Southeast Asia and a man who had met the North Vietnamese leader only two years earlier, ABC journalists ignored the implications of their contradiction. Thus, Fall could say of Ho Chi Minh:

I would say next to Khrushchev, he's probably the most personable Communist leader. An interesting thing, the man for example doesn't picture himself as the father of his country as Mao Tse-tung does or Stalin did. He's called Uncle Ho. He's the uncle. You know in the Chinese way of looking at things uncle is surely a senior person, but not someone whom you have to obey as implicitly as your father.

ABC correspondent Keith McBee, however, never asked Fall to reconcile that assessment with Ron Cochran's anti-Communist stereotype of the North Vietnamese leader.

When Professor Zbigniew Brzezinski appeared to offer his assessment, the newsmen seemed less interested in his first point—that the incident might have resulted from a war psychosis in North Vietnam, and that the attacks upon American ships were mistakes made in panic—than in his second and third points—that this might have been an effort by Hanoi to force an American response and thereby "get the Chinese involved," or that it could have been "a premeditated action on the part of the Vietnamese and the Chinese jointly to give themselves an excuse for doing something."

The only journalist to approach the truth on this ABC news program was Howard K. Smith. He stumbled over it in his editorial comment. After describing how LBJ had emerged from his first international crisis "smelling like roses," Smith seemed bewildered over why North Vietnam would attack the U.S. Navy in international waters, where the ratio of force is "about 10 million to one which the United States possesses over Vietnam and Red China together at sea." According to Smith,

> The only logical explanation for a peanut-sized sea power assailing the world's strongest on an element where U.S. power is almost unanswerable—the ocean—is to assume that Mr. Johnson was commanding those PT boats. Since he was not, we saw him here in Washington, there is no good explanation except for Dr. Brzezinski's surmises.

The Tonkin Gulf resolution—or, as it was known officially, the Joint Resolution on Southeast Asia—was a watershed for Johnson and the war in Vietnam. It was a brief statement—only three short sections—but it gave the president carte blanche in prosecuting the war. Because the bombing raids on North Vietnam predated the resolution by three days, the resolution actually sanctioned extension of the American military initiative, even to the point of spreading the conflict to new countries. The essence of the Tonkin Gulf resolution read: "Congress approves and supports the determination of the

President as commander-in-chief to take all necessary measures to repel any armed attack against the forces of the United States and to prevent further aggression."

Also inherent in the resolution was the surrender of the American population to the will of Lyndon Johnson. Whether he acted as peace-maker or as warrior, few now questioned the chief executive. Having absorbed years of moralizing, anti-Communist television, the public could easily accept a war. Somehow Johnson's escalations in Vietnam were equatable with those inevitable reactions to immorality and wrongdoing that every hero of every video drama experienced. Just as surely as those TV champions thwarted villainy and won the gratitude of all, LBJ would win in Vietnam and leave Southeast Asia an honored man. It was a familiar scenario.

The American people approved of their leader's militancy. In the month before the Tonkin Gulf incident, 58 percent of the public was critical of Johnson's handling of the war. But 85 percent favored the retaliatory bombing of North Vietnam. A poll on August 10 showed the president's entire war policy was now approved by 72 percent of the American people. Less than three months before the presidential elections, by a margin of 71 percent to 29 percent Americans felt Johnson could conduct the war better than Goldwater. "In a single stroke," wrote pollster Lou Harris, "Mr. Johnson has, at least temporarily, turned his greatest political vulnerability in foreign policy into one of his strongest assets."[80]

With his reputation for toughness now established, LBJ could approach his presidential election campaign as one who wanted peace. Although he and his closest advisers were already drafting secret plans for a dramatic escalation of the U.S. military role in Vietnam, LBJ could be accepted as a sincere opponent of anything except an advisory role for Americans in the war. On September 25, he told an audience in Eufaula, Oklahoma, "We don't want our American boys to do the fighting for the Asian boys. We don't want to get involved in a nation with 700 million people [Communist China] and get tied down in a land war in Asia." On October 21, the president spoke at the University of Akron and pledged that "We are going to continue to try to make these people [South Vietnamese] more effective and more efficient, and do our best to resolve that situation where the aggressors will leave their neighbors alone, and they will finally learn to live together in other parts of the world." On election eve, November 2, the president spoke to a national television audience and made a thinly disguised attack upon Barry Goldwater's reputation as a quick-on-the-trigger militarist:

Let there be no mistake. There is no check or protection against error or foolhardiness by the President of the United States. He, alone, makes basic decisions which can lead us toward peace or toward mounting danger. In his hands is the power which can lay waste in hours a civilization that took a thousand years to build. In your hands is the decision to choose the man that you will entrust with this responsibility for your survival.

More dramatic in their depiction of LBJ as a peace-loving protector of civilization—and his Republican opponent as an irresponsible militarist—were two television commercials aired in September. One ad exploited Goldwater's opposition to the nuclear test-ban treaty signed in August 1963 by the United States, Great Britain, and the Soviet Union. This ad showed a little girl licking an ice cream cone while a female announcer suggested that if Goldwater were elected, that ice cream might soon be tainted by radioactive poisons.

Do you know what people used to do? They used to explode atomic bombs in the air. Now, children should have lots of vitamin A and calcium. But they shouldn't have any strontium 90 or cesium 137. These things come from atomic bombs, and they're radioactive. They can make you die. Do you know what people finally did? They got together and signed a nuclear test-ban treaty, and then the radioactive poison started to go away. But now, there's a man who wants to be President of the United States, and he doesn't like this treaty. He fought against it. He even voted against it. He wants to go on testing more bombs. His name is Barry Goldwater. And if he's elected, they might start testing all over again.

Aimed primarily at women voters and aired on NBC's "Saturday Night at the Movies" on September 12, the starkness of the message was enhanced by the feature film being telecast—"The Diary of Anne Frank," an intense study of Nazi military fanaticism and its fatal impact on a Jewish girl and her family in Amsterdam.

Before the ice-cream-cone advertisement, however, Johnson's reelection committee aired an even more impressive commercial visualizing the president's rational trustworthiness and Goldwater's perceived nuclear irrationality. Presented on September 7 during NBC's "Monday Night at the Movies"—this time showing the Biblical feature *David and Bathsheba*, and thereby lending an aura of Old Testament forewarning to the commercial—this ad showed a young girl plucking and incorrectly counting petals from a daisy while an announcer precisely counted off the seconds before a nuclear blast. Although the name of the Republican candidate was not mentioned, the anti-Goldwater message was powerfully communicated:

Child in field: 1-2-3-4-5-7-6-6-8-9-9.

Announcer (voice-over): 10-9-8-7-6-5-4-3-2-1-0.

Nuclear explosion with LBJ's voice: These are the stakes. To make a world in which all of God's children can live, or go into the dark. We must either love each other, or we must die.

Slide reading: "Vote for President Johnson on November 3."

Announcer: Vote for President Johnson on November 3rd. The stakes are too high for you to stay home.[81]

The American people chose to entrust LBJ with responsibility for their survival. He received 15,951,296 votes, 61.1 percent of the total. He gained 486 electoral votes to 52 for Goldwater. It was, to that date, the greatest plurality ever won by a presidential candidate.

The candidate of peace and firmness was inaugurated in his own right on January 20, 1965. Eighteen days later Johnson began the process of massive escalation that would take the United States fully into the Asian war he seemed so earnestly to abhor. The pretext for escalation this time was a guerrilla attack—with 8 dead and 108 wounded —on an American military billet in Pleiku, 240 miles northeast of Saigon. TV covered the story in great detail.

Actually, throughout the election campaign Johnson and his assistants had been planning a dramatic, phased increase in the U.S. military role in Vietnam. Now that he was safely elected, as Eric Goldman has written, LBJ "readied public opinion, kept up a stream of congressional conferences, and waited for the right moment."

Quickly the president ordered bombing raids against what he felt was the real culprit, North Vietnam. American jets flew 160 sorties north of the seventeenth parallel in February. The raids were justified as punishment for specific acts of Viet Cong terrorism. In April, U.S. bombers conducted 1,500 strikes against North Vietnam and 3,200 air attacks against enemy targets in South Vietnam. Now, however, the strikes were no longer explained as reactive. They were an integral part of American offensive military strategy for winning, propping up the weakening South Vietnamese military, interdicting the increased infiltration of South Vietnam by regular units of the North Vietnamese Army, and for winning a victory against Communism in Southeast Asia. Except for an occasional "pause" or "limitation," Johnson's bombing campaign against North Vietnam—code name "Operation Rolling Thunder"—would continue until October 1968.

The size and scope of the war now expanded. In response to bourgeoning U.S. military participation, the government of North Vietnam increased its flow of men and matériel to the south. Whereas an estimated 12,400 North Vietnamese soldiers had entered the war in 1964, 36,300 came south in 1965; 92,287 in 1966; and 101,263 the following year.[82] The anti-Communist side also increased; in 1965 small contingents of troops from Australia, New Zealand, South Korea, Thailand, and the Philippines joined the Americans and South Vietnamese.

Most dramatic, however, was the increase in American troop strength. Where there had been 21,000 troops in Vietnam when Johnson was elected, by June 1965 there were 75,000 men. Two months later the total was 125,000, excluding Navy personnel and support units stationed in Thailand. In July the president raised the monthly Selective Service call from 17,000 to 35,000 men. By the end of 1965 there were 184,000 troops in Vietnam—on the way to a peak of 540,000 by the time Richard M. Nixon replaced Johnson in January 1969. Before the war concluded in January 1973, it would engage 8,744,000 American military personnel.

Escalation of the Vietnam War by the president became immediately evident in a rising death toll. While there had been 246 Americans killed in Vietnam between 1961 and 1964, during the first year of full-scale conflict 1,363 Americans were slain. Before it ended, there were 58,003 U.S. troops dead and 303,704 wounded. There were, moreover, countless Vietnamese killed and wounded.

The president enjoyed lavish popular support during his first year of expanded war, his approval rate in Harris and Gallup polls fluctuating between 61 and 71 percent. Significantly, although 54 percent of the citizenry felt in October 1965 that the war would continue for a long time, only 24 percent considered it a mistake for the United States to be involved.[83]

At his televised news conference on July 28, 1965, President Johnson read a letter from a Midwestern woman. It was a short note, but it asked a profound question.

Dear Mr. President:

In my humble way I am writing to you about the crisis in Vietnam. I have a son who is now in Vietnam. My husband served in World War II. Our country was at war, but now, this time, it is just something that I don't understand. Why?

The chief executive responded to the writer with slogans. Rather than a complex, honest answer, Johnson spoke of fighting for freedom, the Chinese desire "to extend the Asiatic dominion of Communism," the lessons of "Hitler at Munich," the honor of the American "word," and the bloodbath that would follow abandonment of "those who believed in us and trusted us." It was a language of clichés and stereotypes that Americans understood. They had learned it on TV.

The journey from demobilization and peace following World War II to full-scale hostilities in Vietnam had been a long one. A people who well understood the meaning of World War II now wondered why combat in Vietnam was required. Importantly, however, they did not refuse to meet that requirement. Americans went to battle with little complaint.

Simultaneously with that political evolution, video entered American life and was overwhelmingly accepted. From it flowed news and entertainment replete with values, ideals, attitudes, fantasies, and morality. Americans soon defined themselves according to TV. They found heroes and role models on the medium. They bought because of TV, and thought according to TV. As an influence upon American social reality, video was more powerful than any other national medium of communication.

Television shaped and directed a generation of Americans to accept something as absurd as an inadequately explained, undeclared war halfway around the globe, costing billions of dollars each year, losing thousands of young lives monthly, and ultimately wrenching the moral fiber of American civilization. The war was justified because it was familiar. The images transmitted over all those years offered explanation enough. Americans could answer that quizzical Midwestern mother, for they all had the TV experience of Good versus Evil, freedom against slavery, and moral, manly honor in mortal struggle with the forces of wickedness. A shared common conductor, video spread its monotonous political message and educated the nation. That it was effective was obvious in the reality of the war in Vietnam.

EPILOGUE: TOWARD A
MORE RESPONSIBLE MEDIUM

In his study of the inner workings of the TV industry, Robert MacNeil discussed the failure of the networks to develop commentary in their newscasts. In his view, commercial television was fearful of boring audiences with a "talking head" for two continuous minutes, and it was anxious not to alienate viewers who might disagree with opinions expressed. Above all, MacNeil contended, "Television does not want people to be angry." While "occasional squints of opinion do penetrate the blandness," he reiterated that "what television abhors is controversy."[1]

But the networks did present opinion. In all genres of TV programming there was always an implicit or explicit point of view. And years of exposure to such representation explains in great part the uncritical public acceptance of the Vietnam War. Without controversy, millions of Americans fought in a war that few of them ever fully understood. For a people priding itself on self-reliance and independence from government control, millions gave themselves to the state without question. For a nation free to think and say what it wanted, few thought or said differently from their political leaders. Those who did react differently often faced harassment or ostracism.

Persuaded? conditioned? manipulated? indoctrinated? brainwashed? Whatever the reality, primarily through video Americans learned of themselves and their role in the world. If the information communicated for decades via TV was inaccurate or biased or insufficient, it was ultimately the shortcoming of those who operated the medium.

What MacNeil should have stressed was not the absence of commentary, but the failure of television to promote a range of opinion that challenged conformity and offered alternative interpretations, that broadcast ideas questioning stereotypes and establishing a variety of perspectives from which to understand the United States and the world. As operators of the people's airways, the networks were pledged to provide audiences nothing less. As a free people seeking information with which to make wise decisions, the citizenry had the right to expect as much.

Importantly, however, in the mid-1960s there emerged in commercial television a critical mentality that would lead the medium and the nation to a more independent attitude in assessing the direction of life in the United States. While not a fully developed spectrum of opinion, it was a mentality capable of seeing through hollow rhetoric and of presenting more honest appraisal. This development was the product of two distinct sources: the critique of government and society that emerged with the civil rights movement, and the coverage of antiwar critics whose popular support and/or national prestige commanded objective consideration.

For many Americans the civil rights movement was a TV program.[2] Although its roots were deep in American history, its modern embodiment took shape in the mid-1950s and matured on television in the first years of the following decade. Its most renowned personality was the Reverend Martin Luther King, Jr., a handsome, well-educated, eloquent, and idealistic young man. Significantly, King was also telegenic. As early as 1955, when he led a boycott of city buses in Montgomery, Alabama, this Baptist preacher was on national TV articulating his values. By the early 1960s video made King and the civil rights movement practically synonymous.

In covering the vicissitudes of the black protest, American television inevitably reported glaring ironies: poverty in the richest nation on earth, discrimination and segregation in a land of free people, nonviolent black protest to obtain rights taken for granted by white citizens. Out of this situation came fearless TV journalism. To report on school integration, sit-ins, and freedom rides, network correspondents risked bodily injury. Neither TV journalists nor viewers could overlook the inequities they encountered as agents of local and state governments obstructed enforcement of the law; as police turned dogs and fire hoses on chanting marchers; as electrified cattle prods were used to control protesters; as screaming bigots threatened blacks wanting to enter schools and universities; and as firebombings of protesters' churches and homes, and the murder of black children and civil rights leaders, raised irresistible questions about the realities of American civilization.

Television did not create the civil rights movement. But video coverage of the complexities of the movement turned regional protest into national crusade. In documentaries, newscasts, and increasingly in entertainment programs, TV compelled Americans to understand the goals of the movement and to reach informed decisions on the future direction of national life. In this way, television catalyzed a national debate, the end result of which was a fundamental reevaluation of policies and moral attitudes.

The civil rights movement was also a learning experience for television. It set a precedent in social criticism. Video suggested there was something terribly wrong with society, and forthright exposure created mounting pressure to remedy the problem. While the precedent was not yet recognizable in coverage of policies in Southeast Asia, the medium was not without important critical potential as the war escalated in the mid-1960s.

TV treatment of organized protest against the Vietnam War contributed to the medium's maturing sensibilities. At first antiwar protesters received scant coverage. Small bands of progressive students on college campuses seldom attracted TV cameras. Even the May 2 Movement (M2M), a product of the police suppression of antiwar demonstrations in New York City in 1964, received no national attention, in part because the M2M was organized by the Maoist-inspired Progressive Labor Party. And the small Students for a Democratic Society (SDS), with 29 chapters and 1,000 members in June 1964, received no TV coverage when it criticized the war in Southeast Asia. As Todd Gitlin noted in his perceptive analysis, *The Whole World Is Watching*, in mid-1964 "SDS did not perform photogenically; it did not mobilize large numbers of people; it did not undertake flamboyant actions. It was not, in a word, newsworthy."[3]

By the end of the year, however, matters had changed, and student protests became acceptably newsworthy. Thousands of university students had spent the summer of 1964 working in the South to register blacks to vote. This "Mississippi Summer" had elements irresistible to television: middle-class white youths assisting exploited blacks, dangerous threats from local white intransigents, and the scenario of a "children's crusade" that turned to tragedy with the murder in Mississippi of three civil rights workers by the Ku Klux Klan.

That fall, moreover, the Free Speech Movement at the University of California at Berkeley commanded national TV coverage. Here, with angry demonstrations and that creative educational alternative, the university "teach-in," network television perforce treated the anti-war attitudes of student activists.

Throughout 1965, the year of massive escalation in Vietnam, TV continued to focus on student protests. It was definitely not sympathetic coverage. In the first months of patriotic swell, TV correspondents tended to trivialize or otherwise disparage the significance of such demonstrations. They also added "balance" to their coverage by identifying Communists among the students, by emphasizing symbols (North Vietnamese flags) and actions (violence) at such protests, and by giving government officials time to denounce such un-patriotic activities.[4] The critical, institutional attitude of TV toward antiwar protesters was epitomized by NBC newsman Dean Brelis on "Projection '66," televised December 26, 1965.

> The one thing that all American troops in the field say repeatedly is, "What about these demonstrators? Why are they doing this?" They're hurt by it. And they feel that it is a profound form of betrayal of them, because they feel in truth that, "Fine! O.K. Let these people demonstrate. But when they take on the role of calling up their families here in the United States, and telling their families that the people in Vietnam are in error for fighting, then these people are hitting below the belt."
>
> And the other thing that the Americans in Vietnam feel about this protest is this: they say, "Why don't these people mention that the Viet Cong in North Vietnam, when it came to killing the two American prisoners of war, they killed them without any trial."
>
> I for one feel—as a personal, human being involved—that the demonstrations are unfortunate, but perhaps they indicate what kind of a country we are because there is demonstration. It would be better not to have demonstration. But I think that the people themselves who demonstrate, demonstrate irrationally.

Importantly, both Brelis and John Rich on the same program agreed that the North Vietnamese and the Chinese were exploiting American domestic protest in hopes, according to Rich, "that they may be able to win a victory in the United States that has been denied them on the battlefield in Vietnam." In this manner, demonstrators were explained as aiding and abetting the enemy. Nonetheless, TV coverage was publicity, and no matter how negatively demonstrators were displayed, video exposure expanded popular awareness of domestic opposition to the war. Now, as television confronted the antiwar movement, new, less stereotypical views emerged. This was noticable, for example, in the assessment of veteran journalist Edward P. Morgan on "Year in, Year out," the annual news summary on ABC aired December 26, 1965.

> Lou Cioffi: The GIs in Vietnam ... have been made furious and depressed by the peace marches, the peace protests, end the war in Vietnam. If they should spread, if they should become more common, more violent, the GIs who are fighting and dying in Vietnam are going to start wondering what in the world they're fighting and dying for.

> Edward P. Morgan: The demonstrations, I suspect, will spread. It is too glib to believe that they are generated entirely by kooks and/or Communists. Both elements are in them. Both elements in some instances have aspects of leadership. But the bulk of this protest— is what I would call a thoughtful one. It includes not only the new radicals on the campus, it includes middle-aged, middle-income people with children who have one thing in common, a hatred of war.

> Ned Calmer: Well, these people ought to be a lot more constructive than they have been. They ought to direct their protests not only to the American government, but to the governments in Hanoi and Peking and in Moscow, even if it doesn't do any good. I think that'd be heartening to the people in Vietnam that Cioffi was talking about and also the people all over the world.

> John Scali: Ned, it's important that we keep in perspective just how much a minority movement the peace marchers represent. It's important to remember that all polls and surveys show that more than 70 percent of the American people support the President on Vietnam. And this 70 percent includes many intellectuals and many people who are capable of independent thought.

> Edward P. Morgan: This is true. But sadly I predict, John, that that support will erode as the casualty lists increase.

Reconsideration of U.S. foreign policy also emerged among network newsmen assigned to foreign, especially European, capitals. Abroad, where heads of state and public opinion frequently attacked Johnson's escalatory actions, a few American reporters evidenced early disenchantment with the Vietnam War. Such attitudes ranged from a general cynicism to outright condemnation.

Joseph C. Harsch for many years had been the NBC diplomatic correspondent stationed in London. After a year of escalation, he was less than supportive as he delineated official attitudes on the war. Speaking on "Projection '66," Harsch seemed cynical when he contended that the "government in Washington does not truly know how it did get sucked into a minor war in Vietnam which gets bigger day by day, or how to get out of it." He argued that officials feared a pullout would enhance Communist Chinese prestige. He spoke of the domino theory and the national-honor argument. He also mentioned "a small but vigorous minority of policymakers, mostly at the Pentagon and CIA, which believes that we are going to have a war with Communist China someday. So, why not use the Vietnam War as the occasion for getting on with it." The policy of escalating while bolstering weak governments in Saigon, according to Harsch, could create domestic impatience within the United States. This in turn, he argued, "could force the government into continuing escalation, until we were at war, certainly with Communist China, and in the end perhaps even with Russia."

More openly hostile to the American policy in Southeast Asia was John Rolfson, the ABC newsman stationed in Paris. Exposed to the rhetoric of Charles de Gaulle and French opposition to the war, Rolfson on "Year in, Year out," in December 1965, called for the removal of U.S. troops from Vietnam. Citing the views of "a big majority" in France, Rolfson noted that "The overwhelming fact to them is that we are intervening in an internal revolution, running a puppet government that has no popular support." But he interjected his own opinions when he continued:

And that means being bogged down permanently in a hopeless war that's constantly in danger of escalating. And the alternative is the magnanimous gesture: to pull out. It's the one offer that can bring the enemy to talks, and also can get the rest of the world to help us there, to take some responsibility. And I don't think we have to worry anymore about loss of face, or loss of confidence. The whole world knows we have the power to destroy anything we want. We've proved that we can wipe that country off the map if we want to, but I don't think that means we've got to do it to have a consistent policy.

Neither Harsch's cynicism nor Rolfson's call for complete withdrawal was an opinion shared in 1965 by other correspondents in the year-end news summaries. Rolfson, for example, was ridiculed by Bill Lawrence. "Magnanimous gesture!" he retorted sarcastically. "It sounds to me more like an invitation to sign our own death warrant." John Scali argued that a withdrawal now "would be perhaps the biggest disaster of the century for the Free World." Lou Cioffi contended, "We cannot withdraw." His formula for the future was simple: "Maintain our troops there as long as possible; avoid negotiations, if you will, that could pull troops out; and during this period hold the country militarily long enough to create some kind of a government around which the Vietnamese people could rally."

Still another situation in which TV journalists tested past slogans and found them inadequate involved American military intervention in the Dominican Republic in the spring of 1965. A crisis in Dominican politics developed when conservative and military leaders resisted rebel efforts to reinstall Juan Bosch as president of the country. Two years earlier a military coup had deposed Bosch, the duly elected head of state. Now, in April 1965, Bosch supporters—mostly from the left and including Dominican Communists—sought his restoration.

At the height of his power and enjoying overwhelming popular support, LBJ dispatched 21,000 Marines to the West Indies nation, ostensibly to protect American lives and property but also to prevent "another Cuba." The president was on television twice in the midst of the crisis to explain his decisions. On April 30, he said U.S. troops were being used to evacuate American citizens and other foreign nationals. He added, "There are signs that people trained outside the Dominican Republic are seeking to gain control."

In a fuller explanation of his decision, on May 2, Johnson again spoke to the nation. The speech was filled with Cold War phrases about "the forces of tyranny," "Communist conspirators," "another Cuba in this hemisphere," and "those who fight only for liberty and justice and progress." This time the president used more visceral imagery, falsely quoting a dispatch from the American ambassador in Santo Domingo as saying, "Mr. President, if you do not send forces immediately, men and women—Americans and those of other lands—will die in the streets."[5]

Used to reporting frankly on dictatorships and the crushing of democracy, the network newsmen in Latin America almost unanimously clashed with the interpretations from the White House. When the government declared it operated with "impartiality" to save American lives, Don Farmer on ABC reported, "It's been obvious for some time that nationalist Dominican troops are using American forces to help defeat the rebels." Tom Streithorst on "The Huntley-Brinkley Report" told of American soldiers firing on Bosch supporters "who hadn't fired first." Other correspondents, such as Richard Valeriani, Bert Quint, and Lew Wood, broadcast reports that similarly belied official explanations in Washington.[6]

The Dominican experience left a lasting mark on network TV news. *Variety* called it a "refreshing show of independence . . . by the network news departments vis-à-vis the Washington officialese" and "an uncommon depth of journalistic judgment" by a medium "often accused, and often justifiably, of winging with the Administration 'party line'. . . ."[7] The experience also created division within the network news operations; for example, the clash between the idealist Bert Quint and the more experienced Eric Sevareid on a CBS special, "Santo Domingo: Why Are We There?," telecast May 31. Quint argued that the intervention increased hatred of the United States in Latin America, that the Johnson administration had not yet proven Communists controlled the Bosch rebellion, and that Washington repeatedly lied to newsmen. Sevareid responded that if Johnson was willing to fight Communists in Vietnam, he surely could be expected to do so in the West Indies, and that tough decisions like this were part of the agony of being a great power.[8]

Months later, on "Year in, Year out," similar divisiveness was noticeable among ABC journalists. Here the discussants were the correspondent for Latin America, Merwyn Sigale, and John Scali, the diplomatic correspondent. Sigale was blunt:

> Our intervention was wrong and should never have happened. It created a lot of anti-American feeling in a country that had been basically friendly to the United States. . . . it shook the inter-American system to its very foundations. I think that intervention was based on faulty intelligence that confused a popular uprising with a Communist coup. And I think it was also based on inept diplomacy in which our embassy bungled an opportunity to mediate in the very early days of the crisis.

Scali, however, clung to the rationalization sketched by LBJ in his speech of May 2. Eight months later, Scali still spoke of a "pro-Castro-style government" had LBJ not acted when he did. He argued that "pro-democratic" leaders had abandoned the rebellion and left the field to "Communist toughs and hoods in the streets." He lauded the president for having reacted quickly and decisively.

The Dominican intervention was significant not just as a learning experience for network newsmen. As Alexander Kendrick, formerly of CBS, has indicated, for Senator J. William Fulbright "It began his disillusionment with the Johnson administration and the war policy."[9]

Except for the independent-minded Wayne Morse of Oregon and Ernest Gruening of Alaska, no other senators or congressmen voted against the Tonkin Gulf resolution. A year later there were doubters, but outspoken opposition on Capitol Hill had not increased appreciably. The defection of Fulbright in late 1965 was a major blow to the president's military policy. A fellow Democrat and Southerner, Fulbright of Arkansas was also chairman of the powerful Senate Foreign Relations Committee. He had shepherded the Tonkin Gulf resolution through the Senate. He was also a close friend of LBJ. His opposition lent great prestige and credibility to those protesting the war. It also created another situation in which network newsmen took steps toward a more balanced, critical perspective in reporting government activities.

Through live television coverage of his committee's hearings into a relatively minor foreign aid bill, Fulbright in January and February 1966 precipitated the national Vietnam War debate that government never wanted and broadcast journalists had avoided. Before the committee came leading administration "hawks" like Dean Rusk and General Maxwell D. Taylor, ambassador to Saigon since 1964. But Fulbright also invited prominent "doves" and critics like retired General James Gavin and George F. Kennan. While the committee had its own blend of prowar and antiwar advocates, the hearings were clearly dominated by senators critical of the war and experts testifying against escalation.

General Gavin, a hero of World War II, in which he had headed the 82nd Airborne Division, blasted the inefficiency of Johnson's escalatory policy. He called for a more defensive approach to the war through the establishment and defense of strategic enclaves along the Vietnamese coast. Gavin was especially caustic when he told the senators that administration leaders were wrong in their calculations about manpower and money needed to win in Vietnam. "If I were a businessman looking at a potential market and found such miscalculations," he remarked, "I would have to do something about it. I couldn't long survive."[10]

In sometimes heated dialogue with administration witnesses, Senator Morse was, as Roger Mudd of CBS described him, "indefatigible; imperviously, startlingly blunt; abrasive." In a particularly confrontational exchange with General Taylor, Morse cut though the rhetoric to make his point:

Morse: Now, we're engaged in an historic debate in this country—our honest differences of opinion. I happen to hold with the point of view that it isn't going to be too long before the American people, as a people, will repudiate our war in Southeast Asia.

Taylor: That, of course, is good news to Hanoi, senator.

Morse: Oh, I know that that's the smear artist that you militarists give to those of us that have honest differences of opinion with you. But I don't intend to get down in the gutter with you and engage in that kind of debate, General. All I'm asking is, if the people decide that this war should be stopped in Southeast Asia, are you going to take the position: that's weakness on the homefront in a democracy?

Taylor: I would feel that our people were badly misguided, and did not understand the consequences of such a disaster.

Morse: Well, we agree on one thing, that they can be badly misguided. And you and the President, in my judgment, have been misguiding them for a long time in this war.

As an intellectual and diplomat, George F. Kennan was a formidable critic of Johnson's war policies. University professor, former ambassador to Yugoslavia and the Soviet Union, Kennan had written in 1947 the seminal essay on containment that enunciated the idea of containing Russia within present boundaries to prevent the spread of Communism. Thus, it was a strong indictment of American ignorance and arrogance in Southeast Asia when Kennan exchanged ideas with Senator Fulbright on the impossibility of winning in Vietnam.

Fulbright: I take it by this you mean that this is simply not a practicable objective, as I understand it, in this country. We can't achieve it, even with the best of will.

Kennan: This is correct. And I have a fear that our thinking about this whole problem is still affected by some sort of illusions about invincibility on our part. That there is no problem, a feeling that there is no problem in the world which we—if we wanted to devote enough of our resources to it—could not solve. I disbelieve in this most profoundly. I do not think that we can order the political realities of areas in a great many other parts of the world.

Television coverage of the hearings was not an unqualified success. All networks missed Dean Rusk's heated testimony on the first day,

January 28. They offered a few minutes of summary on the evening news. When the hearings resumed on February 4, however, CBS and NBC carried the proceedings live while ABC settled for three "bulletin" summaries. NBC and ABC carried the remaining four days live. But CBS raised a professional uproar when it canceled George F. Kennan's testimony on February 10. Instead, it showed, as scheduled, reruns of "I Love Lucy" (the fifth showing), "The Real McCoys" (the eighth airing), and "The Andy Griffith Show." The executive decision not to telecast the hearings saved CBS $175,000 in advertising revenue. But it cost the network considerable prestige and one of its greatest journalists, as Fred W. Friendly resigned in protest of the shortsightedness of his corporate superiors.[11]

Further, President Johnson tried with some success to overshadow the Fulbright hearings. On February 5 he flew to Honolulu for a surprise three-day conference with leaders of the Saigon government—among them Nguyen Van Thieu and Nguyen Cao Ky. There was much talk about the solidarity of the United States and South Vietnam in the struggle against aggression and social destruction in South Vietnam. There was also extensive television exposure for LBJ. When he returned to the mainland, moreover, network cameras were in Los Angeles, where he stopped long enough to praise the meeting. And his arrival in Washington on February 9 was covered live by network video.

However imperfect or compromised the coverage, the networks did broadcast much of the Foreign Relations Committee hearings live. Evening news programs and special summaries presented edited highlights of the testimonies. In the midst of a war, with the chief executive still enjoying massive national support for his military policies, it was a mark of the maturation of television journalism—due particularly to the broadcast journalists who fought management to obtain coverage—that the medium broadcast lengthy, profound criticism of the Vietnam War. Sentator Fulbright seemed pleased with the results. According to him, "The televising of our committee hearings gave them a great deal more impact and a lot more educational value. I think it was a real public service."[12]

The hearings also raised further doubts about video journalists and their function in a society at war. Television was crucial to the American people. As William R. McAndrew, president of NBC News wrote in mid-1966, network TV was now "the primary source of all information on all facets of the struggle in Vietnam—military, political, economic."[13] Indeed, years before, it had become, statistically, the

principal news medium in American life. But it was beginning to pon-
der its interpretative silence in the face of rising public and government
protest. There was, of course, the example of integrity established by
Fred W. Friendly. His departure severed CBS and TV journalism from
the last direct link with the legacy of Edward R. Murrow. But among
those who stayed in the profession, questions arose. Following a summation of the Fulbright hearings on "Vietnam Perspective: The Senate Hearings and the War," televised February 18, Eric Sevareid pondered this "debate between men who question power." The contest
between ideas, he suggested, "has come late in the day. It should
have come at least a year ago, because the argument is not merely on
how to win the war or how to negotiate peace, it questions the very
reasons for our presence in Vietnam."

In a thoughtful article in *Variety* in January 1966, former CBS
foreign correspondent David Schoenbrun discussed the failure of
American television, as well as other media, to present a comprehensive interpretation of the war. "The great radio-television networks
have given considerable time and effort in reporting the war," noted
Schoenbrun, "but mainly in its pictorial aspects and with much cir-
cumspection and discretion about discussing the gut issues." Above
all, he continued, the problem was that the reporters were being asked
to cover a war that was not officially declared, a war in which "there
are no rules other than the conscience of each reporter and editor
and the fortitude with which he can resist pressures to accept wartime rules without a war officially existing."

This presented a dilemma: on the one hand, the inclination to
close ranks because American soldiers were fighting and dying; on
the other, the temptation to report as fully as possible, even if it
caused upset or prolonged the war. Still, in this period of incubating
professional debate within TV news, Schoenbrun reminded his colleagues, "Close ranks, yes, but to close ranks does not mean to close
our minds."[14]

Nowhere was the tension between closed ranks and closed minds
more pronounced than among those television journalists assigned to
South Vietnam. Here, where news personnel met and befriended
American troops and command personnel, there were pressures to report what the government wanted reported and as favorably as the
government wished. Still, there were professional and personal inclinations that directed journalists toward reporting the entire Vietnam story, even if it offended viewers, government officials, and network executives.

In Vietnam, reporters confronted many problems. There were, of course, predictable hardships due to the brutality of war. Being captured, wounded or killed was always a possibility. Many reporters suffered such fates. There were also technical problems. As Charles Arnot of ABC suggested, covering the war was 90 percent logistics and 10 percent journalism. This meant not only concern about the story, but worry about meeting flight schedules. It also entailed problems getting to, and especially from, the battle front. Further, there were inconveniences of climate, and boredom.[15]

Network correspondents endured pressure in Vietnam and from home when their reports ran counter to the upbeat picture projected by U.S. government officials. But with escalation of the war in 1965, it became increasingly difficult to resist controversial news. The networks bolstered their staffs in Vietnam. By mid-1965, NBC had 22 news professionals covering the war. This represented the largest concentration of network personnel in one foreign country since World War II. CBS and ABC assigned a smaller but enhanced number of newsmen and newswomen.[16]

The buildup of network journalists made it more difficult for the military and the White House to manage reporters. But they tried. Press briefings by the military in Saigon were derisively called the "Five o'Clock Follies" by reporters. These were no-comment sessions in which Pentagon press officers passed out government statistics and presented explanations favorable to the American war effort. Walter Cronkite, who first visited Vietnam in mid-1965, later described "the skepticism of the reporters at the press conferences in Saigon." According to the CBS anchorman, "They were accepting nothing at the five o'clock follies. More than seeking information, they were indulging in what I considered self-centered bearbaiting, pleasing their own egos, showing how much they knew."[17]

Beyond Saigon there was also news management by the Pentagon. In February 1971, in the powerful CBS exposé of the self-promotion practices of the American military establishment, "The Selling of the Pentagon," narrator Roger Mudd described the U.S. Army's Hometown News Center in Kansas City. From this office, he contended, "a blizzard of press releases is turned out in all seasons." Annually, 12,000 radio and TV tapes were mailed from the center to 2,700 radio stations and 546 television outlets. More than 6,500 daily and weekly local newspapers received over 2 million printed releases. While the thrust of such materials was news about promotions, awards, and achievements of community residents, Mudd noted, "The News Center also functions as a publicity agency for American forces abroad. The only news from the Center is good news."

In "The Selling of the Pentagon," moreover, a former military cameraman described the manner in which he staged events, beautified situations, and edited film to get propagandistic images for American television. And a military information officer revealed how he prese-lected interviewees for looks, coached them on "a one-voice concept," and otherwise prepared them for a visiting CBS news crew doing a report on the air war in North Vietnam. After the finished product aired on American television, the military press officer concluded, "Frankly, it was just great! . . . It was as good as if we had done it our-selves." In concluding, he conceded the preeminence of the military's management of information in Southeast Asia:

> I feel that the military information arm is so vast, has been able to be-come so pervasive by the variety and the amounts and the way and the sheer numbers, it's able to present its viewpoint to the American people. I think that this attitude that it was able to develop allowed Vietnam to happen. Had we not been able to convince the American people prior to Vietnam that a military solution was a correct solution, without a doubt and not to be questioned, that we couldn't have had a Vietnam.

Whenever a TV journalist produced a report the Pentagon or White House did not like, he was roundly criticized. To make field com-manders aware of what the correspondents were saying on U.S. tele-vision, the Pentagon compiled kinescopes of network war reportage and sent them weekly to Vietnam for study. Thus, when CBS report-ers Peter Fromson in Vietnam and Martin Agronsky in Washington aired reports that were accurate, but embarrassing to the official mili-tary effort, in February 1966, government representatives berated the networks and publicly denounced the stories as "highly inaccur-ate."[18] Robert MacNeil has written of how "on many occasions" White House officials complained to NBC News about its reportage. Whether a complaint was rejected, disclosed MacNeil, "depends very much on the individual who is approached in the network and how senior is the official making the approach from the White House."[19]

The most renowned instance of TV coverage upsetting to the Pen-tagon was a report filed by Morley Safer on the "CBS Evening News with Walter Cronkite" on August 5, 1965. Safer showed U.S. Marines using cigarette lighters to torch thatched huts in the village of Cam Ne. The image of old South Vietnamese running away while their American protectors mechanically burned their homes and meager possessions made for controversial TV. According to Alexander Kendrick, these images on the video screen "undid six months of . . . briefings and offical handouts."[20] And Safer's accompanying audio description intensified the visual impact. In language reminiscent of Murrow in Korea, Safer remarked:

> The day's operation . . . netted those four prisoners. Four old men who could not answer questions put to them in English. Four old men who had no idea what an I.D. card was. Today's operation is the frustration of Vietnam in miniature. There is little doubt that American firepower can win a victory here. But to a Vietnamese peasant whose home means a lifetime of back-breaking labor, it will take more than presidential promises to convince him that we are on his side.[21]

Government reaction to Safer was quick and heavy-handed. The president saw the report and ordered a background check on the CBS newsman. The investigation revealed that Safer was not a Communist, but that he was a Canadian. For years government officials used his nationality to impugn Safer's objectivity. For instance, Arthur Sylvester, the assistant secretary of defense for public affairs, told CBS News executives that Safer was a "cheap Canadian." He wondered, "Maybe a Canadian has no interest in our efforts in Vietnam and no realization that the Vietnam conflict is not World War II or Korea, but a new type of political, economic, military action."[22] As Fred W. Friendly at the time described it, "The vilification of Morley Safer by people high in government and in the Pentagon has been a case of assassination by words."[23]

As TV journalists came increasingly into contact with the aggressive military policies of the U.S. government, they inevitably began to exercise a more independent judgment. No longer willing to see the world through the eyes of the White House and the Pentagon, a small number of journalists in the mid-1960s began to report more critically on what they experienced. Writing in mid-1965 about "the maturing of electronic news," Jack Pitman in *Variety* praised this "emergence lately of independent reportorial judgments that in the past were a rarity."[24]

Skepticism, however, was not a contagion among broadcast journalists in Vietnam. Charges of "no-guts journalism" continued to be hurled at video correspondents, especially by print newsmen. For many newspaper and magazine writers, TV coverage of Vietnam was filled with courage in gathering pictures, but it lacked interpretative depth. By early 1966, John Gregory Dunne in *The New Republic* dismissed all documentaries on Vietnam as "a puff of nothing." Hal

Humphrey of the *Los Angeles Times* complained about television's imbalance, where reporters were not allowed to editorialize or offer interpretive remarks, but "how frequently Washington has had unmolested opportunities to air its views." Most effectively, critic Brock Brower in *Life* complained that despite the heroics of reporters and cameramen, "Difficult war aims and delicate policies are simply not rendered any clearer. . . ." And, he noted, "For all their courage and 'toughness' the TV correspondents have not been able to extract much sense from their string of stark vignettes."[25]

Nonetheless, the national debate commenced in the Fulbright committee hearings was not dead in TV. Television did offer more diversity in its war coverage. Certainly, the government still exercised powerful influence over the medium. Johnson still requisitioned free network time, and he held frequent news conferences in which he stated his opinions. And other administration spokesmen—from White House advisers to General William C. Westmoreland, commander of U.S. forces in Vietnam—appeared regularly on TV to explain how matters were progressing. Secretaries Rusk and McNamara were especially accessible and effective when interviewed on shows like "Meet the Press," "Face the Nation," and "Issues and Answers." They also contributed to many documentaries and made countless short statements for evening newscasts.

Further, as the networks developed actuality series dealing specifically with the war, administration representatives were always invited to participate. And often they were given considerably more time than antiwar critics. In late 1965, ABC devoted its prestigious—if not widely televised[26]—"ABC Scope" exclusively to the war in Southeast Asia. This network commitment lasted until January 1968—107 half-hour programs later. Several ABC newsmen anchored the programs, but especially when the hawkish Howard K. Smith handled the feature, "ABC Scope" demonstrated a discernibly sympathetic bent toward the Johnson administration. Typically, on the broadcast of July 16, 1966, Smith attacked American intellectuals opposed to the war. "They feel guilty," he surmised. "They can stand it only if they periodically curse themselves, strive to be weak, declare their rich nation to be mankind's enemy, demand that it yield, simply because the foe happens to be poor—whether he's aggressive or not doesn't seem to matter."[27]

"Vietnam Perspective" was conceived by CBS as a forum in which to debate the issues of the Vietnam War. But from its beginnings in August 1965, the series was more a vehicle for well-prepared White

House spokesmen to justify the conflict in Asia. By early 1967, critic Michael J. Arlen could criticize one "Vietnam Perspective" presentation, "Air War in the North," as "an allegedly serious examination" that was actually "childish and unaware and fundamentally chicken [as] a piece of journalism." As Arlen described the program, it failed to deliver the critical balance originally intended for the series: "CBS took one of the most controversial and important political-emotional issues of the moment, made a few brief stammers at 'objectivity,' presented government propaganda for fifty minutes, then gave us some hurried, underweighted glimpses at the 'opposition' for a final five minutes, and that was it."[28]

In his critique of "no-guts journalism," Brock Brower wrote of the documentaries and news reports projecting war as hell—but as a challenge Americans were heartily meeting. "Their footage *in toto* runs together as an appalling record of surprise and death," wrote Brower, "Its only coherence being the Kilroyesque figure of the groggy GI slogging through the unfriendly terrain of any war, calmly convinced that he is getting a job done, the sooner the better."[29] There were many such images in network documentaries. Typical was "Same Mud, Same Blood" an "NBC News Special" on December 1, 1967, supposedly about black American soldiers in Vietnam, Instead of asking profound questions about the black struggle for freedom in Vietnam and Watts, or the high proportion of blacks on the front lines relative to their percentage in the American population, the program became an uplifting lesson where black and white together fought an Oriental enemy whose designs made brothers at last of Caucasian and Negro.[30]

Another familiar theme for the networks was Communist China. As the United States intensified and expanded its bombing in North Vietnam, TV speculated about possible Chinese entry into the war. The theme was probed in "CBS News Special: Inside Red China," broadcast November 22, 1966. CBS aired "Morley Safer's Red China Diary" on August 15, 1967. On January 15 and 30, 1967, NBC presented a two-part documentary, "The China Crisis." On April 27, 1966, ABC News offered "Red China: The Year of the Gun?" Here, where American journalists were forbidden to travel by order of the U.S. State Department and the Peking government—Safer entered the country on a Canadian visa—the anti-Communist stereotype endured. Thus, John Scali could conclude "Red China: The Year of the Gun?" with speculation about "Mao Tse-tung's blueprint for expanding Chinese power." He spoke of the 20,000 Chinese troops now in North

Vietnam manning anti-aircraft batteries and guarding the railroad route between Peking and Hanoi. He concluded:

> There is every prospect 1966 will become a year of confronting Chinese military power in North Vietnam as our bombers step up their attacks against targets there. We can and we will meet this threat. But inevitably we will kill Chinese, taking us another step closer to the larger war we wish to avoid. The question thus arises, if we intend to pursue the war in Vietnam as I think we should: is it time to consider some safety-valve gestures to give the Chinese a face-saving retreat, even as we gave Nikita Khrushchev a way out of the Cuban missile dilemma.

Hollywood stars, especially those with military credentials, entered the picture. In 1966, ABC aired "Operation Sea War: Vietnam" (March 10), narrated by Navy Commander Glenn Ford. WCAU-TV—the CBS-owned station in Philadelphia—broadcast "Louder Than Guns" (March 28), a personal view of the war by ex-Marine Hugh O'Brian. The following year on NBC, "Raymond Burr Visits Vietnam" (October 6) presented TV's Perry Mason interpreting the war favorably for the government. And "Our Time in Hell" (March 21) on ABC, hosted by ex-Marine Lee Marvin, was so flattering to Marine Corps actions in the Pacific during World War II that Morry Roth in *Variety* questioned the motives of the documentary. Roth decided "This was less a documentary and more an hour-long public relations plug for the Marines paid for by 3M [the sponsor]—and ultimately by the taxpayers through defense contracts."[31]

While network and independent films supportive of the Vietnam War appeared regularly on television, the medium was inhospitable toward productions condemning the war. However, these films existed, the creations of foreign filmmakers, and shown around the globe. As Erik Barnouw has pointed out, in the 1960s "film about Vietnam erupted in a chain explosion around the world." From Communist nations, but also from Canada, France, Great Britain, Japan, Syria, Sweden, and elsewhere, these documentaries offered "a picture of the war very different from what Americans saw."[32] It was extremely difficult, if not impossible, to televise such films in the United States.

One such production was "Inside North Vietnam," an 85-minute report on the enemy compiled by British journalist Felix Greene. Originally commissioned by CBS but then rejected, the film was edited to 49 minutes and shown on the 131 stations of the National Education Television network on January 22, 1968, on the prestigous "NET Journal" series. The documentary challenged U.S. government claims about the Asian enemy. Contrary to reports from Washington, the North Vietnamese exhibited confidence and high morale. There were also scenes of civilian devastation and loss of life caused by U.S. antipersonnel bombing, although the Department of Defense reported bombing only military targets. In all, the film was the most complete look at the North Vietnamese ever seen on national TV. But placing it on television created a political furor.

An influential group of congressmen wrote to the NET chairman threatening a cessation of government funding. Some attacked Greene's loyalties, while others explained the film as pure Communist propaganda. Although most critics reacted before ever seeing the documentary, NET sought balance by following the telecast with a debate between "dove" journalist David Schoenbrun and "hawk" political scientist Robert Scalapino of the University of California at Berkeley.[33]

But there were unmistakable signs that TV journalists were developing and demonstrating independent judgment. This was particularly the case at CBS. It was seen in the year-end discussion program "Where We Stand in Vietnam" (December 14, 1965) when correspondents questioned the administration's view of the war. It was noticeable in "In the Pay of the CIA: An American Dilemma" (March 13, 1967), which probed the actions of that secret government organization. And, again, this new professionalism was seen in "The People of South Vietnam: How They Feel About the War" (March 21, 1967), for which CBS commissioned a poll of South Vietnamese and concluded that 46 percent wanted the bombing stopped, 48 percent felt life was worse now than the year before, and a sizable number blamed the Americans for destroying their villages and saw no U.S. motives in Vietnam except "to colonize it or to save face."[34]

Slowly, several of the most prestigious broadcast journalists began to reevaluate their support of the war, and to state in network specials their opinions that American policy in Southeast Asia was inadequate. On "Vietnam Perspective: Eric Sevareid's Personal Report" (June 21, 1966), the distinguished CBS correspondent painted a dismal picture of President Johnson's predicament in Vietnam. Sevareid argued that the United States had involved itself in a civil war in Vietnam, but that now involvement was spreading to Laos, Cambodia, and Thailand. The administration, according to Sevareid, was speaking from faith, not facts, when it considered the war, for even if the United States actually won the war, it would be faced with the specter of impoverished South Vietnam. Further, Sevareid criticized American military operations, pointing out that there was little lasting gain from U.S. combat operation, and that given the small number of Americans who actually fought in Vietnam, U.S. troops were incurring high numbers of casualties.

Where Sevareid's report was rational and confessional, "Morley Safer's Vietnam: A Personal Report" (April 4, 1967) was an emotional tour through the savagery of the Vietnam War. Safer employed graphic images and the words of American soldiers to underscore the ironies of the conflict. Here was singer Nancy Sinatra performing her hit song, "These Boots Are Made for Walking," while hospitalized GIs, some with legs bandaged or amputated, looked on. Safer interviewed a young soldier, then announced his death shortly after the filming had been completed. Most striking, however, was the human insensitivity created by the war. One fatalistic soldier explained, "I'd be lying if I said I was glad to be here, but since I'm here I'm glad to be doing what I'm doing." And the crew of an attack helicopter—now drinking beer in a service club—answered Safer's question "How do you feel when you make a kill like that?"

> PILOT: I feel sort of detached from the whole thing. It's not personal. . . .
>
> CAPTAIN: I feel real good when we do it. It's kind of a feeling of accomplishment. It's the only way you're going to win, I guess, is to kill 'em.
>
> THIRD PILOT: I just feel like it's another target. You know, like in the States you shoot at dummies, over here you shoot at Vietnamese. Viet Cong.
>
> ANOTHER PILOT'S VOICE (interrupting): Cong. You shoot at Cong. You don't shoot at Vietnamese.
>
> THIRD PILOT (laughing): All right. You shoot at Cong. Anyway, when you come out on the run and then you see them, and they come into your sights, it's just like a wooden dummy or something there, you just thumb off a couple pair of rockets. Like they weren't people at all.[35]

The doubts of major network newsmen also appeared in media other than television. In 1967, Mike Wallace wrote in *The Nation* of matters he still could not discuss on CBS Television. His topic was the South Vietnamese Army, and he compared its dispirited, unpatriotic attitude with the dedication of the Viet Cong.[36] In the same publication Ted Koppel of ABC treated the irony of bigoted American soldiers hoping to win the hearts and minds of Asian peasants.

"The time is perhaps long overdue," wrote Koppel, "for us to give up the naive assumption that the bigot from Bayonne, the dropout from Dayton, the hood from Hattiesburg, and the plain uninterested Marine from Montgomery have, in the long trip to Southeast Asia, been magically transformed into effective good-will ambassadors."[37]

When he learned from Adlai Stevenson that the North Vietnamese twice made overtures to the United States to negotiate peace, only to be turned down by the Johnson administration, Eric Sevareid kept the information away from CBS, preferring to explain it in a *Look* magazine article in 1965.[38] And while Chet Huntley remained undaunted in his support of the president's policies, his NBC partner, David Brinkley, in 1967 chose *TV Guide* as his outlet for announcing:

> We should stop the bombing—there's not much evidence that it has ever been as effective as the Air Force thinks it is, in this or any war—and I think we should take the first settlement that is even remotely decent and get out, without insisting on any kind of "victory."[39]

Speaking before the International Radio and Television Society (IRTS) in January 1967, anchormen Walter Cronkite of CBS and Peter Jennings of ABC, as well as correspondent Edwin Newman of NBC, criticized the bombing of North Vietnam.[40] The same month the King Broadcasting Company began editorializing against escalation and arguing against the basic premises of the American commitment.[41]

Of particular significance were the views of Cronkite. Long a supporter of government military policy, as late as January 1966, he had disagreed before the IRTS with Jennings, who spoke even then against the bombing. But by early 1967, Cronkite had become a strong vocal critic of the government's war policies—although he never voiced his opinions on TV. By February 1967, while speaking at Johns Hopkins University, Cronkite assailed the "news obscuration" by the government, characterized the right wing of American politics as "wounded bears of know-nothingism," and criticized the dishonesty in all sectors of American life that "has brought almost unparalleled cynicism to threaten faith in our democracy at home and in our integrity abroad."[42]

The climax of this self-evaluation by TV newsmen was reached in early 1968. In the wake of the Tet offensive, in which enemy troops overran much of South Vietnam—even sending guerrillas inside the U.S. embassy in Saigon—Cronkite finally spoke his new views on television. Although the Viet Cong and North Vietnamese lost their military bid in the Tet offensive, they undermined the faith among Americans at home that after all those years the war in Vietnam was near an end. On the special "Report from Vietnam by Walter Cronkite" (February 27, 1968), the well-respected CBS newsman told a prime-time audience:

> We have been too often disappointed by the optimism of the American leaders, both in Vietnam and Washington, to have faith any longer in the silver linings they find in the darkest clouds. . . . To say we are closer to victory today is to believe, in the face of the evidence, the optimists who have been wrong in the past. . . . But it is increasingly clear to this reporter that the only rational way out then will be to negotiate, not as victors, but as an honorable people who lived up to their pledge to defend democracy, and did the best they could.[43]

On network radio, a medium always more open to informed commentary than was television, the critique of Johnson's policies in Vietnam was even more intense. Howard Tuckner of NBC, back from 20 months covering the war, blasted the American military effort. "Militarily and politically, it is not going well for the United States," Tuckner reported in February, "no matter how hard Washington tries to rationalize the situation." He attacked the credibility of Pentagon figures coming from Vietnam as being "as believable as a Saigon bar girl." He also raised a new theme, suggesting that for the first time American military officers in South Vietnam felt the United States could lose the war militarily.[44]

David Brinkley on NBC radio was similarly cynical and disenchanted with the Vietnam War. It had taken many bloody years for American broadcast journalism to reach this point of independence in judging the actions of government leaders, but Brinkley's commentary on February 15 epitomized the new professionalism emerging among network news personnel:

> For either a hawk or dove it is hard to see any point in continuing the war at its present level since it's achieving nothing. It actually is doing harm. It is destroying South Vietnam in the process of saving it. And even if victory were achieved by the present military level, it is doubtful there would be much left worth saving. . . . more and more of South Vietnam is being destroyed. Its civilian population—men, women, children and even babies—are being killed by the thousands. A very large proportion of the American money sent in there winds up somehow in the pockets of local officials. . . . And after three years of a huge, costly American effort, including more bombing than Germany got in the whole of World War II, the enemy forces are stronger than they were

when we started, and certainly more aggressive, as in the attacks on the cities in the last two weeks. . . . It is clear to all, or should be, that fighting the war at the present level is accomplishing nothing.[45]

While news-related television experienced a professional reappraisal, TV as entertainment demonstrated few critical breakthroughs. This was still an escapist medium of spies, comic and serious soldiers, Western champions, and syndicated reruns of anti-Communist heroics from the previous decade. Entertainment TV in the 1960s projected values supportive of the American military effort in Southeast Asia. Not until the 1970s—in popular series such as "All in the Family," "M.A.S.H.," and "Saturday Night Live"—did widely accepted programs offer cynical attitudes about war. By that time, moreover, the U.S. role in Vietnam was moving toward a peace arrangement and American withdrawal in January 1973.

Nevertheless, in two important comedy shows of the 1960s—"That Was the Week That Was" ("TW3") and "The Smothers Brothers Comedy Hour"—video realized its potential as an entertainment forum able to be critical of government policies. During its 16 months on NBC (January to July 1964, and September 1964 to May 1965), "TW3" was not a popular series. In its last weeks it was ninety-fourth in the network ratings. Copied from a program successful in Great Britain, it was, nevertheless, a landmark series in American television because it relied heavily upon political satire.

In its gags, sketches, blackouts, and songs, "That Was the Week That Was" often tossed barbs at the war in South Vietnam. One skit involved "Bernie the bookie," a Las Vegas gambler taking bets on political developments in Southeast Asia. He gave 9 to 5 odds that the North Vietnamese and Viet Cong would overrun Saigon by closing day at Hialeah race track. Chinese ground intervention was 4 to 1; Chinese air support for North Vietnam was even odds; the chances of the present Saigon government lasting until the All-Star baseball game was 99 to 1 against. Bernie even took bets on World War III—war with Russia was 9 to 1; with China was 7 to 1; and use of atomic weapons was Us 12 to 1, Them 6 to 1.

Because the half-hour program lampooned a wide range of social and political realities, the humor directed at the Vietnam War appeared as part of a nonstop parade of jokes. Its sting was thereby dissipated, for it appeared with wisecracks about religion, civil rights, Congress, pornography, and other social concerns. There was in the satire of "TW3," however, political criticism of the Vietnam War. And that was new to entertainment television. It was nowhere better exemplified than when Buck Henry, on the program of January 26, 1965, gave a short, sarcastic history of government in South Vietnam:

> Trouble here began in November '63 with the overthrow of the Diem regime. Madame Nhu left the country and the regime was ousted by the military in a coup. Madame Nhu has since gone on to become a Miss Universe loser. Power was then in the hands of Major General Duong Van Minh. But in January '64, Major General Nguyen Khanh led a bloodless coup which made him premier, but still impossible to pronounce. In March '64, after threats, Khanh stepped down and Nguyen Xuan Oanh was made acting premier. In September a bloodless coup installed Tran Van Huong as premier, replacing Khanh, and giving rise to the saying, "Khanh today, Huong tomorrow." In December, the Young Turks of the Army staged a demi-coup against civilian rule and Huong brought four military leaders into his cabinet. Then this week another coup, the fifth, deposed Huong and put Khanh back as premier. Khanh's first public statement was that Vietnam has had its final coup. It would be a pity if the South Vietnamese stopped now. They're just getting good at it.

Far more successful and provocative than "TW3" however, was the CBS musical-variety program "The Smothers Brothers Comedy Hour." Between February 1967 and June 1969, this mix of songs, guest stars, and irreverent topical humor often addressed the Vietnam War and related issues of social protest. Tom and Dick Smothers several times had Pete Seeger as their guest. On his first appearance, September 10, 1967—Seeger's first network TV performance in 17 years—he performed "Waist Deep in Big Muddy," a satirical song about a stubborn military officer compelling his men to wade into a muddy, impassable river. The "big fool" officer was clearly a reference to the president and his attitude about the Vietnam War. Although Columbia Records (a division of CBS) had recently recorded this Seeger tune, CBS Television edited it from the video-tape of the program. This created such an adverse reaction, however, that Seeger returned on February 25, 1968, and was permitted to perform the song uncensored.[46]

Another controversial folksinger, Joan Baez, was also censored by CBS. An activist and wife of a convicted draft resister, Baez was hired to sing on the program of March 9, 1969. The videotape of the show was so heavily abridged by network executives that a fully edited copy was not ready in time for airing. The program with Baez was postponed for three weeks. Among the cuts from the show were Baez's complete explanation of the significance of her forthcoming record album, "David's Album." The record was dedicated to her husband, David Harris, who was about to enter federal prison for refusing induction into the Army. Network censors allowed her to say the album was "kind of a gift to David because he's going to be going to prison probably in June. And he'll be there for three years." CBS then cut from the videotape her remaining words: "The reason he is going to prison is that he resisted Selective Service and the draft and militarism in general. Anybody who lays it out in front like that generally gets busted, especially if you organize, which he did."[47]

The Smothers brothers themselves were not averse to political satire. On the program of April 23, 1967, their opening dialogue centered on a recent coup in Greece that brought a repressive military regime to power and crushed Greek democracy. The brothers used that experience to make pointed statements about government in the United States.

> Tom: This past week, if you were reading the papers and everything, I think you read about a revolution in Greece. The army threw out the premier and took over the government. . . . And we'd like to be the first TV show to recognize that new government in Greece. . . .
>
> Dick: It is true, it's really true. Over the weekend—or not really the weekend—last week, the Greek army did overthrow the Greek government. That's true. . . .
>
> Tom: Now, this is very important, 'cause the people should have the right to overthrow their government and change. Like even right here in this country. If there's something that we don't like, we have the right as members of this country to stand right up and throw the government right out. You know, march right over and throw 'em out.
>
> Dick: Now, wait a minute, Tommy, you love this country.
>
> Tom: I know I love this country. I'm not too sure about the government.
>
> Dick: Now wait a minute. That is not how he feels. And Tommy does not advocate throwing over the government. You don't, do you?
>
> Tom: I don't advocate throwing over the government. I was just saying that—to keep 'em on their toes.

The critical attitude of the brothers toward the Vietnam War also prompted CBS censorship. For their Mothers Day broadcast in 1968, they planned to show a Mother's Day card reading "War is not healthy for children and other living things. . . . I don't want candy or flowers.

I want an end to the killing. We who have given life must be dedicated to preserving it. Please talk peace." The censors cut the entire segment, explaining that the mothers' group distributing the card might be subversive, and that in an entertainment program, "We do not permit political positions."[48]

"The Smothers Brothers Comedy Hour" was dropped by CBS in the spring of 1969—only days after it had announced a 26-week extension of the program. Cancellation of the show stemmed not from any specific act of censorship, but from Tom Smothers' professional "indiscretion" of complaining in person to senators and FCC officials about CBS expurgations and what he felt to be network inhibition of his artistic freedom. Both network and talent had lived successfully for two years with the deletion of program segments and controversial jokes. But, as Robert Metz noted in his controversial book, *CBS: Reflections in a Bloodshot Eye*, "Name calling, even if it reaches the press, is forgivable. But going to the Feds—whether the FCC or Congress—is not playing the game."[49]

Despite two years of battling CBS executives, "The Smothers Brothers Comedy Hour" was pivotal in the history of television. It brought "political positions" to entertainment TV. It sprang from a liberal, anti-establishment mentality, and the consistently high ratings it received proved that there was an audience for such programming. More than "That Was the Week That Was"—and certainly much more than the slapstick comedy of "Rowan & Martin's Laugh-In"—the Smothers brothers' show opened video to a new type of humor. In the 1960s it was an oasis of liberal commentary. In the next decade its satire paled before the irreverence of Hawkeye Pierce and B. J. Hunnicut, as well as the indictments from Mike and Gloria Stivic as they fought for antiwar values against Archie Bunker.

In the years since presidents Kennedy and Johnson plunged the nation into an Asian land war, commercial television had exhibited small, but expanding, political diversity in its reportage. Where the medium had been the principal means of persuading the nation to accept unquestioningly a conflict against Communism thousands of miles from the United States, it began now to pay attention to political voices critical of government in general—and of the Vietnam War in particular. Some of its most popular stars—in entertainment, but more so in journalism—now began to speak out against the war.

Ironically, several days before Tom and Dick Smothers were canceled by CBS, a Roper poll showed again that more Americans received more news from TV than from any other medium of information, but by the widest margin—44 percent to 21 percent for newspapers, 11 percent for magazines, and 8 percent for radio—they now rated TV the "most reliable" news medium.[50]

In the following decades the importance of television to the nation would increase. There would be more war in Vietnam to cover. There would be the Watergate scandal and the resignation of an incumbent president. And in the 1980s, there was the growing threat of war in the Middle East and Central America. In all cases, however, network television acted as it had not in the past, to present a balance of opinion and a willingness to investigate without bias. It was a crucial function for TV to perform. Unfortunately, it took a costly war in Asia for television to recognize its responsibility to American society and to perform with integrity, independence, balance, and relative thoroughness its function as the most important medium of communication in the nation.

NOTES

PREFACE

1. John E. Mueller, *War, Presidents and Public Opinion* (New York: John Wiley and Sons, 1973), p. 63.

CHAPTER 1

1. Jeanette Sayre [Smith], "An Analysis of the Radiobroadcasting Activities of Federal Agencies," *Studies in the Control of Radio* no. 3 (June 1941): 65; reprinted in *Studies in the Control of Radio*, nos. 1-6 (New York: Arno, 1971).

2. Carl J. Friedrich and Evelyn Sternberg, "Congress and the Control of Radio-broadcasting," *Studies in the Control of Radio* no. 5 (Oct. 1943): 14; reprinted in *Studies in the Control of Radio*, nos. 1-6 (New York: Arno, 1971).

3. Sayre [Smith], "An Analysis of Radiobroadcasting Activities," p. 12.

4. Friedrich and Sternberg, "Congress and the Control of Radio-broadcasting," p. 3.

5. Ibid., p. 28.

6. J. Fred MacDonald, *Don't Touch That Dial! Radio Programming in American Life, 1920-1960* (Chicago: Nelson-Hall, 1979), pp. 264-67.

7. J. Fred MacDonald, "Government Propaganda in Commercial Radio— The Case of *Treasury Star Parade*, 1942-1943," *Journal of Popular Culture* 12, no. 2 (1978): 285-304.

8. *Variety*, Sept. 9, 1942, p. 47.

9. *Broadcasting*, July 3, 1950, p. 15.

CHAPTER 2

1. *Variety*, Jan. 4, 1950, p. 113.

2. Ibid., Jan. 3, 1951, p. 112.

3. Ibid., Sept. 26, 1951, p. 29.

4. Ibid., Mar. 28, 1951, p. 26.

5. Ibid., Apr. 4, 1951, pp. 1, 54.

6. Ibid., Aug. 8, 1951, pp. 1, 40.

7. Ibid., Jan. 6, 1954, p. 91; For similar views from Weaver, see *Variety*, Nov. 23, 1955, p. 26.

8. *Variety*, May 12, 1948, pp. 1, 61. For Sarnoff's views on this subject during the Korean War, see *New York Times*, July 13, 1950. See also, *Broadcasting*, Aug. 16, 1954, pp. 85, 90.

9. *Broadcasting*, July 10, 1950, p. 15; Sept. 4, 1950, p. 34.

10. *Variety*, May 11, 1955, pp. 2, 44. Sarnoff's idea of free radios for Iron Curtain countries was advanced as early as 1950. See *Broadcasting*, Aug. 7, 1950, p. 21. See also Eugene Lyons, *David Sarnoff*. (New York: Harper & Row, 1966), pp. 324-28.

11. Senator Alexander Wiley of Wisconsin admitted that this idea sounded "Buck Rogersish," but he felt "the fantasy of yesterday has become the reality of today." *Variety*, Nov. 23, 1949, p. 34; *Broadcasting*, Dec. 5, 1949, p. 61.

12. *Variety*, Feb. 9, 1949, p. 61.

13. Ibid., Jan. 21, 1948, p. 27.

14. Ibid., June 7, 1950, p. 29.

15. *Broadcasting*, Apr. 24, 1950, p. 32.

16. David Caute, *The Great Fear. The Anti-Communist Purge under Truman and Eisenhower* (New York: Simon and Schuster, 1978), p. 21.

17. *Broadcasting*, Sept. 25, 1950, p. 27.

18. *New York Times*, Dec. 21, 1950.

19. David G. Yellin, *Special. Fred Freed and the Television Documentary* (New York: Macmillan, 1972 and 1973), p. 49.

20. Erik Barnouw, *The Golden Web. A History of Broadcasting in the United States 1933-1953* (New York: Oxford University Press, 1968), p. 266; *Variety*, Sept. 10, 1952, p. 2.

21. *Variety*, Aug. 30, 1950, pp. 1, 54; Sept. 13, 1950, p. 29; Aug. 29, 1951, p. 25.

22. Barnouw, *The Golden Web*, p. 264; *Variety*, Jan. 25, 1950, p. 38, and Nov. 17, 1954, p. 2; Stefan Kanfer, *A Journal of the Plague Years* (New York: Atheneum, 1973), pp. 100-01.

23. Muir was not allowed to speak on TV about her blacklist experience. On an installment of the women's discussion program "Girl Talk," scheduled for Dec. 27, 1965, she named the sponsor and advertising agency—General Foods and Young & Rubicam—responsible for dropping her from "The Aldrich Family." ABC deleted these remarks from the final videotape. See *Variety*, Dec. 29, 1965, p. 2.

24. Barnouw, *The Golden Web*, pp. 266-67.

25. *Variety*, Mar. 11, 1959, p. 1.

26. *Broadcasting*, Apr. 30, 1951, p. 64.

27. *Variety*, Apr. 29, 1953, p. 30.

28. Ibid., Nov. 17, 1948, p. 29.

29. Ibid., July 28, 1948, p. 31.

30. Ibid., July 22, 1953, p. 27.

31. Ibid., Dec. 4, 1957, p. 39.

32. Ibid., July 27, 1949, p. 44.

33. Ibid., Dec. 18, 1957, pp. 1, 34.

34. Ibid., Feb. 14, 1951, p. 23; Mar. 21, 1951, p. 33.

35. Ibid., July 11, 1951, p. 44.

36. Francis H. Heller, ed., *The Korean War. A 25-Year Perspective* (Lawrence: Regents Press of Kansas, 1977), pp. 169-70; John E. Mueller, *War, Presidents and Public Opinion* (New York: Wiley, 1973), pp. 42-65.

37. *Variety*, July 5, 1950, p. 1.

38. *Broadcasting*, Dec. 25, 1950, pp. 28-29; July 24, 1950, p. 19.

39. Ibid., Dec. 15, 1952, p. 30.

40. *Variety*, Aug. 16, 1950, p. 32.

41. Ibid., Mar. 28, 1951, p. 30.

42. Edward R. Murrow, *In Search of Light. The Broadcasts of Edward R. Murrow 1938-1961* (London: Macmillan, 1968), pp. 154-56, 160-61.

43. Alexander Kendrick, *Prime Time. The Life of Edward R. Murrow* (Boston: Little, Brown, 1969), p. 327.

44. Edward R. Murrow and Fred W. Friendly, eds., *See It Now* (New York: Simon and Schuster, 1955), pp. 1-29.

45. *Variety*, Dec. 31, 1952, p. 24.

46. Ibid., Sept. 16, 1953, p. 42.

47. Ibid., Dec. 6, 1950, p. 34.

48. *Broadcasting*, Oct. 22, 1951, p. 87; Nov. 5, 1951, p. 80; Dec. 10, 1951, p. 52. See also Erik Barnouw, *Documentary. A History of the Non-Fiction Film*, 2nd ed. (New York: Oxford University Press, 1983), p. 300. For an overview of the atomic bomb as the focus of TV programming, see *Broadcasting*, Oct. 8, 1951, pp. 26, 76.

49. *Broadcasting*, May 24, 1954, p. 18.

50. Ibid., Mar. 23, 1953, pp. 14-15.

51. *Chicago Sun-Times*, Aug. 10, 1977; Howard L. Rosenberg, *Atomic Soldiers. American Victims of Nuclear Experiments* (Boston: Beacon, 1980), p. 117.

52. *TV Guide*, May 21, 1955, p. 18.

53. Ibid., Feb. 7, 1959, p. 29.

54. *New York Times*, Aug. 7, 1957.

55. Ibid., June 15, 1955; June 16, 1955.

56. Caute, *The Great Fear*, p. 47.

57. *Variety*, June 24, 1953, p. 31.

58. *New York Times*, Apr. 25, 1954.

59. *Variety*, Jan. 27, 1954, p. 29.

60. Ibid., Oct. 28, 1959, p. 22.

61. Ibid., May 5, 1954, p. 23. See also Michael Straight, *Trial by Television* (Boston: Beacon, 1954), pp. 255-76.

62. Barnouw, *The Golden Web*, p. 299.

63. Erik Barnouw, *The Image Empire. A History of Broadcasting in the United States since 1953* (New York, Oxford University Press, 1970), pp. 17-18.

64. *TV Guide*, Oct. 30, 1954, pp. 5-7; John C. O'Brian, "The President and Television—An Interview with James C. Hagerty," ibid., Dec. 27, 1958, pp. 4-7.

65. *New York Times*, Feb. 3, 1951.

66. *Variety*, Mar. 28, 1956, p. 32.

67. Ibid., Jan. 15, 1958, p. 1.

68. Townsend Hoopes, *The Devil and John Foster Dulles* (Boston: Little, Brown, 1973), p. 491.

69. James Shipley, "How Dulles Averted War," *Life*, Jan. 16, 1956, p. 78.

70. *New York Times*, Dec. 24, 1957.

71. Blanche Wiesen Cook, *The Declassified Eisenhower. A Divided Legacy* (New York: Doubleday, 1981), pp. 218-62. Barnouw, *The Image Empire*, pp. 97-98.

72. *New York Times*, July 1, 1954.

73. Alexander Kendrick, *The Wound Within. America in the Vietnam Years, 1945-1974* (Boston: Little, Brown, 1974), p. 131; James Pinckney Harrison, *The Endless War. Fifty Years of Struggle in Vietnam* (New York: The Free Press, 1982), pp. 244-45.

74. *New York Times*, Mar. 30, 1954.

75. Ibid., May 8, 1954.

76. Ibid., Mar. 9, 1955.

77. George McTurnan Kahin and John W. Lewis, *The United States in Vietnam* (New York: Dial Press, 1967), pp. 107-20; Harrison, *The Endless War*, pp. 220-26; Guenter Lewy, *America in Vietnam* (New York: Oxford University Press, 1977), pp. 14-18.

78. *New York Times*, Mar. 9. 1955.

79. Robert MacNeil, *The People Machine. The Influence of Television on American Politics* (New York: Harper and Row, 1968), pp. 307-08.

80. Hoopes, *The Devil and John Foster Dulles*, p. 257.

81. Transcript of the telecast of "The Camel News Caravan" is from Irving Settel, ed., *Top TV Shows of the Year 1954-1955* (New York: Hastings House, 1955), pp. 177-81. Reprinted by permission of R. J. Reynold Tobacco Company.

82. A. William Bluem, *Documentary in American Television. Form-Function-Method* (New York: Hastings House, 1965), pp. 149-63.

83. *Variety*, Oct. 19, 1955, pp. 1, 15. See also Peter C. Rollins, "*Nightmare in Red*: A Cold War View of the Communist Revolution," in John E. O'Connor, ed., *American History/American Television. Interpreting the Video Past* (New York: Frederick Ungar, 1983), pp. 134-58.

84. *Variety*, June 12, 1957, p. 30.

85. Ibid., July 3, 1957, p. 17. For an overview of the diverse reactions to the interview with Khrushchev, see *Broadcasting*, June 10, 1957, pp. 60, 64.

86. Fred W. Friendly, *Due to Circumstances Beyond Our Control . . .* (New York: Random House, 1967), p. 86; *Variety*, Oct. 15, 1958, p. 46.

87. *Variety*, Aug. 22, 1956, p. 26; Robert Stahl, "Do Newscasters Have Freedom of Speech?" *TV Guide*, Aug. 3, 1957, pp. 8-10.

88. David Halberstam, *The Powers That Be* (New York: Knopf, 1979), p. 416.

89. *Broadcasting*, Mar. 29, 1954, p. 62.

90. Robert Cunniff, "There's Nobody, but Nobody, Like Walter," *TV Forecast*, Nov. 1, 1952, p. 36.

91. *Variety*, Jan. 15, 1958, p. 37; *Television Magazine*, Apr. 1958, pp. 44-47, 91; Sig Mickelson, "TV Accepts Its Greatest Challenge," ibid., May 1958, pp. 44-47, 82-84. For a capsulized history of broadcast editorializing, see *Broadcasting*, July 18, 1962, pp. 58-64.

92. *Variety*, May 6, 1959, p. 20; *Broadcasting*, May 4, 1959, p. 9. Compare the Cuban response discussed in *Broadcasting*, June 1, 1959, p. 79.

93. *Variety*, Oct. 5, 1960, pp. 25, 56.

94. Ibid., Dec. 31, 1958, pp. 17, 32.

95. Kendrick, *Prime Time*, p. 445.

96. *Variety*, July 30, 1958, p. 1.

97. *TV Guide*, May 10, 1958, pp. 25-26; Herman Land, "It's Time to Take Stock," *Television Magazine*, July 1957, p. 42.

98. Edward R. Murrow, "How TV Can Help Us Survive," *TV Guide*, Dec. 13, 1958, pp. 22, 25. This article comprises excerpts from Murrow's speech in Chicago on Oct. 15, 1958, before a national convention of the Radio-Television News Directors Association. See *Variety*, Oct. 15, 1958, pp. 23, 46.

99. Murrow, "How TV Can Help Us Survive," p. 27.

CHAPTER 3

1. Dennis Joseph Rinzel, "A Description of the Ziv Television Series: 'I Led 3 Lives,'" Masters thesis (University of Wisconsin, Madison, 1975), pp. 218, 228.

2. *Series, Serials & Packages. A TV Film/Tape Source Book*, Loretta Hanley, ed., New York: Broadcast Information Bureau, 1974.

3. Ibid., p. 209. Compare the denials of political intent made by writer Jon Epstein and actor Richard Carlson, ibid., pp. 169-71, 194. See also comments by Carlson in *New York Times*, May 9, 1954; and see *TV Guide*, Dec. 4, 1953, pp. 5-7.

4. *Broadcasting*, Apr. 12, 1954, p. 33.

5. *Variety*, May 8, 1957, p. 21.

6. Ibid., Jan. 11, 1956, pp. 32-33.

7. In the Feb. 1953 issue of *TV Writer*, a publication of the Television Writers of America, as cited in *Variety*, Feb. 25, 1953, p. 25.

8. *Series, Serials & Packages*.

9. *Variety*, May 11, 1949, p. 29.

10. As cited in Peter C. Rollins, "*Victory at Sea*: Cold War Epic," *Journal of Popular Culture* 6, no. 4 (1973): 467. See also *Broadcasting*, Jan. 13, 1958, p. 52.

11. J. William Fulbright, *The Pentagon Propaganda Machine* (New York: Liverright, 1970), p. 38.

12. *Broadcasting*, Apr. 5, 1954, p. 32; Apr. 19, 1954, p. 33.

13. Ibid., Nov. 14, 1949, p. 63.

14. *Variety*, Dec. 23, 1953, p. 26.

15. Ibid., July 30, 1958, p. 26; Dec. 3, 1958, p. 36.

16. "Uncle Sam to the Rescue," *TV Guide*, June 11, 1954, pp. 18-19.

17. Compiled by author.

18. Harry T. Paxton, "Football's Biggest Show," *Saturday Evening Post*, Nov. 26, 1955, p. 28.

19. Neil Hickey, "The Army-Navy Football Battle," *TV Guide*, Nov. 27, 1965, p. 33.

20. Donald F. Glut and Jim Harmon, *The Great Television Heroes* (New York: Doubleday, 1975), p. 86.

21. For an interesting discussion of "faith" songs in the middle of the era of rock and roll music, see *Variety*, July 4, 1956, p. 1. On feature films with Biblical themes, see *Variety*, June 17, 1953, pp. 4, 16.

22. Fulton J. Sheen, *Liberty under Communism* (New York: Paulist Press, 1937), pp. 22-23.

23. Citations from Sheen's TV programs are from Fulton J. Sheen, *Life Is Worth Living*, I (New York: McGraw-Hill, 1953), pp. 211, 132, 149, 270-71.

24. For a fuller list of wartime feature films suspect in the Cold War see John Cogley, *Report on Blacklisting. I: Movies* (New York: Fund for the Republic, 1956), pp. 234-64.

25. *Variety*, July 26, 1950, p. 35.

26. Ibid., Aug. 30, 1950, p. 19; *Broadcasting*, Aug. 28, 1950, p. 28.

27. *Variety*, Oct. 10, 1956, p. 33.

28. Ibid., Oct. 29, 1958, p. 21.

29. *New York Times*, Feb. 18, 1955.

30. Words of the editor of *Top Western* magazine, as cited in John P. Sisk, "The Western Hero," *Commonweal*, July 12, 1957, p. 367. See also Robert P. Ellis, "The Appeal of the Western Movie Thriller," *America*, May 17, 1958, p. 229; and *Time*, Mar. 30, 1959, p. 53. For an excellent discussion of Cold War themes in Western movies, see John H. Lenihan, *Showdown. Confronting Modern America in the Western Film* (Urbana: University of Illinois Press, 1980), pp. 24-54.

31. Gene Autry, "Gene Autry's Prize Round-up," *Radio and Television Mirror*, July 1952, p. 25.

32. David Willson Parker, "A Descriptive Analysis of The Lone Ranger as a Form of Popular Art," Ph.D. dissertation (Northwestern University, 1955), p. 213.

33. *Newsweek*, Feb. 2, 1953, p. 75; Parker, "A Descriptive Analysis of The Lone Ranger," pp. 192-94.

34. *Variety*, Feb. 8, 1950, p. 32; David Rothel, *Who Was That Masked Man?* (South Brunswick, N.J.: A. S. Barnes, 1976), p. 86.

35. Parker, "A Descriptive Analysis of The Lone Ranger," p. 208.

36. *Variety*, Nov. 27, 1957, p. 38.

37. Ibid., Feb. 4, 1959, p. 27. Reprinted courtesy of A. C. Nielsen Company.

38. *Series, Serials & Packages*.

39. William F. Rickenbacker, "60,000,000 Westerners Can't Be Wrong," *National Review*, Oct. 23, 1962, pp. 324-25.

40. David Shea Teeple, "TV Westerns Tell a Story," *American Mercury*, Apr. 1958, pp. 116-17.

41. Peter Homans, "The Western. The Legend and the Cardboard Hero," *Look*, Mar. 13, 1962, p. 89.

42. Alexander Miller, "The Western—A Theological Note," *The Christian Century*, Nov. 27, 1957, p. 1410.

43. *TV Guide*, Jan. 23, 1965, p. 8.

44. Rickenbacker, "60,000,000 Westerns Can't Be Wrong," p. 322.

45. *TV Guide* (Minneapolis-St. Paul Edition), Feb. 1, 1958.

46. *Variety*, Oct. 6, 1954, p. 23.

47. Ibid., Mar. 8, 1961, pp. 1, 78.

CHAPTER 4

1. *Information Please Almanac 1976*, Ann Golenpaul, ed. (New York: Dan Golenpaul Associates, 1975), p. 76; *International Television Almanac 1962*, Charles S. Aaronson, ed. (New York: Quigley Publications, 1961), pp. 9A, 22A-26A.

2. *Variety*, Dec. 23, 1959, p. 39; *Broadcasting*, Feb. 12, 1962, pp. 27-29. Reprinted courtesy of the Roper Organization.

3. John F. Kennedy, "Television: A Force in Politics," *TV Guide*, Nov. 14, 1959, pp. 6-7.

4. Henry Fairlie, *The Kennedy Promise. The Politics of Expectation* (New York: Doubleday, 1973), pp. 58-59.

5. Alexander Kendrick, *The Wound Within. America in the Vietnam Years, 1945-1974* (Boston: Little, Brown, 1974), pp. 85-86.

6. *Vital Speeches of the Day*, Aug. 16, 1956, pp. 617-19.

7. Robert Lardine, "Kennedy: They Loved Him on TV," *TV Radio Mirror*, Mar. 1961, p. 78.

8. *TV Guide*, Feb. 10, 1962, p. 23.

9. *Variety*, Mar. 7, 1962, p. 1. For a complete listing of Kennedy's live TV appearances, see *Broadcasting*, Nov. 8, 1965, p. 56.

10. Arthur M. Schlesinger, Jr., *A Thousand Days. John F. Kennedy in the White House* (Boston: Houghton Mifflin, 1965), p. 717; Merriman Smith, "The Presidential Press Conference," *TV Guide*, Apr. 29, 1961, pp. 4-6.

11. Theodore C. Sorensen, *Kennedy* (New York: Harper and Row, 1965), pp. 322, 325. For Salinger's description of Kennedy's purposes, see Pierre Salinger, *With Kennedy* (New York: Avon, 1967), pp. 79, 83.

12. Pierre Salinger, "Introduction" to Harold W. Chase and Allen H. Lerman, eds., *Kennedy and the Press. The News Conferences* (New York: Crowell, 1965), p. x; *Broadcasting*, Oct. 23, 1961, p. 71; Newton P. Minow, John Bartlow Martin and Lee M. Mitchell, *Presidential Television* (New York: Basic Books, 1973), p. 39.

13. *Broadcasting*, Feb. 5, 1962, p. 45.

14. William H. Lawrence, "Presidential Press Conference," *TV Guide*, May 4, 1963, p. 6.

15. Henry Harding, "Conducting President Kennedy's Press Conferences," *TV Guide*, Apr. 21, 1962, p. A-3.

16. William Small, *To Kill A Messenger. Television News and the Real World* (New York: Hastings House, 1970), p. 227.

17. Allen Kirschner and Linda Kirschner, eds., *Radio and Television. Readings in the Mass Media* (New York: Bobbs-Merrill, 1971), pp. 208-09.

18. *Broadcasting*, July 17, 1961, p. 50; *Variety*, July 19, 1961, p. 35.

19. *Variety*, Apr. 12, 1961, p. 31.

20. Garry Wills, *The Kennedy Imprisonment. A Meditation on Power* (Boston: Little, Brown, 1982), p. 149.

21. Peter Wyden, *Bay of Pigs. The Untold Story* (New York: Simon and Schuster, 1979), pp. 289-311; Erik Barnouw, *The Image Empire. A History of Broadcasting in the United States since 1953* (New York: Oxford University Press, 1970), pp. 185-95.

22. *Variety*, Apr. 26, 1961, p. 176.

23. Ibid., May 24, 1961, p. 1.

24. *The New Republic*, Oct. 9, 1961, p. 3.

25. Fairlie, *The Kennedy Promise*, pp. 125-27.

26. Ibid., p. 187.

27. Phillip Katcher, *Armies of the Vietnam War 1962-1975* (London: Osprey, 1980), pp. 19-21.

28. Wills, *The Kennedy Imprisonment*, pp. 280-81.

29. *Variety*, Apr. 28, 1962, p. 29.

30. Ibid., May 16, 1962, p. 33.

31. Albert Paul Klose, "Howard K. Smith Comments on the News. A Comparative Analysis of the Use of Television and Print." Ph.D. dissertation (Northwestern University, 1970), pp. 104-06, 121.

32. Alexander Kendrick, *Prime Time. The Life of Edward R. Murrow* (Boston: Little, Brown, 1969), p. 13.

33. David Halberstam, *The Powers That Be* (New York: Knopf, 1979), pp. 433, 438-41.

34. *Broadcasting*, Jan. 1, 1962, p. 48; Apr. 9, 1962, p. 34.

35. Robert MacNeil, *The People Machine. The Influence of Television on American Politics* (New York: Harper and Row, 1968), p. 19.

36. Ibid., pp. 19-20.

37. *Variety*, May 30, 1956, p. 1.

38. Ibid., Dec. 25, 1968, p. 23.

39. Information on war contractors comes from *Variety*, Feb. 23, 1966, pp. 1, 46; June 7, 1967, p. 29. See also Robert F. Kaufman, *The War Profiteers* (Indianapolis: Bobbs-Merrill, 1970), pp. 42-55.

40. *Variety*, Feb. 23, 1966, p. 46. Permission to reprint chart courtesy of Variety, Inc.

41. *Variety*, Feb. 23, 1966, p. 1, 46.

42. Ibid., June 7, 1967, p. 29. See also Erik Barnouw, *The Sponsor: Notes on a Modern Potentate* (New York: Oxford University Press, 1978), pp. 117-19.

43. *Variety*, Dec. 25, 1968, p. 23.

44. Nicholas Johnson, "The Silent Screen," *TV Guide*, July 5, 1969, p. 8.

45. Gary A. Steiner, *The People Look at Television. A Study of Audience Attitudes* (New York: Knopf, 1963), pp. 172-94.

46. *Variety*, July 6, 1960, pp. 29, 47.

47. *Broadcasting*, Sept. 28, 1959, p. 90.

48. Ibid., Jan. 1, 1962, p. 5. See also Darrell Yoshito Hamamoto, "Television Situation Comdy and Post-War Liberalism: 1950-1980" (Ph.D. dissertation) University of California, Irvine, 1981, pp. 180-81.

49. *Broadcasting*, Jan. 22, 1962, p. 27; Oct. 16, 1961, p. 10.

50. William R. McAndrew, prefatory remarks to *NBC News: Profile on Communism* (New York: National Broadcasting Company, 1963).

51. *Series, Serials & Packages. A TV Film/Tape Source Book*, Loretta Hanley, ed. (New York: Broadcast Information Bureau, Inc. 1974).

52. *Variety*, July 4, 1962, p. 66.

53. Hamamoto, "Television Situation Comedy," pp. 145-50.

54. *Series, Serials & Packages*.

55. *Series, Serials & Packages*.

56. Paul Hoch, *Rip off the Big Game. The Exploitation of Sports by the Power Elite* (New York: Doubleday, 1972), pp. 70-99.

57. Barnouw, *The Image Empire*, p. 261; Barnouw, *The Sponsor*, p. 117.

58. Gary H. Grossman, *Saturday Morning TV* (New York: Dell, 1981), p. 336.

59. Victor S. Navasky, *Naming Names* (New York: Viking, 1980), p. 328.

60. *Variety*, Jan. 17, 1962, p. 29. The Weavers had been blacklisted from TV as early as 1951; see Stefan Kanfer, *A Journal of the Plague Years* (New York: Atheneum, 1973), p. 150.

61. *Variety*, Mar. 27, 1963, p. 35.

62. Ibid., Jan. 15, 1964, p. 27.

63. Ibid., Jan. 17, 1968, p. 27.

64. Ibid., Apr. 22, 1964, p. 117. A year earlier Lisa Howard had interviewed Fidel Castro for an ABC documentary aired May 10, 1963; see ibid., May 15, 1963, p. 39.

65. Barnouw, *The Image Empire*, p. 243. Note that Barnouw misdates this documentary. The program was broadcast Apr. 19, not Aug. 19.

66. MacNeil, *The People Machine*, p. 310.

67. Minow et al., *Presidential Television*, p. 171; *Broadcasting*, Nov. 6, 1965, pp. 54-58.

68. Eric F. Goldman, *The Tragedy of Lyndon Johnson* (New York: Knopf, 1969), p. 8.

69. MacNeil, *The People Machine*, p. 300.

70. Minow et al., *Presidential Television*, p. 19.

71. Ibid., p. 25; MacNeil, *The People Machine*, pp. 308-11; *Variety*, May 12, 1965, p. 2; Robert Goralski, "Television and the President," *TV Guide*, July 4, 1964, pp. 3-5.

72. *Broadcasting*, Jan. 27, 1964, pp. 70-72.

73. Doris Kearns, *Lyndon Johnson and the American Dream* (New York: Harper and Row, 1976), p. 252.

74. Goldman, *The Tragedy of Lyndon Johnson*, pp. 380-81.

75. John Galloway, *The Gulf of Tonkin Resolution* (Rutherford, N.J.: Fairleigh Dickenson University Press, 1970), p. 52.

76. Joseph C. Goulden, *Truth Is the First Casualty. The Gulf of Tonkin Affair—Illusion and Reality* (Chicago: Rand McNally, 1969), p. 142; Eugene G. Windchy, *Tonkin Gulf* (New York: Doubleday, 1971), pp. 211ff.; Anthony Austin, *The President's War. The Story of the Tonkin Gulf Resolution and How the Nation Was Trapped in Vietnam* (Philadelphia: J. B. Lippincott, 1971), p. 205; Guenter Lewy, *America in Vietnam* (New York: Oxford University Press, 1977), pp. 32-36.

77. *Variety*, Oct. 17, 1962, p. 23.

78. Ibid., Nov. 6, 1963, p. 27.

79. Goulden, *Truth Is the First Casualty*, pp. 24-25.

80. Ibid., p. 77.

81. *Broadcasting*, Sept. 21, 1964, p. 30; *Variety*, Sept. 16, 1964, p. 1, and Sept. 23, 1964, p. 35.

82. Lewy, *America in Vietnam*, p. 66.

83. Walt Whitman Rostow, *The Diffusion of Power. An Essay in Recent History* (New York: Macmillan, 1972), p. 479.

EPILOGUE

1. Robert MacNeil, *The People Machine. The Influence of Television on American Politics* (New York: Harper and Row, 1968), p. 38.

2. J. Fred MacDonald, *Blacks and White TV. Afro-Americans in Television since 1948* (Chicago: Nelson-Hall, 1983), pp. 83-100.

3. Todd Gitlin, *The Whole World Is Watching. Mass Media in the Making and Unmaking of the New Left* (Berkeley: University of California Press, 1980), p. 26.

4. Ibid., pp. 27-28.

5. These are the words cited in *Public Papers of the Presidents of the United States*. Compare the more emotional text in Eric F. Goldman, *The Tragedy of Lyndon Johnson* (New York: Knopf, 1969), p. 396.

6. *Variety*, May 26, 1965, p. 28.

7. Ibid.

8. Ibid., June 2, 1965, p. 42.

9. Alexander Kendrick, *The Wound Within. America in the Vietnam Years, 1945-1974* (Boston: Little Brown, 1974), p. 204.

10. Quotations from hearings were transcribed by the author from a recording of the CBS-TV special report, "Vietnam Perspective: The Senate Hearings and the War," broadcast Feb. 18, 1966.

11. Fred W. Friendly, *Due to Circumstances Beyond Our Control . . .* (New York: Random House, 1967), pp. 213-65. For a much less flattering interpretation of Friendly's departure from CBS, see Gary Paul Gates, *Air Time. The Inside Story of CBS News* (New York: Harper and Row, 1978), pp. 123-25.

12. *Variety*, Mar. 9, 1966, p. 1.

13. Ibid., June 15, 1966, p. 28.

14. Ibid., Jan. 5, 1966, pp. 101, 160.

15. Ibid., Nov. 18, 1966, p. 25.

16. Ibid., July 28, 1965, p. 1; Aug. 4, 1965, p. 38.

17. Walter Cronkite, "Playboy Interview: Walter Cronkite," *Playboy*, June 1973, p. 78.

18. *Variety*, Feb. 9, 1966, pp. 27, 38.

19. MacNeil, *The People Machine*, pp. 315-16. See also Erik Barnouw, *The Image Empire. A History of Broadcasting in the United States since 1953* (New York: Oxford University Press, 1970), pp. 271-81.

20. Kendrick, *The Wound Within*, p. 214.

21. Gates, *Air Time*, p. 160.

22. William Small, *To Kill a Messenger. Television News and the Real World* (New York: Hastings House, 1970), pp. 101-02.

23. *Variety*, Dec. 22, 1965, p. 42; Apr. 27, 1966, p. 33; May 25, 1966, p. 28; June 29, 1966, p. 1.

24. Ibid., Aug. 11, 1965, p. 36.

25. Ibid., Feb. 2, 1966, pp. 31, 36. See also Francis D. Faulkner, "Bao Chi: The American News Media in Vietnam, 1960-1980" (Ph.D. dissertation, University of Massachusetts, 1981), pp. 151-55.

26. On the failure of ABC affiliates to air "ABC Scope" as the network intended, see ibid., Aug. 16, 1967, p. 38; Jan. 24, 1968, p. 32.

27. Ibid., July 20, 1966, p. 42. See also May 25, 1966, p. 38.

28. Michael J. Arlen, *Living-Room War* (New York: Viking, 1969), p. 45. More than likely the CBS program mentioned in "The Selling of the Pentagon" as manipulated by U.S. military personnel was this installment of "Vietnam Perspective."

29. Brock Brower, "Worthy Try at Covering a Big Story," *Life*, Jan. 21, 1966, p. 15.

30. Arlen, *Living-Room War*, pp. 144-48.

31. *Variety*, Mar. 29, 1967, p. 46.

32. Erik Barnouw, *Documentary. A History of the Non-Fiction Film* (New York: Oxford University Press, 1974), pp. 274-75.

33. *Variety*, Jan. 24, 1968, p. 31; Arlen, *Living Room War*, pp. 160-67; Barnouw, *The Image Empire*, pp. 291-93.

34. Ibid., p. 48; Charles Montgomery Hammond, Jr., *The Image Decade. Television Documentary 1965-1975* (New York: Hastings House, 1981), p. 207.

35. Arlen, *Living-Room War*, pp. 64-65.

36. Mike Wallace, "The Deserters," *The Nation*, June 26, 1967, pp. 811-12.

37. Ted Koppel, "Wham!," *The Nation*, June 26, 1967, pp. 812-13.

38. Eric Sevareid, "The Final Troubled Hours of Adlai Stevenson," *Look*, Nov. 30, 1965, pp. 81-84. For criticism of the article, see *Variety*, Dec. 29, 1965, p. 1; and Sevareid's reply in ibid., Jan. 12, 1966, p. 38.

39. Joan Barthel, "Huntley and Brinkley 10 Years Later," *TV Guide*, July 1, 1967, p. 19.

40. *Variety*, Jan. 11, 1967, p. 38. Compare Cronkite's views a year earlier, in ibid., Jan. 12, 1966, p. 39. On Jennings' early views, see ibid., Sept. 1, 1965, pp. 26, 42.

41. Ibid., May 10, 1967, p. 39.

42. Ibid., Feb. 15, 1967, pp. 25, 40.

43. Peter Braestrup, *Big Story. How the American Press and Television Reported and Interpreted the Crisis of Tet 1968 in Vietnam and Washington*, II (Boulder, Colo.: Westview Press, 1977), pp. 188-89; Walter Cronkite, "Playboy Interview: Walter Cronkite," p. 80.

44. *Variety*, Feb. 28, 1968, pp. 29, 40.

45. Ibid., Feb. 21, 1968, pp. 1, 79.

46. Ibid., Sept. 13, 1967, p. 1; Feb. 21, 1968, p. 48; Feb. 28, 1968, p. 30; Mar. 6, 1968, p. 39; Pete Seeger, "How *Waist Deep in Big Muddy* Finally Got on Network Television in 1968," in Marianne Philbin, ed., *Give Peace a Chance. Music and the Struggle for Peace* (Chicago: Chicago Review Press, 1983), pp. 71-74; Bert Spector, "A Clash of Cultures: The Smothers Brothers vs. CBS Television," in John E. O'Connor, ed., *American History/American Television. Interpreting the Video Past* (New York: Frederick Ungar, 1983), pp. 159-83.

47. *Variety*, Mar. 12, 1969, p. 78.

48. Robert Metz, *CBS: Reflections in a Bloodshot Eye* (New York: New American Library, 1975), p. 299.

49. Ibid., p. 303.

50. *Variety*, Apr. 2, 1969, p. 38.

BIBLIOGRAPHY

There is no doubt that radio and television programming has been an important influence upon American society in the twentieth century. Nonetheless, historians have yet to place broadcasting in its proper historical focus—to assess such programming for the social, political, intellectual, moral, and economic impact it has had upon the American citizenry. The greatest obstacle to rectifying this oversight is the lack of well-developed audiovisual archives. In recent years such collections have been started, but they remain generally underdeveloped and lacking in breadth and depth. As beginnings, these archives must be applauded. But until they are comprehensive and accessible to scholars, historians will remain hampered in their attempt to reassess old programs and series.

This present study of Cold War television is based in great part upon the author's personal audiovisual collection. Most specific references to radio and television programs cited herein are drawn from this private archive of vintage films, kinescopes, and sound recordings. In all but a few instances, program titles and broadcast dates have been cited in the text. Thus, footnoting of television and radio quotations is generally absent.

As for materials related to the Cold War as a political phenomenon, there is an abundance of primary sources and secondary interpretations. An especially rich resource is the *Public Papers of the Presidents of the United States*. The many volumes of this government publication contain all official public communications of the presidents of the United States. These communications are arranged in chronological order. In this present study it has not been necessary to footnote official statements by presidents Truman, Eisenhower, Kennedy, and Johnson. Because they were drawn from the *Public Papers*, they are cited herein with reference only to dates of delivery.

The printed materials cited in this book are as follows:

UNPUBLISHED SOURCES

Faulkner, Francis D. "Bao Chi: The American News Media in Vietnam, 1960-1975." Ph.D. dissertation. University of Massachusetts, 1981.

Hamamoto, Darrell Yoshito, "Television Situation Comedy and Post-War Liberal Ideology: 1950-1980." Ph.D. dissertation. University of California, Irvine, 1981.

Klose, Albert Paul. "Howard K. Smith Comments on the News. A Comparative Analysis of the Use of Television and Print." Ph.D. dissertation. Northwestern University, 1970.

Parker, David Willson. "A Descriptive Analysis of The Lone Ranger as a Form of Popular Art." Ph.D. dissertation. Northwestern University, 1955.

Rinzel, Dennis Joseph. "A Description of the Ziv Television Series: 'I Led 3 Lives.'" Masters thesis. University of Wisconsin, Madison, 1975.

NEWSPAPERS AND MAGAZINES

Broadcasting, 1948-68.
Chicago Sun-Times, 1977.
Life, 1950.
The New Republic, 1961.
New York Times.
Newsweek, 1953.
Television Magazine, 1957-58.
Time, 1955, 1959.
TV Forecast, 1952.
TV Guide, 1953-68.
Variety, 1930-68.
Vital Speeches of the Day, 1956.

ALMANACS

Information Please Almanac 1976. Edited by Ann Golenpaul. New York: Dan Golenpaul Associates, 1975.

International Television Almanac 1962. Edited by Charles S. Aaronson. New York: Quigley Publications, 1961.

Series, Serials & Packages. A TV Film/Tape Source Book. Edited by Loretta Hanley. New York: Broadcast Information Bureau, Inc., 1974.

PRIMARY SOURCES—BOOKS

Arlen, Michael J. *Living-Room War*. New York: Viking, 1969.

Friendly, Fred W. *Due to Circumstances Beyond Our Control....* New York: Random House, 1967.

Kirschner, Allen, and Linda Kirschner, eds. *Radio and Television. Readings in the Mass Media*. New York, Bobbs-Merrill, 1971.

Murrow, Edward R. *In Search of Light. The Broadcasts of Edward R. Murrow 1938-1961*. London: Macmillan, 1968.

Murrow, Edward R., and Fred W. Friendly, eds. *See It Now*. New York: Simon and Schuster, 1955.

Salinger, Pierre. *With Kennedy*. New York: Avon, 1967.
Settel, Irving, ed. *Top TV Shows of the Year 1954-1955*. New York: Hastings House, 1955.
Sheen, Fulton J. *Life Is Worth Living*. Volume I. New York: McGraw-Hill, 1953.
_____. *Liberty under Communism*. New York: Paulist Press, [1937].
Sorensen, Theodore C. *Kennedy*. New York: Harper and Row, 1965.

PRIMARY SOURCES—ARTICLES

Cronkite, Walter. "Playboy Interview: Walter Cronkite." *Playboy*, June 1973, pp. 67-90.
Goralski, Robert. "Television and the President." *TV Guide*, July 4, 1964, pp. 3-5.
Johnson, Nicholas. "The Silent Screen." *TV Guide*, July 5, 1969, pp. 6-13.
Kennedy, John F. "Television: A Force in Politics." *TV Guide*, November 14, 1959, pp. 5-7.
Koppel, Ted. "Wham!" *The Nation*, June 26, 1967, pp. 812-13.
McAndrew, William R. Prefatory remarks. In *NBC News: Profile on Communism*. New York: National Broadcasting Company, 1963.
Mickelson, Sig. "TV Accepts Its Greatest Challenge." *Television Magazine*, May 1958, pp. 44-47, 82-84.
Murrow, Edward R. "How TV Can Help Us Survive." *TV Guide*, December 13, 1958, pp. 22-27.
O'Brien, John C. "The President and Television—An Interview with James C. Hagerty." *TV Guide*, December 27, 1958, pp. 4-7.
Salinger, Pierre. Introduction. In *Kennedy and the Press. The News Conference*. Edited by Harold W. Chase and Allen H. Lerman. New York: Crowell, 1965, pp. ix-xi.
Seeger, Pete. "How *Waist Deep in Big Muddy* Finally Got on Network Television in 1968." In *Give Peace a Chance. Music and the Struggle for Peace*. Edited by Marianne Philbin. Chicago: Chicago Review Press, 1983, pp. 71-74.
Sevareid, Eric. "The Final Troubled Hours of Adlai Stevenson." *Look*, November 30, 1965, pp. 81-86.
Wallace, Mike. "The Deserters." *The Nation*, June 26, 1967, pp. 811-12.

SECONDARY MATERIALS—BOOKS

Austin, Anthony. *The President's War. The Story of the Tonkin Gulf Resolution and How the Nation Was Trapped in Vietnam*. Philadelphia: J. B. Lippincott, 1971.
Barnouw, Erik. *Documentary. A History of the Non-Fiction Film*. Second edition. New York: Oxford University Press, 1983.
_____. *The Sponsor. Notes on a Modern Potentate*. New York: Oxford University Press, 1978.
_____. *The Image Empire. A History of Broadcasting in the United States since 1953*. New York: Oxford University Press, 1970.

Barnouw, Erik. *The Golden Web. A History of Broadcasting in the United States 1933-1953*. New York: Oxford University Press, 1968.

Bluem, A. William. *Documentary in American Television. Form-Function-Method*. New York: Hastings House, 1965.

Braestrup, Peter. *Big Story. How the American Press and Television Reported and Interpreted the Crisis of Tet 1968 in Vietnam and Washington*. 2 volumes. Boulder, Colorado: Westview Press, 1977.

Brauer, Ralph, with Donna Brauer. *The Horse, the Gun and the Piece of Property*: *Changing Images of the TV Western*. Bowling Green, Ohio: Bowling Green University Popular Press, 1975.

Caridi, Ronald J. *The Korean War and American Politics: The Republican Party as a Case Study*. Philadelphia: University of Pennsylvania Press, 1968.

Caute, David. *The Great Fear. The Anti-Communist Purge under Truman and Eisenhower*. New York: Simon and Schuster, 1978.

Cogley, John. *Report on Blacklisting. I: Movies*. New York: Fund for the Republic, 1956.

Cook, Blanche Wiesen. *The Declassified Eisenhower. A Divided Legacy*. New York: Doubleday, 1981.

Fairlie, Henry. *The Kennedy Promise. The Politics of Expectation*. New York: Doubleday, 1973.

Friedrich, Carl J., and Evelyn Sternberg. "Congress and the Control of Radio-broadcasting." *Studies in the Control of Radio* no. 5 (October 1943). Reprinted in *Studies in the Control of Radio*, nos. 1-6. New York: Arno, 1971.

Fulbright, J. William. *The Pentagon Propaganda Machine*. New York: Liverright, 1970.

Galloway, John. *The Gulf of Tonkin Resolution*. Rutherford, New Jersey: Fairleigh Dickenson University Press, 1970.

Gates, Gary Paul. *Air Time. The Inside Story of CBS News*. New York: Harper and Row, 1978.

Gitlin, Todd. *The Whole World Is Watching. Mass Media in the Making and Unmaking of the New Left*. Berkeley: University of California Press, 1980.

Glut, Donald F., and Jim Harmon. *The Great Television Heroes*. New York: Doubleday, 1975.

Goldman, Eric F. *The Tragedy of Lyndon Johnson*. New York: Knopf, 1969.

Goulden, Joseph C. *Truth Is the First Casualty. The Gulf of Tonkin Affair—Illusion and Reality*. Chicago: Rand McNally, 1969.

Grossman, Gary H. *Saturday Morning TV*. New York: Dell, 1981.

Halberstam, David. *The Powers That Be*. New York: Knopf, 1979.

Hammond, Charles Montgomery, Jr. *The Image Decade. Television Documentary 1965-1975*. New York: Hastings House, 1981.

Harrison, James Pinckney. *The Endless War. Fifty Years of Struggle in Vietnam*. New York: The Free Press, 1982.

Heller, Francis H., ed. *The Korean War. A 25-Year Perspective*. Lawrence: Regents Press of Kansas, 1977.

Hoch, Paul. *Rip off the Big Game. The Exploitation of Sports by the Power Elite*. New York: Doubleday, 1972.

Hoopes, Townsend. *The Devil and John Foster Dulles*. Boston: Little, Brown, 1973.

Kahin, George McTurnan, and John W. Lewis. *The United States in Vietnam*. New York: Dial Press, 1967.

Kanfer, Stefan. *A Journal of the Plague Years*. New York: Atheneum, 1973.

Kaufman, Richard F. *The War Profiteers*. Indianapolis: Bobbs-Merrill, 1970.

Katcher, Phillip. *Armies of the Vietnam War 1962-1975*. London: Osprey, 1980.

Kearns, Doris. *Lyndon Johnson and the American Dream*. New York: Harper and Row, 1976.

Kendrick, Alexander. *The Wound Within. America in the Vietnam Years, 1945-1974*. Boston: Little, Brown, 1974.

_____. *Prime Time. The Life of Edward R. Murrow*. Boston: Little, Brown, 1969.

Lenihan, John H. *Showdown. Confronting Modern America in the Western Film*. Urbana: University of Illinois Press, 1980.

Lewy, Guenter. *America in Vietnam*. New York: Oxford University Press, 1977.

Lyon, Eugene, *David Sarnoff*. New York: Harper and Row, 1966.

MacDonald, J. Fred. *Blacks and White TV. Afro-Americans in Television since 1948*. Chicago: Nelson-Hall, 1983.

_____. *Don't Touch That Dial! Radio Programming in American Life, 1920-1960*. Chicago: Nelson-Hall, 1979.

MacNeil, Robert. *The People Machine. The Influence of Television on American Politics*. New York: Harper and Row., 1968.

Maltin, Leonard. *The Disney Films*. New York: Crown, 1973.

Metz, Robert. *CBS: Reflections in a Bloodshot Eye*. New York: New American Library, 1975.

Minow, Newton P., John Bartlow Martin, and Lee M. Mitchell. *Presidential Television*. New York: Basic Books, 1973.

Mueller, John E. *War, Presidents and Public Opinion*. New York: John Wiley and Sons, 1973.

Navasky, Victor S. *Naming Names*. New York: Viking Press, 1980.

Rosenberg, Howard L. *Atomic Soldiers. American Victims of Nuclear Experiments*. Boston: Beacon, 1980.

Rostow, Walt Whitman. *The Diffusion of Power. An Essay in Recent History*. New York: Macmillan, 1972.

Rothel, David. *Who Was That Masked Man?* South Brunswick, New Jersey: A. S. Barnes, 1976.

Sayre [Smith], Jeanette. "An Analysis of the Radiobroadcasting Activities of Federal Agencies." *Studies in the Control of Radio* no. 3 (June 1941). Reprinted in *Studies in the Control of Radio*, nos. 1-6. New York: Arno, 1971.

Schlesinger, Arthur M., Jr. *A Thousand Days. John F. Kennedy in the White House*. Boston: Houghton Mifflin, 1965.

Small, William. *To Kill a Messenger. Television News and the Real World*. New York: Hastings House, 1970.

Steiner, Gary A. *The People Look at Television. A Study of Audience Attitudes.* New York: Knopf, 1963.

Straight, Michael. *Trial by Television.* Boston: Beacon, 1954.

Wills, Gary. *The Kennedy Imprisonment. A Meditation on Power.* Boston: Little, Brown, 1982.

Windchy, Eugene G. *Tonkin Gulf.* New York: Doubleday, 1971.

Wyden, Peter. *Bay of Pigs. The Untold Story.* New York: Simon and Schuster, 1979.

Yellin, David G. *Special. Fred Freed and the Television Documentary.* New York: Macmillan, 1972 and 1973.

SECONDARY MATERIALS—ARTICLES

Autry, Gene, "Gene Autry's Prize Round-up," *Radio and Television Mirror*, July 1951, pp. 46, 86.

Barthel, Joan, "Huntley and Brinkley 10 Years Later," *TV Guide*, July 1, 1967, pp. 15-19.

Brower, Brock, "Worthy Try at Covering a Big Story," *Life*, January 21, 1966, p. 17.

Cunniff, Robert, "There's Nobody, but Nobody, Like Walter," *TV Forecast*, November 1, 1952, pp. 8-9, 36.

Ellis, Robert P., "The Appeal of the Western Movie Thriller," *America*, May 17, 1958, pp. 228-29.

Harding, Henry, "Conducting President Kennedy's Press Conferences," *TV Guide*, April 21, 1962, p. A-3.

Hickey, Neil. "The Army-Navy Football Battle." *TV Guide*, November 27, 1965, pp. 32-35.

Homans, Peter. "The Western. The Legend and the Cardboard Hero." *Look*, March 13, 1962, pp. 82-90.

Land, Herman. "It's Time to Take Stock." *Television Magazine*, July 1957, pp. 42-45, 109.

Lardine, Robert. "Kennedy: They Loved Him on TV." *TV Radio Mirror*, March 1961, pp. 26-27, 77-78.

Lawrence, William H. "Presidential Press Conference." *TV Guide*, May 4, 1963, pp. 4-7.

MacDonald, J. Fred. "Government Propaganda in Commerical Radio—The Case of *Treasury Star Parade*, 1942-1943." *Journal of Popular Culture* 12, no. 2 (1978): 285-304.

Miller, Alexander. "The Western—A Theological Note." *The Christian Century*, November 27, 1957, pp. 1409-10.

Paxton, Harry T. "Football's Biggest Show." *Saturday Evening Post*, November 26, 1955, pp. 28-29, 120-124.

Rickenbacker, William F. "60,000,000 Westerners Can't Be Wrong." *National Review*, October 23, 1962, pp. 322-25.

Rollins, Peter C. "*Nightmare in Red*: A Cold War View of the Communist Revolution." In *American History/American Television. Interpreting the Video Past*. Edited by John E. O'Connor. New York: Frederick Ungar, 1983, pp. 134-58.

————. "*Television's Vietnam*: The Visual Language of Television News." *Journal of American Culture* 4, no. 2 (1981), pp. 114-35.

————. "*Victory at Sea*: Cold War Epic." *Journal of Popular Culture* 6, no. 3 (1973), pp. 463-82.

Sahl, Mort. "The Comics Prove It's Hard to Be Funny on TV." *TV Guide*, May 2, 1959, pp. 17-19.

Shipley, James. "How Dulles Averted War." *Life*, January 16, 1956, pp. 70-80.

Sisk, John P. "The Western Heroes." *Commonweal*, July 12, 1957, pp. 367-69.

Smith, Merriman. "The Presidential Press Conference." *TV Guide*, April 29, 1961, pp. 4-6.

Spector, Bert. "A Clash of Cultures: The Smothers Brothers vs. CBS Television." In *American History/American Television. Interpreting the Video Past*. Edited by John E. O'Connor. New York: Frederick Ungar, 1983, pp. 159-83.

Stahl, Bob. "Do Newscasters Have Freedom of Speech?" *TV Guide*, August 3, 1957, pp. 8-10.

Teeple, David Shea. "TV Westerns Tell a Story." *American Mercury*, April 1958, pp. 115-17.

INDEX

ABOUT THE AUTHOR

J. Fred MacDonald is professor of history at Northeastern Illinois University in Chicago.

Dr. MacDonald is a recognized authority on the social and cultural history of the mass media. His articles have appeared in *Journal of Popular Culture, Phylon,* and *American Quarterly.* He is the author of *Don't Touch That Dial! Radio Programming in American Life, 1920-1960* (1979) and *Blacks and White TV: Afro-Americans in Television since 1948* (1983). He is also a past president of the Popular Culture Association.

Dr. MacDonald holds B.A. and M.A. degrees from the University of California at Berkeley and a Ph.D. from the University of California at Los Angeles.

WITHDRAWN